Cool Papas and Double Duties

Cool Papas and Double Duties

*The All-Time Greats
of the Negro Leagues*

by WILLIAM F. MCNEIL

McFarland & Company, Inc., Publishers
Jefferson, North Carolina, and London

Library of Congress Cataloguing-in-Publication Data

McNeil, William
    Cool papas and double duties : the all-time greats of the Negro
Leagues / by William F. McNeil.
        p.   cm.
    Includes bibliographical references and index.   ∞
    ISBN 0-7864-1074-4 (illustrated case binding : 50# alkaline paper)
    1. African American baseball players— Biography.   2. Baseball
players— United States— Biography.   3. Negro leagues.   I. Title.
GV865.A1M379   2001
796.357'092'396073 — dc21   2001037059
[B]

British Library cataloguing data are available

Manufactured in the United States of America

On the cover: Satchel Paige

*McFarland & Company, Inc., Publishers
    Box 611, Jefferson, North Carolina 28640
    www.mcfarlandpub.com*

This book is gratefully dedicated to the memories of all former Negro League players, the legendary players and Hall of Fame candidates, as well as the average players and the journeymen players who helped keep Negro League baseball in the public eye during the 65 years that the major leagues practiced their heinous whites-only policy.

All Negro League veterans were true pioneers. They made a major contribution toward turning this country into a land we can all be proud of.

Acknowledgments

John Holway was a tremendous help in the preparation of this work. He contributed many photographs, authorized the use of other photographs in the author's possession, and gave permission to use many of the batting and pitching statistics he developed over 30 years of devoted research into the careers of former Negro League players. The complete statistics for these Negro League players can be found in his latest book, *The Complete Book of the Negro Leagues*. John also gave me valuable information about individual Negro League players and provided me with his insight into the league, its players, the National Baseball Hall of Fame, and baseball in general. Much of the biographical material in this book was gleaned from Holway's numerous books and articles.

Many other people also contributed photographs for the book, or authorized the use of their photographs in the author's possession. These include Jay Sanford, Frank Keetz, Robert W. Peterson, Dr. Lawrence D. Hogan, the Robert W. Peterson Collection in the National Baseball Hall of Fame, Dick Clark, Larry Lester, Todd Bolton, Luis Alvelo, and Jim Riley.

Jim Riley's excellent book, *The Biographical Encyclopedia of the Negro Baseball Leagues*, was used quite extensively to obtain biographical information about former Negro League players. Other books used for biographical research included *The Negro Leagues Book*, *Only the Ball Was White*, *Voices from the Great Black Baseball League*, *Blackball Stars*, *Black Diamonds*, and *Voices from the Negro Leagues*.

The author is deeply indebted to all the respondents to the survey, the dozens of Negro League veterans, as well as the Negro League authors and historians, and members of the Society for American Baseball Research

(SABR). The SABR directory was used to obtain biographical information about many of the historians and authors who participated in the surveys.

Statistical information came from many sources, which are listed in
the bibliography.

Contents

Introduction: The Baseball Hall of Fame's Missing Members

Baseball, or one or another of its ancestors, has been played in the civilized world for more than 4000 years. A round leather ball, now in the British Museum, was found in Egypt and dated to 2000 B.C. Numerous temple paintings and other artwork in ancient Egypt and Greece and books from medieval Europe depict field games being played with a bat and ball. A drawing from fourteenth-century England shows a man, perhaps a pitcher, in the process of throwing a ball, another man with a bat waiting to hit it, and several men standing behind the pitcher apparently waiting to catch the ball after it is hit. The American game of baseball, which has been in vogue since 1845, when the Knickerbocker Baseball Club was formed in New York City, evolved from these early games of bat and ball.

Baseball spread up and down the eastern seaboard of the United States during the 1860s, was transmitted to soldiers from both the Confederate and Union Armies during the Civil War, and became the "National Pastime" in the 1870s. Some photographs of the period show blacks and whites playing the game together. By the 1880s, blacks were playing professional baseball in several leagues in the eastern half of the country. The first black player in organized baseball was reportedly John W. "Bud" Fowler, who pitched for the Chelsea, Massachusetts, team in 1878. Six years later, Moses "Fleet" Walker and his brother Welday played major league baseball for the Toledo Blue Stockings of the American Association.

According to SABR's *Minor League Baseball Stars*, (Vol. 3), "At least

75 blacks played one or more games in the minors between 1878 and 1899." Many of the black players were of major league quality and several of them were potential Hall of Fame candidates. Included in that list was Frank Grant, who may have been the greatest second baseman, black or white,

to play professional baseball in the nineteenth century; George Stovey, a 34-game winner with Newark of the International League in 1887; and Sol White, who had a career .356 batting average in the minors and never hit less than .300 in any minor league.

Blacks were beginning to make their mark in professional baseball until Cap Anson, one of the most influential players and managers in the major leagues, refused to let his team take the field against the Newark team if Stovey was in uniform. His action, and his subsequent politicking with club owners, contributed to blacks being systematically banished from organized baseball completely by the early 1890s. The unwritten rule of "whites only" stayed in effect for more than 50 years, until Branch Rickey, Happy Chandler, and Jackie Robinson destroyed it forever.

It is now known that the game of baseball was erroneously attributed to Abner Doubleday, who supposedly invented the game in Cooperstown, New York, in 1839. There is no record, in Doubleday's autobiography or in any other writing, that he even played the game, let alone

Before Babe Ruth became the world's greatest home run hitter, he was the best southpaw pitcher in the major leagues, winner of 94 career games.

invented it. Nevertheless, based on the Doubleday myth, the Cooperstown Chamber of Commerce purchased the land that included the legendary baseball field in 1919. Eventually, the site was expanded to include the National Baseball Museum and the National Baseball Hall of Fame, which was built to honor the greatest players ever to play the game. One of the requirements for election to the Hall was that the player had a minimum of ten years experience at the major league level. The first four members of the Hall of Fame, elected in 1936, were Ty Cobb, Walter Johnson, Babe Ruth, and Honus Wagner.

Today, the National Baseball Hall of Fame has a total of 251 members, of which 206 were players. The remaining 45 inductees were managers, executives, and umpires. The Hall of Fame was exclusively a white club for 26 years, until Jackie Robinson marched through its doors in 1962. Robinson, of course, was admitted for his major league achievements. Four years later, in 1966, Ted Williams, in his induction speech, brought the injustices against former Negro League players to the attention of all Americans when he said, "Baseball gives every American boy a chance to excel. Not just to be as good as someone else, but to be better. This is the nature of man and the name of the game. I hope that some day, Satchel Paige and Josh Gibson will be voted into the Hall of Fame as symbols of the great Negro players who are not here only because they weren't given the chance."

Satchel Paige said he was appreciative of the fine compliment paid him by Williams, but he reminded everyone that he and Josh weren't the only Negro League stars deserving of induction into the Hall of Fame. As he said, "There were many Satchels. There were many Joshs."

The pressure to admit former Negro League players to the Hall of Fame grew from that day on. Eventually, the Hall of Fame was forced to recognize Satchel Paige and his teammates. At first, the Hall offered to admit Satchel into a "special section" set aside to recognize Negro League greats. Paige declined the offer, saying he and his fellow Negro League veterans deserved equal recognition alongside their major league counterparts.

In 1971, the Baseball Hall of Fame relented. A committee was established to study the Negro Leagues and to recommend players from those leagues that deserved induction into the Hall. Quite naturally, the first Negro League player to be admitted was Satchel Paige. Subsequent selections by the Negro League Committee included Josh Gibson (1972), Buck Leonard (1972), Monte Irvin (1973), Cool Papa Bell (1974), Judy Johnson (1975), Oscar Charleston (1976), John Henry Lloyd (1977), and Martin Dihigo (1977).

The Negro League Committee was then disbanded, with the token

Ty Cobb not only owns the major league record for the highest career batting average (.367), he is also first in runs scored and fifth in RBIs, and held the single season and career stolen base record for decades.

admittance of nine former Negro League players. But the baseball public would not accept that weak gesture on the part of the baseball establishment. They kept the pressure on to admit more deserving black players. The review process was assigned to the Veterans Committee and, after a lapse of four years, Rube Foster, the legendary Negro League pitcher and founder of the Negro National League, was admitted in 1981. He was followed by Ray Dandridge in 1987. Once again, the National Baseball Hall of Fame, feeling it had done its duty by electing 11 Negro League stars, stopped reviewing possible Negro League candidates.

It didn't end there, however. In 1995, once again under pressure to admit more Negro League players, the Veterans Committee announced they would elect five more Negro Leaguers, one a year for five years. The inductees were Leon Day (1995), Willie Foster (1996), Willie Wells (1997), Bullet Joe Rogan (1998), and Smokey Joe Williams (1999).

The major problem over the past 28 years seems to be that the National Baseball Hall of Fame has repeatedly tried to establish a quota for Negro League inductees to pacify the various elements in the baseball world who are pushing hard for recognition of the Negro League greats. But quotas are not the answer. If there is only one former Negro League player that is deserving of induction into the Hall of Fame, then only one player should be admitted. But if 100 players are of Hall of Fame caliber, then all 100 should be admitted. Surely none of the current Negro League inductees — Paige, Gibson, Bell, Leonard, others — would want to be known as the token Negro Leaguer in the HOF.

When the members of the Veterans Committee meet each year to consider new candidates, they do not work against a quota for former major league players. It is only when they sit down to evaluate potential candidates from the old Negro Leagues that the word "quota" rears its ugly head. One of the arguments the establishment uses to keep from having to consider Negro League players for induction into the Hall is that there are very few statistics available for the players. They also question the quality of the opposition. And finally, they argue that no one is around today who saw most of them play. To begin with, many statistics have been compiled over the past 20 years, thanks to people like John Holway, the dedicated researcher who has spent the better part of 20 years digging out old box scores, so that argument is no longer completely valid. It is true that the old-time players, prior to the formation of the Negro National League 1920, have fewer statistics to support their case. But there are some statistics available from the highly rated Cuban Winter League, where whites and blacks played side by side, as well as from the California Winter League, where Negro teams competed against white teams composed of both major and minor league players, from late October through late March every year from the early 1900s through the late 1940s. The final argument that no one is around who saw them play is, for the most part, correct, but irrelevant. The Veterans Committee elected George Davis to the Hall of Fame in 1999 and Bid McPhee in 2000. Both players starred in the major leagues in the nineteenth century. There is no one alive today who saw them play either, but that didn't stop the committee from electing them.

The only thing black players, and their friends and relatives, are looking for is equality. Blacks have been looking for equality in all segments of American society for 200 years. It is time they found it. The National Baseball Hall of Fame can be a leader in that fight. Since the Hall has admitted that Negro League players are eligible for induction into Cooperstown, they should now cast off all semblances of discrimination and let the Veterans Committee evaluate both major league players and Negro League players on an equal basis each and every year. Let those players deserving of recognition walk proudly through the front door, regardless of color or league affiliation. Get rid of the quota system, once and for all.

Smokey Joe Williams's election to the Hall of Fame in 1999 did not complete the recognition of qualified Negro League players in the Hall. That year, the Veterans Committee announced that two more Negro Leaguers would be elected in the years 2000 and 2001. The first inductee of the twenty-first century was long overdue. Norman "Turkey" Stearnes was a superstar of mythical proportions. As Cool Papa Bell noted on his election, "Turkey Stearnes is the man who should be in the Hall of Fame. If he isn't in, no one should be in." Well, Turkey finally made it. The only regret is that he couldn't have been elected when he was still around to appreciate it. Unfortunately, Turkey Stearnes died in 1979, at the age of 78 Also Hilton Smith, who died in 1983, was elected in 2001.

How many more Turkey Stearneses or Hilton Smiths are there, standing in the shadows, or looking down from above, waiting for their call? This book will investigate that question and will try to answer it by the most satisfactory method available — by polling former Negro League players, most of whom are now in their 70s, 80s, and 90s, plus Negro League historians and authors, the people who are most familiar with the careers and baseball skills of the legendary black players of yesteryear.

1

From Jackie Robinson to the New Millennium: The Long Struggle for Recognition

The National Baseball Hall of Fame has been struggling with its responsibilities for the past 28 years. To the baseball public, the Hall seems less than dedicated in reaching out to the world-class athletes from professional baseball leagues outside the major leagues, specifically the players from the old Negro Leagues. The Hall of Fame has made token gestures to the black community from time to time, admitting a few Negro League players over the years, to pacify the indignation of the black baseball world. At first, they tried to hide Satchel Paige away in a "special" section. After being forced to admit him through the front door, they opened the doors to eight more Negro League legends during the seventies. Begrudgingly, they let in two more during the eighties. Then, they went back to treading water, hoping the token recognition would satisfy the baseball public. When that didn't work, they established another quota — five more Negro Leaguers would be admitted, one a year from 1995 through 1999. They then extended that quota for two more years, with players to be admitted in 2000 and 2001. And so it goes, seemingly ad infinitum.

The record shows that since 1962, when Jackie Robinson was elected to the National Baseball Hall of Fame for his accomplishments in the major leagues, 58 players have been elected to the Hall by the Baseball Writers Association of America through 2000. Another 99 players have been elected by the Veterans Committee. Of the 58 players elected by the BBWAA, all for their major league contributions, 41 were white and 17 (or 29 percent) were black. The black players included such outstanding Negro League veterans as Roy Campanella, Hank Aaron, Ernie Banks, and Willie Mays. These, and the other 12 black players, were stars of mythical proportions. They would have been baseball legends whether they played in the major leagues or the Negro Leagues. And they would have deserved admittance into the National Baseball Hall of Fame regardless of which league they played in. Campanella, in fact, had a long and productive career in both the Negro Leagues and the major leagues.

There were many other Hall of Fame–caliber players who showcased their skills in the Negro Leagues before integration. They were still great, even though they were not permitted to play with their white neighbors in the major leagues. Remember, the decision to bar them from playing in the majors was not theirs. It was made by the white major league owners and enforced by the baseball commissioner, Kenesaw Mountain Landis. Now, once again, they are being prevented, by the existing baseball establishment, from achieving the recognition they so richly deserve.

Prior to 1962, a total of 147 players, all white, were elected into the Hall of Fame by the Baseball Writers Association of America. If the percentage of black players to white players deserving election into the Hall was the same, both before and after 1962, there should have been 43 black players (29 percent of the honorees) elected to the Hall between 1936 and 1961. The first question to be asked is whether or not 29 percent is a realistic percentage of black players to white players.

A study of today's major league baseball teams indicates that approximately 30 percent of the rosters are black, which is in agreement with the above figures. The U.S. population is approximately 10 percent black, but the major leagues also have a heavy incidence of foreign-born players. A recent survey showed that between 35 percent and 43 percent of 1999 major league spring training rosters were foreign-born. The Los Angeles Dodgers' roster, for instance, had 17 foreign born players out of a total of 40, a 43 percent representation. Eight of the foreign-born players were black, 9 were white. There were also four black players who were American born (10 percent of the roster). The Dodger roster, therefore, was 30 percent black, of which 10 percent were American-born blacks.

Assuming that the above figures from the Hall of Fame, supported by the present major league personnel makeup, are realistic, then 43 Negro League veterans should now be members in good standing in the National Baseball Hall of Fame. As noted earlier, 16 Negro League players, representing the great Negro League stars of the first half of the twentieth century

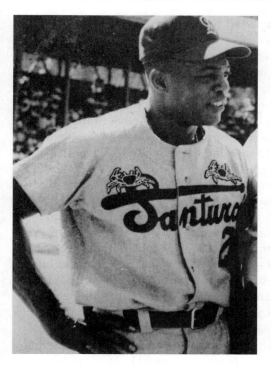

Willie Mays is regarded by many experts as the greatest all-around player in baseball history. (**Photograph courtesy Yuyo Ruiz.**)

and led by Satchel Paige and Josh Gibson, presently reside in the hallowed halls of Cooperstown. That leaves another 27 deserving players on the outside looking in.

To get some idea of the quality of the players in the old Negro Leagues, it is only necessary to review the established Negro League stars who broke into the major leagues in the years immediately following Jackie Robinson's signing. From 1946 through 1952, the black trailblazers, in addition to Robinson, included Roy Campanella, Satchel Paige, Larry Doby, Monte Irvin, Willie Mays, Ernie Banks, Hank Aaron, Luke Easter, Sam Jethroe, Don Newcombe, and Joe Black. Eight of the twelve are now members of baseball's Hall of Fame.

Those players represented the best of the Negro Leagues during the 40s and early 50s, except for old Satch who was a legend as far back as 1935. When Paige broke into the Cleveland Indian lineup in 1948, he was a 42-year-old, battle-scarred veteran with 21 years of professional baseball behind him. That didn't stop him, however. He proceeded to help Cleveland win the American League pennant, by racking up a 6–1 record with a 2.47 ERA in 21 games. The tall, lanky flamethrower shocked the baseball world by throwing two complete-game shutouts at the Chicago White Sox over an eight-day span. At 42 years old, he was the American League's oldest Rookie of the Year.

Some of the other players were also past their primes when they entered the major leagues, but they still went on to have outstanding careers in the big show. Roy Campanella was a nine-year Negro League veteran when Branch Rickey brought him into the Brooklyn organization, but Campy went on to have a 10-year Hall of Fame career with the Dodgers. He was voted the National League's Most Valuable Player three times, capable of hitting .300, banging out 30–40 homers, and driving in over 100 runs, when healthy. He was also the league's best defensive catcher, gunning down two out of every three would-be base stealers, a feat unheard of in today's game. He may well be the greatest all-around catcher in major league history.

Monte Irvin was a 30-year-old veteran, with 12 years of professional baseball behind him, when he joined the New York Giants in 1949. In his third year with Leo Durocher's troops, he led the team to the National League flag, batting a timely .312 with 24 home runs and a league-leading 121 RBIs. He finished his eight-year major league career with a .293 career batting average, although he most likely would have been a lifetime .300 hitter if he had played in the major leagues during his prime.

Luke Easter, the big 6' 4", 240-pound slugger, didn't begin playing professional baseball until he was 32 years old. Prior to that time, he played amateur and semi-pro ball around St. Louis and Cincinnati. After a short two-year career in the Negro League, he was signed by the Cleveland Indians, where he flexed his muscles until his 39th birthday. Then he went on to play AAA ball in the International League for another 11 years. He finally retired in 1964 at the age of 50 after having hit 424 home runs as a professional, all of them after his 32nd birthday!

Larry Doby was one of the top hitters in the Negro Leagues, pounding the ball at a .384 clip for four years. He was a pioneer, like Jackie Robinson, joining the Cleveland Indians in 1947, just a couple of months after Jackie joined Brooklyn. Doby was a sensation in Cleveland, playing a spectacular center field, in addition to averaging 25 home runs and 100 RBIs with a .283 batting average, over a 13-year major league career. He helped Bill Veeck's team capture two American League pennants and one World Championship.

Sam "Jet" Jethroe was another Negro League all-star who set the major leaguers on their heels. After raking Negro League pitchers for a .340 batting average over a seven-year period, he joined the Boston Braves outfield in 1950 at the age of 28 and walked off with the National League's Rookie of the Year honors, by rapping the ball at a .273 clip, with 18 home runs and a league-leading 35 stolen bases.

Don Newcombe pitched the Brooklyn Dodgers to three National League flags in 1949, 1955, and 1956, with records of 17–8, 20–5, and 27–7. He also batted a sizzling .359 with 7 home runs in just 117 at-bats in '55. Five years earlier, the big right-hander pitched both ends of a double-header against the Philadelphia Phillies, winning the opener 2–0 and leaving the nightcap after seven innings, trailing 2–0. The Dodgers pulled out the second game with three runs in the ninth.

Joe Black, at 28 years old and an eight-year veteran of the Negro Leagues, won National League Rookie of the Year honors with the Brooklyn Dodgers in 1952, after leading the Brooks to the pennant. He marched out of the bullpen 56 times, winning 15 games against only four losses and saving another 14 games, while compiling a minuscule 2.15 earned run average. He went on to stun the baseball world by starting the opening game of the World Series, and he justified his manager's gamble by whipping the New York Yankees 4–2. He was the only black pitcher to win a World Series game until Mudcat Grant took the Dodgers to task 14 years later.

In the 1950s, younger Negro League stars paraded across the major league stage. Willie Mays, the Giants all-world center fielder, with 660 career major league home runs, 1903 RBIs, and a .302 batting average, was a three-year Negro League veteran when he first appeared in organized baseball. Hank Aaron, who went on to become the major league's all-time career home-run king with 755 circuit blasts, began his career with the Indianapolis Clowns of the Negro American League. "Hammerin'" Hank set a new major league record for runs batted in with 2,297, to go along with a .305 batting average. And Ernie "Let's Play Two" Banks, the Chicago Cubs great shortstop, played two years with the Kansas City Monarchs before joining the Cubs. When the dust had cleared from his 19-year major league career, his stats showed a .274 batting average, with 2,583 base hits, 512 home runs, and 1,636 RBIs. If integration had not been accomplished, Hank Aaron would be an unknown Negro League baseball player, and Babe Ruth would still be the home-run king, with 714 career round trippers. And people would never have heard of Willie Mays or Ernie Banks.

To date, 16 major league players have accumulated 500 or more career home runs. Seven of them (44 percent), are black, and three of them were veterans of the Negro Leagues. Two of the three players with more than 600 home runs are Negro League veterans, as is one of the two with more than 700. The other black players with more than 500 home runs are Frank Robinson, Reggie Jackson, Willie McCovey, and Eddie Murray.

Over an 11-year period, from 1949 through 1959, Negro League veterans won 9 of 22 Most Valuable Player awards (41 percent), with Campy taking three, Ernie Banks two, and Jackie Robinson, Willie Mays, Don Newcombe, and Hank Aaron capturing one apiece. They also won 6 of 12 Rookie of the Year awards (50 percent) between 1947 and 1953 (J. Robinson, D. Newcombe, S. Jethroe, W. Mays, J. Black, and J. Gilliam), and the first Cy Young award (Don Newcombe).

These great players are not aberrations. They are typical of the players that displayed their talents in the Negro Leagues from the turn of the century through the 1940s. The Ken Griffeys of the 90s are descendants of the Eddie Murrays of the 80s, the Rod Carews of the 70s, the Roberto Clementes of the 60s, and the Aarons, Mayses, and Bankses of the 50s. Prior to the Robinson era, there were the Monte Irvins and Larry Dobys of the 40s, the Josh Gibsons and Satchel Paiges of the 30s, the Chino Smiths and Bullet Joe Rogans of the 20s, the John Henry Lloyds and Smokey Joe Williams of the teens, and the Pete Hills and Rube Fosters of the first decade of the century. There has been a continuous line of black baseball talent from one end of the twentieth century to the other. The missing link is the recognition due both the black major league players and the exciting pioneers of the first half of the century.

The Hall of Fame has not been the only culprit in the melodrama. They have been ably supported by a bevy of baseball writers and historians. This situation has been, and continues to be, indelibly recorded in the written works of the last thirty years. Jackie Robinson broke the color barrier in 1946, but 55 years later black players, past and present, are still striving to achieve adequate recognition for their significant contributions to the game. Over the last half century, numerous all-star teams have been selected by fans, players, media representatives, and historians and, in most cases, black players have come up short when compared to their white counterparts. The slight is not restricted to the Negro League pioneers of the first half of the twentieth century. A review of the annual major league all-star teams since 1947 will verify that black players have been a formidable force in the game. Yet when all-time all-star teams are selected, the black players are generally ignored.

The first all-star team of note can be found in Gerald Secor Couzens's book, A Baseball Album. It reported a 1969 survey of baseball fans, writers, and sportscasters, conducted by the major league offices. The 27 finalists included four black players—Jackie Robinson, Ernie Banks, Roy Campanella, and Willie Mays. None of them made the final cut, not even Mays who is generally regarded as one of the two greatest all-around players in baseball history. Forty-three years after Branch Rickey ended segregation in organized baseball, this survey showed that the disease of ignorance and discrimination still had not been completely eradicated in white America.

Street and Smiths, celebrating 50 years of publishing their annual baseball magazine, approached baseball players, both active and retired, as well as coaches, managers, executives, and the media, to select their "Dream Team," the greatest baseball players of the period, 1941 through 1991. Two teams were chosen, an American League all-star team and its National League counterpart. This poll presented an even-handed evaluation of the players and gave the black players considerable recognition.

The National League team consisted of eight position players and three pitchers. Only four of the players were white, indicating that some progress has been made in racial recognition over the years. The seven black players were Bob Gibson, Willie McCovey, Joe Morgan, Ozzie Smith, Willie Mays, Hank Aaron, and Roberto Clemente. Noticeably absent were Jackie Robinson and Roy Campanella. Mays was selected as the best player of the period, while Stan Musial was chosen as the best hitter.

The American League team, however, presented a different face. All 11 players were white. That was not an unexpected result, since the National League had pioneered integration.

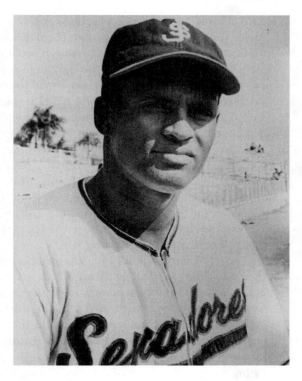

Roberto Clemente was a superstar who could hit for average, hit with power, run, field, and throw. (**Photograph courtesy Yuyo Ruiz.**)

American League teams, like the New York Yankees and the Boston Red Sox, maintained their white posture for several years. The Yanks finally added Elston Howard to their roster in 1955, while the Red Sox, the last team to relent, brought Pumpsie Green up in 1959. Black stars like Frank Robinson, Rickey Henderson, Eddie Murray, and Rod Carew were on the candidate list but failed to make the final team. Joe DiMaggio was voted the best all-around player, while Ted Williams was selected as the best hitter.

Additionally, there were four pinch hitters, two utility players, and two pinch runners selected for the two leagues. Four of the eight were black. And the two smartest players chosen by the panel were also black, Joe Morgan and Jackie Robinson.

Overall, 11 black players were chosen for the two major league all-star teams, out of 30 players, a 37 percent black representation. This was an equitable balance between blacks and whites, even though there were major differences between the two leagues. One team was predominantly black and the other team was predominantly white.

This difference between the National League and American League is evident in another all-star exercise. David Nemec, in his fascinating, informative, and entertaining book on major league baseball, *The Great American Baseball Team Book*, presented all-time all-star teams for each major league franchise. As might be expected, the Brooklyn-L.A. Dodgers team included seven black players on their 24-man squad (30 percent). Other National League squads were similar. The Giants of New York and San Francisco had four blacks on the team, while the Pittsburgh Pirates had six. In the American League, the New York Yankees had only one black player on the 24-man team, while the Boston Red Sox had none. In fact, none of the eight original American League franchises had more than four black players on their 24-man roster.

In 1997, the Baseball Writers Association of America (BBWAA) picked their all-time major league all-star team, with interesting results. The team consisted of thirty-two players from the turn of the twentieth century to the end of the century. Seven of the thirty-two players (22 percent) were black — Roy Campanella, Lee Smith, Joe Morgan, Jackie Robinson, Willie Mays, Hank Aaron, and Harold Baines. Of those players whose careers began after 1946, 11 were white and 7 were black. It is interesting to note that four of the seven black players were graduates of the Negro Leagues. That being the case, it is not unreasonable to assume that as many as six Negro League players from the period 1900 to 1946 could also have been members of the team if they had been permitted to play in the majors.

Although the overall team was reasonably well integrated, the starting lineup was predominantly white. Eleven of the twelve players, consisting of eight position players, two starting pitchers, one relief pitcher, and a designated hitter were white, with just Willie Mays cracking the color barrier.

As the twentieth century came to a close, it became a popular exercise to select the top 100 baseball players of the century. Major League Baseball decided to present an All-Century team by polling of the fans. The results were what you might expect from a fan poll. Major league legends like Honus Wagner, Christy Mathewson, and Lefty Grove were not selected. They were beaten out by modern players like Cal Ripken, Roger Clemens, and Nolan Ryan. In order to bring a little credibility to the poll, Major League Baseball added a special selections committee, to recognize those deserving players who were ignored by the fans. The special committee selected Wagner, Mathewson, and Grove, plus Stan Musial and Warren Spahn, who also failed to generate any fan support.

This poll was one of the first to include both major league players and Negro League players. A ballot containing 100 professional baseball candidates was made available to baseball fans across the country. The list included — as police captain Renaud in *Casablanca* would say, "the usual suspects" — Negro Leaguers Josh Gibson, Satchel Paige, Buck Leonard, Cool Papa Bell, and Oscar Charleston. Those five players were the most visible names from the Negro Leagues, having been well publicized by authors like John Holway, James A. Riley, and Robert W. Peterson, but whether they were the greatest Negro League players is open to debate. Polls taken over the years by various black media and Negro League historians generally rated Smokey Joe Williams to be Paige's equal, if not his superior. Bullet Joe Rogan also received strong support as the Negro League's all-time greatest pitcher. Many of the polls also voted Norman "Turkey" Stearnes, Martin Dihigo, or John Henry Lloyd as the greatest all-around player in Negro League history. Yet, none of the five, Williams, Rogan, Stearnes, Dihigo, or Lloyd, were even on the candidate list. It would appear from the above list that the architects of the poll were not familiar with the Negro Leagues or its players, but they needed to include a few Negro League players to be politically correct.

The final All-Century team consisted of 30 players. Guess how many Negro Leaguers made the team? Right. None. Zero. Nada. How many fans do you think had even heard of the Negro League players, other than Paige and Gibson. If you said about 5 percent, you were probably too high. The team did include six black players— Jackie Robinson, Hank Aaron, Willie Mays, Ken Griffey, Jr., Bob Gibson, and Ernie Banks— a 20 percent black presence, which is a minimum spread across ethnic lines. One problem with a fan poll is that fans, in general, are not familiar with a wide range of baseball talent. Their choices are often limited to the major leagues and to the period from 1970 to the present. Many of them are not familiar with players from other generations. They know very little about the white legends of the game and nothing at all about the Negro League stars. It was only because of the special selections committee that icons like Honus Wagner and Christy Mathewson were included, and they didn't make the starting nine. And even the special selections committee bypassed the Negro League greats like Josh Gibson and Satchel Paige.

The final 30-player team not only did not include any former Negro League players, except for the four who also had major league experience, it also did not include any Hispanics. The starting nine, the players with the highest vote total by position, had seven white players and two black players.

The All-Century Team

Catcher: Johnny Bench
Pitcher: Nolan Ryan
First Base: Lou Gehrig
Second Base: Jackie Robinson
Shortstop: Cal Ripken
Third Base: Mike Schmidt
Outfield: Babe Ruth, Hank Aaron, Ted Williams

Willie Mays once again failed to make the starting lineup, as he had in Couzens' poll. All in all, there was some recognition of black major league stars in this poll, but a continued ignorance of the black players of old who, in addition to showcasing their skills in the major metropolitan areas like New York, Pittsburgh, and Kansas City, created a legend of their own in the small towns, villages, and hamlets all across this country in the early days of the twentieth century.

Street and Smiths presented their own all-time all-star team in 1999. Their team, selected by a panel of writers and editors, plus the staff of Stats, Inc., picked a starting lineup of nine players, with an additional 16 subs, plus a 25-man second team. The starting nine were all white. The 16 subs included five black players, of which two (Satchel Paige and Josh Gibson) were again the "token" Negro Leaguers. The second squad consisted of 17 white players and eight black players. Again, the total breakdown was reasonable, 13 black players out of 50 players, a 26 percent black representation, but the starting lineup was lily-white.

One of the more interesting, entertaining, and controversial exercises of the period was published early in 2000. The *Spring Training Baseball Yearbook*, in conjunction with the Strat-O-Matic Game Company, selected a major league all-star team for each decade of the twentieth century — ten teams in all. They then played a full 162-game computerized schedule. Naturally the first five all-star teams had no black players since baseball was not integrated at the time. The 25 man all-star squads representing the decades of the '50s (1950–1959), through the '90s, included 6, 8, 12, 5, and 10 black players respectively, a 33 percent black representation.

In the end, the 1930s team captured the league championship, followed by the 1940s, 1990s, 1910s, 1920s, 1950s, 1900s, 1960s, 1980s, and 1970s. There were a number of problems with the computer program, such as comparing the 1990s active players whose batting and pitching averages haven't yet begun to decline with retired players, not adjusting the home runs for the 1900s and 1910s players to the live-ball era, and making injuries part of the program. But the biggest problem with the program centered around the black players.

The All-Tournament team, which is essentially an All-Century team, bypassed black players completely. All eleven players selected for the All-Tournament team were white — Bench, Gehrig, Hornsby, Schmidt, Ripken, Williams, DiMaggio, Ruth, Clemens, Grove, and Franco. Statistically, the black players came out poorly in all batting and pitching categories. Tony Gwynn, the top hitter of his era, had the 16th highest batting average in the tournament and was the lone black player in the top 17. He was outhit by Ted

Ken Griffey, Jr., the modern era's superstar, is on track to hit 800 career home runs. (Photograph courtesy James R. Madden, Jr.)

Kluszewski, Chuck Klein, Cecil Travis, and Jake Daubert. Barry Larkin was tied for 18th place in hitting, with Jake Beckley, at .300. Willie Mays could do no better than .259, Hank Aaron came in at .298, Ernie Banks was at .256, and Ken Griffey Jr. was at .262. Ten of the eleven home-run leaders were white (Willie Stargell was the token black), and ten of the eleven RBI leaders were white (Stargell finished sixth). In the pitching department, only Bob Gibson could crack the white monopoly, finishing sixth in ERA. All ten leaders in victories and all eleven leaders in saves were white. Black pitchers, in general, fared badly. Of the six black pitchers, only one — Pedro Martinez — had a winning record (9–6). The six black pitchers together had a combined record of just 43–56, for a percentage of .434.

The Strat-O-Matic game is an interesting exercise, but it needs to be refined and then run again. Injuries should be eliminated from the computer program. The best decade of the century should not be determined by injuries. The 1990s statistics should be adjusted downward to take into account their declining years. The home runs should be adjusted — up for the 1900s and 1910s and down for the 1990s. Pitching rotations and complete games should reflect the actual strategy of the period, as should the use of relief pitchers. The program also needs to be analyzed carefully to determine why the black players fared so badly.

During the last half of the twentieth century, organized baseball was still somewhat blinded by a whites-only mentality, but the situation seems to be gradually improving. David Nemec's fine book, *The Great American Baseball Team Book* selected all-star teams for three eras after integration — 1942 to 1960, 1961 to 1976, and 1977 to 1992. The American League, which historically trails its senior partner in the number of black players, had one black player on its first era all-star team — Minnie Minoso. The next era included 3 blacks out of 11 players, and the last era had 5 black players on a 12-man roster — Randolph, Puckett, Henderson, Winfield, and Murray. The National League era all-star teams included 4 black players out of 11 on the 1942–1960 team, 10 blacks on the 11-man roster of the 1961–1976 team, and 5 black players on the 12-man roster of the 1976 to 1992 team. In total, the two leagues had 28 black players on the era all-star teams out of a total of 68 players, a 41 percent black representation.

The Associated Press's list of the greatest baseball players of the twentieth century included three black players from a list of the ten greatest — Mays, Aaron, and Jackie Robinson.

And the beat goes on. In Street and Smith's *Guide to Baseball 2000,* 9 of the top 19 players on the 1999 American League's Most Valuable Player list were black. In the National League, there were 9 black players in the top 25. Once again, black players represented 41 percent of the major league's 44 Most Valuable Players.

It does seem as if the black major league players are beginning to receive more recognition now than they did when Couzens's poll was taken in 1969, the Strat-O-Matic computer game notwithstanding. All-star teams in recent years have a much better blend of white players and black players. Some of the problems encountered when selecting major league all-star teams, such as the Street and Smith's 1941–1991 teams, was due, not to the mindset of the voters, but to the makeup of the leagues. The National League was the leader in integration, and their teams had many more black players than American League teams did.

The major problem facing baseball at the present time is lack of appreciation for the immense skills of the old-time Negro League players. The two All-Century team polls discussed above included a few highly visible Negro League players, a no-brainer that the pollsters apparently added to pacify the Negro League supporters. It becomes obvious from polls like those that very few mainstream baseball experts are familiar with the Negro League players. Occasionally, familiar names like Paige and Gibson will be pulled out of a hat to fill out a candidate list, and even names like Bell, Charleston, Leonard, and Dandridge will be bandied about infrequently, but it is all a charade. If you were to ask the experts why those players should be on an all-time all-star baseball team, most of them couldn't give you an intelligent answer.

It is doubtful that the image of the great Negro League ballplayers will change until the baseball experts are educated in Negro League history as well as in the accomplishments of its legendary players. Hopefully the efforts of Negro League authors, historians, and researchers, like John Holway, Robert W. Peterson, Brent Kelley, Dick Clark, Larry Lester, James A. Riley, and others, will help to rectify that situation in the near future.

Hall of Fame Candidates: Players' Selections

Organized baseball has made significant strides in making the game color blind in the past several years, but there is still a long road to travel before it can truly be called "America's Game." The aforementioned polls, and the Negro League blindspot of the National Baseball Hall of Fame, continue to present problems for the fair-minded citizens of this great country.

In order to ascertain how many Negro League players deserve consideration for admittance into the Hall, a survey was sent to more than 150 former Negro League players, Negro League historians, and authors. There were actually two surveys conducted. The first survey asked the respondents to select the 27 players they thought should be in the Hall of Fame. The number of 27 players is not a quota *per se*. It is not an arbitrary number chosen at random, as are the quotas set by the National Baseball Hall of Fame. It is an estimate based on the data presented earlier, which showed a total of 147 players having been elected to the Hall of Fame by the Baseball Writers Association of America prior to 1962. It is as accurate an estimate as can be determined under the circumstances. If the percentage of black players to white players was the same prior to 1962 as it was during the period from 1962 through 1999 (29 percent), then the 147 Hall of Fame inductees should have included 43 black players. Since 16 Negro League veterans were elected to Cooperstown by the Veterans and Negro League Committees prior to 2000, another 27 players deserve recognition.

The second survey requested that the respondents choose their All-Time Negro League All-Star Team.

Surveys were sent to all former Negro League players who were active in the leagues prior to the time that Jackie Robinson broke the color barrier. The survey was actually conducted over a period of about five years, so some of the respondents are now deceased, but their input lives on. Fortunately, some of the greatest players in Negro League history contributed to the survey before they passed on — Buck Leonard, Lou Dials, Cowan "Bubba" Hyde, and Leon Day, as well as Negro League historian Normal "Tweed" Webb, among others. Surveys were also sent to Negro League historians, authors, researchers, and members of the Society for American Baseball Research (SABR) Negro League Committee.

A total of 59 returns were received out of 171 surveys sent, a remarkable 35 percent. A normal return rate would be in the 10–20 percent range.

The 28 Negro League veterans who responded to the survey included four players who are currently members of the National Baseball Hall of Fame — Buck Leonard, Leon Day, Monte Irvin, and Larry Doby — and Negro League legends "Double Duty" Radcliffe, Rodolfo Fernandez, and Buck O'Neil, plus the famous Negro League historian Normal "Tweed" Webb.

On the non-player side, participants included well-known Negro League authors Robert W. Peterson, John Holway, Brent Kelley, Dick Clark, and Larry Lester. Not all the contributors agreed with my request for 27 selections. Brent Kelley, Bob Peterson, and Jim Overmyer objected to a quota system. Their objection is quite valid. As Kelley pointed out, "I don't think a quota system is even marginally valid for Hall of Fame selection." Peterson thought my logic was faulty in selecting 27 players. And Overmyer noted that he wasn't sure he could find 27 men who ought to be in the Hall. Hopefully, the reasoning described above will satisfy the concerns of the respondents. For the record, Kelley selected 19 players, while Peterson chose 9, and Overmyer 12.

John Holway left out some talented Negro League players because they did not play 10 years in the Negro Leagues, and therefore did not meet the 10-year requirement established by the Hall of Fame. For my survey, I did not consider the ten year requirement to be a necessity for Negro League players because many of them played baseball year-round. In the summer, they played league ball in the United States, and in the winter they played in Mexico, Cuba, Puerto Rico, the Dominican Republic, and other countries throughout the western hemisphere. Some even played in an integrated winter league in California against white professionals, many of them from the major leagues. Chino Smith for instance, who is generally considered to be the greatest hitter in Negro League history, had a relatively short Negro League career of just six years. However, he also played five seasons in Cuba which, in my mind, qualifies him for Hall of Fame consideration. Another outstanding Negro Leaguer, Dobie Moore, was one of the four greatest shortstops in Negro League history, along with John Henry Lloyd, Dick Lundy, and Willie Wells. But again, Moore's career was cut short by an accident, leaving him with a brief seven-year career. Once again, I would review his overall career. In addition to his Negro League service, he also played several years in the California Winter league against major league opposition and two years in Cuba. His statistics speak for themselves. His .355 Negro League batting average is sixth all-time, behind Chino Smith's .434, and his Cuban Winter League average of .356 is third behind Jud Wilson (.372) and Oscar Charleston (.365). His combined average of .355 is the third highest batting average of any player who played in both the Negro Leagues and the Cuban Winter League. Chino Smith is first at .378, with Jud Wilson second (.357), Oscar Charleston fourth (.354), and Josh Gibson fifth (.353).

By comparison, a look at the career of Sandy Koufax will expose the fallacy in the Hall of Fame's 10-year service requirement. Koufax was, without a doubt, the greatest pitcher in baseball from 1961 through 1966. His 129–47 won-lost record, a .733 winning percentage, would be Hall of Fame numbers in any era. However, his 36–40 record from 1955 through 1960 was mediocre. Should his record during those years be considered in evaluating Koufax for induction into the Hall? I think not. Sandy Koufax had a Hall of Fame career, but it lasted only six years. Both Dobie Moore and Chino Smith had equally impressive numbers over a longer period of time. By Hall of Fame standards, neither Moore nor Smith would qualify for induction, since their careers did not last the necessary 10 years. However, if either or both of them played another three or four years, even with mediocre results, they would be eligible for induction into the Hall of Fame under the 10-year rule. Ridiculous, isn't it?

The following pages present the Hall of Fame selections made by 28 veterans of the old Negro Leagues. The respondents, who were asked to vote for 27 players, played professional baseball from as early as 1926 to as late as 1952. All of them were members of Negro League teams at some time prior to 1947.

JIMMIE ARMSTEAD

Jimmie Armstead enjoyed a 10-year career in the Negro Leagues between 1938 and 1949. He was a pitcher and an outfielder for the Indianapolis ABCs, the St. Louis Stars, the Baltimore Elite Giants, and the Philadelphia

Stars. According to James A. Riley, Armstead batted .294 in 1940. Some of his more noteworthy teammates included Quincy Trouppe, Roy Campanella, Bill Byrd, Sammy T. Hughes, George Scales, Joe Black, Junior Gilliam, Willie Wells, Bus Clarkson, and Barney Brown.

Armstead, who is now about 80 years old, lives in New Rochelle, New York.

ARMSTEAD'S SELECTIONS

Catcher: Biz Mackey, Louis Santop
Pitcher: Dick Redding, Ray Brown, Hilton Smith, Chet Brewer, Ted Trent, Dizzy Dismukes, Sam Streeter
First Base: Mule Suttles
Second Base: Sammy T. Hughes, George Scales, Newt Allen, Marvin Williams
Shortstop: Sam Bankhead, Bus Clarkson, Pee Wee Butts
Third Base: Oliver Marcelle, Dewey Creacy, Hank Thompson, Dave Malarcher, Felton Snow
Outfield: Turkey Stearnes, Cristobal Torriente, Willard Brown, Jimmy Crutchfield, Wild Bill Wright

Biz Mackey is one of the five greatest catchers in baseball history. (Photograph courtesy John B. Holway.)

HERBERT BARNHILL

Herb Barnhill, another octogenarian, is now enjoying the sunny climes of Jacksonville, Florida, but 60 years ago he was a sturdy backstop for the Jacksonville Red Caps of the Negro American League. His nine-year Negro League career, between 1938 and 1946, included stops with the Cleveland Bears, Kansas City Monarchs, and Chicago American Giants in addition to the Red Caps.

Barnhill's more well-known teammates included Newt Allen, Willard Brown, Buck O'Neil, Satchel Paige, Hilton Smith, Hank Thompson, Chet Brewer, Jimmy Crutchfield, and Art Pennington.

BARNHILL'S SELECTIONS

Catcher: Double Duty Radcliffe
Pitcher: Hilton Smith
First Base: Buck O'Neil
Outfield: Willard Brown

He, as all the respondents were, was requested not to vote for the 16 players who were already installed in the National Baseball Hall of Fame.

JOE BLACK

Joe Black was an outstanding pitcher in the Negro Leagues from 1943 to 1950. He joined the Brooklyn Dodgers in 1952 and was a major factor in their National League championship chase. He pitched 56 games in relief, winning 15, losing 4, and posting a 2.15 earned run average. He was voted the National League's Rookie of the Year. In the World Series that year, Black was a surprise starter in game one and pitched a complete-game six-hitter, winning 4–2.

Black declined to participate in the survey, saying only, "I don't assist anyone with publications unless I know how the Negro League veterans will be compensated."

BILL "READY" CASH

William Walker Cash was born in Round Oak, Georgia, on February 21, 1919. He began an excellent eight-year Negro League career with the Philadelphia Stars in 1943. In 1951, he left the Stars to join organized baseball with Granby of the Provincial League. He retired in 1952, after a season with Waterloo in the III League.

The rugged 6'2", 195-pound catcher played in two Negro League all-star games. His Negro League career batting average was .261. He subsequently hit a solid .296 with 16 home runs in just 321 at-bats for Granby. He also hit .310 in Mexico in 1950 and .330 in two years in the Dominican Summer League.

His teammates included Gene Benson, Barney Brown, Oscar Charleston, Felton Snow, Jim West, Bus Clarkson, Harry "Suitcase" Simpson, and Satchel Paige.

Bill Cash is retired and lives in Philadelphia. He is a member of the

Hilton Smith had the third highest winning percentage in The Negro Leagues. (Photograph courtesy John B. Holway)

Society for American Baseball Research (SABR) and is on their Negro Leagues Committee.

CASH'S SELECTIONS

Catcher: Biz Mackey, Louis Santop

Pitcher: Dick Redding, Hilton Smith, Webster McDonald, Slim Jones

Second Base: Newt Allen

Shortstop: Dick Lundy

Third Base: Hank Thompson

Outfield: Turkey Stearnes, Jimmy Crutchfield, Wild Bill Wright, Gene Benson

ROSS DAVIS

Ross "Satchel" Davis was a right handed pitcher who pitched for the Baltimore Elite Giants, Cleveland Buckeyes, and Boston Blues from 1940 to 1947, with two years out for military service. Davis, who is now 81 years old, lives in Long Beach, California.

His teammates included Chet Brewer, Sam Jethroe, Theolic Smith, Parnell Woods, Quincy Trouppe, Sad Sam Jones, and Al Smith. Jethroe, Jones, and Smith went on to enjoy successful major league careers.

DAVIS' SELECTIONS

Catcher: Biz Mackey, Louis Santop

Pitcher: Ray Brown, Max Manning, Hilton Smith, Chet Brewer, Bill Byrd

First Base: Buck O'Neil, Bob Boyd

Second Base: Sammy T. Hughes, Newt Allen

Shortstop: Artie Wilson, Dick Lundy
Third Base: Hank Thompson, Jud Wilson
Outfield: Turkey Stearnes, Willard Brown, Jelly Gardner, Sam Jethroe, Wild Bill Wright, Vic Harris

---

LARRY DOBY

Lawrence Eugene Doby was born in Camden, South Carolina, on December 13, 1923. He began his Negro League career with the Newark Eagles in 1942. The 17-year-old second baseman teamed up with veteran shortstop Willie Wells to give Abe Manley's team a hard-hitting, smooth-fielding middle infield combination. Doby enjoyed a short but sensational Negro League career, during which he hit a .384 (second all-time), with 27 home runs a year. He led the Eagles to two Negro National League pennants, in 1946 and again in 1947, with averages of .341 and a sizzling .414. The smooth-swinging southpaw slugger was signed to a major league contract by Bill Veeck of the Cleveland Indians midway through the '47 season, just a few short weeks after Jackie Robinson joined the Brooklyn Dodgers. He was the first black to play in the American League, and he had to endure the same intense racist opposition that his National League counterpart did. In spite of the considerable emotional trauma that accompanied his 13-year career, Doby still put up Hall of Fame numbers.

He pounded the ball at a career .283 clip with 253 home runs in 5,348 at-bats. He played in two World Series, was a member of one World Championship club, and was selected for seven American League all-star teams. He had two .300 seasons over his major league career, batted in over 100 runs five times, hit 20 or more homers eight times, and scored more than 100 runs three times. He led the league in runs scored in 1952 (104), home runs in 1952 (32) and 1954 (32), and in RBIs, in 1954 (126). He was inducted into the National Baseball Hall of Fame in 1999.

During his tenure in the Negro Leagues, Larry Doby played with such outstanding players as fellow Hall of Famers Willie Wells, Ray Dandridge, Leon Day, and Monte Irvin, as well as potential Hall of Fame candidates Mule Suttles, Bus Clarkson, and Biz Mackey.

DOBY'S SELECTIONS

Catcher: Biz Mackey, Louis Santop
Pitcher: Dick Redding, Ray Brown, Chet Brewer, Bill Byrd, Slim Jones

First Base: Mule Suttles, Edgar Wesley, Bob Boyd
Second Base: Sammy T. Hughes, George Scales, Newt Allen
Shortstop: Sam Bankhead, Artie Wilson, Dick Lundy
Third Base: Hank Thompson, Jud Wilson
Outfield: Turkey Stearnes, Willard Brown, Jimmy Crutchfield, Rap Dixon, Sam Jethroe, Wild Bill Wright, Vic Harris

MAHLON DUCKETT

Mahlon Duckett played in the Negro Leagues from 1940 to 1950. He joined his hometown Philadelphia Stars as a 17-year-old infielder in 1940. He played both shortstop and third base in his rookie season and did a creditable defensive job at both positions, but he was penalized by a weak bat, hitting just .234. As he matured, he became the regular second baseman, teaming with Frank Austin to give the Stars one of the best double-play combinations in the league. He also raised his batting average into the .250 range and learned how to handle the bat with finesse. Batting in the second slot in the batting order, he became a good bunter and an effective hit-and-run man. He also had outstanding speed and was a good base stealer.

Mahlon Duckett selected only 14 players, but I believe that was the result of a communication problem between us, not that he thought only 14 Negro League players deserved consideration for induction into the Hall of Fame. The asterisk (*) indicates Duckett's first choice at the position.

DUCKETT'S SELECTIONS

Catcher: Biz Mackey* Louis Santop
Pitcher: Max Manning, Hilton Smith*
First Base: Mule Suttles*, Bob Boyd
Second Base: Sammy T. Hughes*, Bill Monroe
Shortstop: Dick Lundy*, Artie Wilson
Third Base: Oliver Marcelle*, Dewey Creacy
Outfield: Wild Bill Wright*, Turkey Stearnes

AL FENNAR

Al "Cleffie" Fennar was born in Wilmington, North Carolina, on May 12, 1911. The stocky infielder joined the Harlem Stars in New York after graduation from high school in that city. He played second base, short-stop, and third base for the Stars, the New York Black Yankees, the Brooklyn Royal Giants, the Atlantic City Bacharach Giants, the Cuban Stars, and the Pennyslvania Red Caps over a four-year period.

Fennar often batted in the leadoff position to take advantage of his outstanding speed. While he was with the Black Yankees, the team wore old New York Yankee uniforms and, according to James A. Riley, Fennar had the honor of wearing the immortal Lou Gehrig's number 4.

While he was with the Harlem Stars, he became close friends with John Beckwith, the Negro League's "bad boy." "The Black Bomber" was a devastating hitter, but he was also a brawler, on and off the field. He took a liking to Fennar however, probably because of Cleffie's aggressive play.

Baseball, particularly Negro League baseball, was not a high-paying profession in the early '30s. In fact, it was usually a hand-to-mouth existence. As a result, Fennar left the Negro Leagues in 1935 to find a permanent job, and he spent the next 12 years playing baseball on industrial teams, and coaching youth baseball. He presently resides in Palm Bay, Florida.

FENNAR'S SELECTIONS

Catcher: Louis Santop, Double Duty Radcliffe
Pitcher: Dick Redding, Hilton Smith, Bill Holland
First Base: Mule Suttles, Huck Rile
Second Base:
Shortstop: Dick Lundy, John Beckwith
Third Base: Oliver Marcelle, Jud Wilson
Outfield: Turkey Stearnes, Jimmy Crutchfield, Clint Thomas

Al Fennar wrote:

> Mr. McNeil:
> I am only marking whom I have played with or against. I can not in good conscience do otherwise.
> The Hall of Fame was originated to have a place where outstanding ballplayers could be recognized. John Beckwith was an outstanding ballplayer. He belongs in the Hall of Fame.
> You have taken on an immense task—case in point, myself—I played under the names Fino, — Dario, and others.
> > Good Luck,
> > Al "Cleffie" Fennar
> P.S. I just turned 88 years of age.

BERNARD FERNANDEZ

Bernard Fernandez was born in Cuba, but played in the Negro Leagues, off and on, from 1938 to 1949. He was a right handed pitcher who was big, fast, and wild. During his 12-year career he played with the Atlanta Black Crackers, Jacksonville Red Caps, Pittsburgh Crawfords, and New York Black Yankees. His teammates included Pee Wee Butts, George Crowe, Marlin Carter, Red Moore, Joe Greene, and Parnell Woods.

FERNANDEZ'S SELECTIONS

Catcher: Biz Mackey, Louis Santop, Double Duty Radcliffe, Robert Clark, Josh Gibson

Pitcher: Dick Redding, Ray Brown, Max Manning, Hilton Smith, Chet Brewer, Bill Byrd, Dave Barnhill

First Base: Mule Suttles, Buck O'Neil, Red Moore

Second Base: Sammy T. Hughes

Shortstop: Sam Bankhead, Artie Wilson, Dick Lundy, Pee Wee Butts

Third Base: Hank Thompson, Jud Wilson

Outfield: Cristobal Torriente, Willard Brown, Jimmy Crutchfield, Sam Jethroe, Wild Bill Wright, Fats Jenkins, Piper Davis

It is obvious from his selections that Bernard Fernandez, like most Negro League players, was a student of baseball history. His selections of Louis Santop and Dick Redding, who had retired before Fernandez began his professional career, reveals a thorough knowledge of the game. Also, his selection of Robert Clark, a sterling defensive catcher but a weak hitter who enjoyed a 26-year career in the Negro Leagues, shows the thought given to his choices.

RODOLFO FERNANDEZ

Rodolfo "Rudy" Fernandez was born in Havana, Cuba, on June 27, 1911, and grew up to be one of the top pitchers in the western hemisphere during the 1930s and 1940s. The 6'1" 190-pounder was a right handed pitcher with excellent speed, a devastating sinker, and pinpoint control. He toiled in the Negro Leagues, with the New York Cubans and the Cuban Stars, for twelve years, from 1932 to 1944. He played winter ball in the Cuban Winter League from 1931 to 1944, compiling a 50–38 record. He

No one hit a baseball any farther than big Mule Suttles. He averaged 40 home runs a year in the Negro Leagues. (Photograph courtesy Dr. Lawrence D. Hogan.)

also pitched in Venezuela and Canada and was a member of the famous Cuidad Trujillo team in the 1937 Dominican Summer League.

James Riley noted that "He was especially effective against major-league teams. In the spring of 1937 in Havana he defeated the defending National League champion New York Giants, 4–0, on 4 hits; defeated the Brooklyn Dodgers, 3–0, in another Cuban exhibition game; and beat the Cincinnati Reds, 2–1, in Puerto Rico."

He was inducted into the Cuban Baseball Hall of Fame in 1983.

Fernandez settled in New York City after leaving baseball and worked in a hospital until his retirement.

FERNANDEZ'S SELECTIONS

Catcher: Biz Mackey, Louis Santop, Double Duty Radcliffe
Pitcher: Max Manning, Jose Mendez, Bill Byrd

First Base: Mule Suttles, Buck O'Neil, George Giles
Second Base: George Scales
Shortstop: Sam Bankhead, Artie Wilson, Dick Lundy
Third Base: Oliver Marcelle
Outfield: Turkey Stearnes, Cristobal Torriente, Valentin Dreke, Jimmy Crutchfield, Rap Dixon, Bernardo Baro, Sam Jethroe, Alejandro Oms, Wild Bill Wright

Rudy Fernandez finished his correspondence with the note: "To me, all of these players should be in the HOF."

WILLIE GRACE

Willie Grace was born in Memphis, Tennessee, on June 30, 1918. He enjoyed a nine-year career in Negro League baseball, from 1942 to 1950, playing with the Cincinnati Buckeyes, Cleveland Buckeyes, Louisville Buckeyes, and Houston Eagles. He played one year of minor league ball, with Erie in the Middle Atlantic League, hitting .299 in 120 games, in 1951.

Grace was a 6', 170-pound switch-hitting outfielder and a good clutch hitter in his prime. He played in two Negro League World Series, hitting .313 in the 1945 classic, as the Buckeyes swept the Homestead Grays four straight. He also appeared in two all-star games. From 1946 through 1948, Grace strung together averages of .305, .301, and .322.

Willie Grace met a girl in Erie, married her, and retired after the 1951 season at the age of 33. He still resides in Erie.

GRACE'S SELECTIONS

Catcher: Biz Mackey
Pitcher: Hilton Smith
First Base: Mule Suttles
Second Base: Newt Allen
Shortstop: Artie Wilson
Third Base: Hank Thompson
Outfield: Jimmy Crutchfield, Willard Brown, Sam Jethroe, Wild Bill Wright

Willie Grace, like many of the others, did not choose 27.

MONTE IRVIN

Monte Irvin was elected to the National Baseball Hall of Fame by the Negro Leagues Committee in 1973 for his achievements in the Negro Leagues, but his career is evidence that he was a Hall of Fame player in the major leagues as well.

Irvin was born in Halesburg, Alabama, on February 25, 1919. He developed into a super athlete in high school in Orange, New Jersey, where he won 16 varsity letters in baseball, football, basketball, and track. Effa Manley signed the 18-year-old slugger to a Newark Eagles Negro League contract in 1937. He went on to star for the Eagles for ten years, with three years out for military service during World War II.

Irvin played all the infield and outfield positions with the Eagles, before settling down in center field. He was an outstanding defensive player, with good range and a strong throwing arm. It was at the plate, however, where the 6'2", 195-pound right handed batter dominated the game. He compiled a .345 career batting average in the Negro Leagues (ninth all-time for players with 1000 or more at-bats), averaging 26 home runs for every 550 at-bats. He captured two batting championships, batting .382 in 1941 and .401 in 1946. He also won two home run titles, with 6 (in 108 at-bats) in 1941 and 14 (in 287 at-bats) in 1946.

Irvin terrorized other leagues around the western hemisphere, in addition to the Negro Leagues. He pounded the ball at a .397 pace in Mexico (with 20 home runs in just 237 at-bats) and a .359 pace in Puerto Rico. His Cuban Winter League average was just .266, but he did lead the league in home runs in 1948–49.

The New York Giants signed Irvin to a major league contract in 1949, at the age of 30. He went on to compile an envious record in organized baseball, even though his prime years were behind him. He hit a tough .293 in the major leagues over an eight-year period, and he destroyed AAA minor league pitching to the tune of .373. He sparked the Giants to two National League pennants and one World Championship. In 1951, as Leo Durocher's troops overcame the Brooklyn Dodgers in the last game of the season, Irvin led the way with 24 home runs, a league-leading 121 runs batted in, and a .312 batting average. He went on to lead the team at the plate in the World Series as well, pounding out 11 base hits in six games, good for a .458 average.

After his playing career ended, Monte Irvin held down a variety of jobs in industry, as well as baseball. He served as assistant to the baseball commissioner for 17 years, was chairman of the National Baseball Hall of Fame's Negro League's Committee for several years, and now serves on the Hall of Fame's Veterans Committee.

His 26 selections include eleven players who are already members of the Hall of Fame.

IRVIN'S SELECTIONS

Catcher: Biz Mackey, Josh Gibson*
Pitcher: Satchel Paige*, Bullet Joe Rogan*, Leon Day*, Dick Redding, Ray Brown, Andy Cooper, Hilton Smith, Webster McDonald, Slim Jones.
First Base: Buck Leonard*, George Giles
Second Base: Sammy T. Hughes, Newt Allen
Shortstop: Willie Wells*, Dick Lundy
Third Base: Ray Dandridge*, Oliver Marcelle
Outfield: Turkey Stearnes, Cristobal Torriente, Pete Hill, Rap Dixon, Wild Bill Wright, Cool Papa Bell*, Oscar Charleston*, Martin Dihigo*

The ten players marked with an asterisk (*) are already members of the National Baseball Hall of Fame and are not part of this study.

Monte Irvin's great respect for the pitchers from the old Negro League is evident in his selections. Nine of his twenty-seven candidates are pitchers.

He had additional comments on some players.

"Dobie Moore was a good shortstop with a great arm, but an injury cut his career short. Willie Wells was better."

"Chino Smith — didn't play long, died early, but was a great left handed hitter that hit mostly to left field, but hit left handed pitchers as well as right handers. Good fielder (LF) with an accurate arm."

"Bullet Rogan — great pitcher and hitter with a fine fastball, real good curve and wonderful control. One of the greatest in the history of Negro baseball."

"Smokey Joe Williams was as good or better than Satchel Paige, his best pitch was his fastball, and he had great control."

"Turkey Stearnes should be in the Hall of Fame. When Cool Papa Bell was alive Turkey's name was mentioned and Cool said 'Take me out of the Hall and put Turkey in.' He could hit, run, throw, field, and hit with power. I only saw him play once, in 1934, against the Eagles. He hit the first pitch for a home run as leadoff."

This study preceded the election of Turkey Stearnes and Hilton Smith into the HOF (in 2000 and 2001 respectively) and so they are commonly named selections.

CHARLES JOHNSON

Not much is known of Charles Johnson. According to the Negro League player listing from the Society for American Baseball Research (SABR), Johnson played for the Chicago American Giants in 1932 and '33. He still resides in Chicago.

Johnson was certainly bullish on the capabilities of the Negro League players. He selected 39 players as potential candidates for the National Baseball Hall of Fame, but his choices do show a considerable amount of thought, as well as expertise in the field of Negro League history. They cover a period of more than 50 years, from Pete Hill's rookie season with the Pittsburgh Keystones in 1899 to Buck O'Neil's final year with the Kansas City Monarchs in 1954.

JOHNSON'S SELECTIONS

Catcher: Biz Mackey, Bruce Petway, Double Duty Radcliffe

Pitcher: Dick Redding, John Donaldson, Max Manning, Andy Cooper, Hilton Smith, Plunk Drake, Frank Wickware, Jose Mendez, Chet Brewer, Ted Trent, Webster McDonald, Sam Streeter

First Base: Mule Suttles, Buck O'Neil, Huck Rile, Ben Taylor, George Giles

Second Base: George Scales, Newt Allen, Bingo DeMoss

Shortstop: Dobie Moore, Artie Wilson, Dick Lundy

Third Base: Oliver Marcelle, Dewey Creacy, Dave Malarcher, Bobby Robinson

Outfield: Turkey Stearnes, Cristobal Torriente, Pete Hill, Jelly Gardner, Jimmy Crutchfield, Jimmy Lyons, Heavy Johnson, Rap Dixon, Sam Jethroe, Vic Harris

JOSH JOHNSON

Josh Johnson was a big, rugged catcher, whose nine-year Negro League career was cut short by World War II. The man known as Brute was a former college football player, who stood 6'1" and weighed in at a steel-hard 195 pounds. He was a formidable force behind the plate and possessed a strong throwing arm. He was not a fast runner, but he hit for average, and with considerable power.

Johnson was an anomaly in the Negro Leagues. He was a college graduate. When he was drafted into the army in World War II, he entered Officers Candidate School (OCS) and graduated as a second lieutenant. He stayed in the army reserve after the war ended, finally retiring with the rank of major. He also returned to college, earning a masters degree in education. He taught school for many years, eventually working his way up to school principal. In later years he was appointed to the position of assistant state superintendent of education in Illinois. During his career, Johnson played with some of the greatest Negro League players ever to step foot on a ballfield — Ray Brown, Buck Leonard, Josh Gibson, Sam Bankhead, Jud Wilson, Barney Brown, Vic Harris, and Bill Holland.

JOHNSON'S SELECTIONS

Catcher: Biz Mackey, Double Duty Radcliffe
Pitcher: Ray Brown, Max Manning, Andy Cooper, Hilton Smith, Chet Brewer, Webster McDonald, Bill Byrd, Bill Holland
First Base: Mule Suttles, George Giles
Second Base: Sammy T. Hughes, George Scales, Newt Allen
Shortstop: Sam Bankhead, Artie Wilson, Dick Lundy
Third Base: Dewey Creacy, Hank Thompson, Jud Wilson
Outfield: Turkey Stearnes, Cristobal Torriente, Willard Brown, Wild Bill Wright, Fats Jenkins, Vic Harris

Josh added the following comments to his survey. "Bullet Joe Rogan, Smokey Joe Williams, and Turkey Stearnes— Hall of Famers. My opinion is that they were just that! Quality par excellence."

Note: All three players were elected to the Hall of Fame subsequent to Johnson's comments.

WILLIAM "RED" LINDSAY

According to SABR's Negro League Player Listing, William H. "Red" Lindsay was a position player for the Hilldale club in the American Negro League in 1931 and 1932. He played with some of the greatest players ever to put on a uniform. His teammates included Martin Dihigo, Judy Johnson, Biz Mackey, Webster McDonald, Nip Winters, and Crush Holloway.

LINDSAY'S SELECTIONS

Catcher: Biz Mackey, Louis Santop, Double Duty Radcliffe
Pitcher: Dick Redding, Chet Brewer, Nip Winters, Webster Mcdonald, Slim Jones

First Base: Mule Suttles, Buck O'Neil
Second Base: George Scales, Newt Allen
Shortstop: Bus Clarkson, Dick Lundy, John Beckwith
Third Base: Hank Thompson, Jud Wilson
Outfield: Turkey Stearnes, Willard Brown, Jelly Gardner, Jimmy Crutchfield, Rap Dixon, Sam Jethroe, Alejandro Oms, Fats Jenkins, Crush Holloway, Vic Harris

Lindsay added: "I played with several of the players on your list, plus several that are already in the Hall of Fame, including Roy Campanella. I am now 94 years old. Had a birthday on April 15th [1999]."

MAX MANNING

Maxwell "Max" Manning was a tall, slim, right handed pitcher who had a full complement of pitches, including a fastball, a curve, and a slider. Known as Dr. Cyclops because of his thick glasses, the 6'4", 185-pounder pitched in the Negro Leagues from 1938 through 1949, with four years out for military service during World War II. He was essentially a low-ball pitcher whose borderline control kept batters from digging in.

He was a member of the 1946 Negro League World Champion Newark Eagles, compiling a season record of 15–1. His career statistics, according to Brent Kelley, showed a 77–36 won-lost record, a brilliant .681 winning percentage.

In addition to his Negro League experience, Manning also pitched four years in Cuba, two years in Mexico, and single seasons in Venezuela, Puerto Rico, Canada, and the Dominican Republic. He also pitched successfully against major league all-star teams. In one game, according to James A. Riley, he fanned 14 big leaguers, including New York Yankee star, Charlie "King Kong" Keller, three times.

A shoulder operation ended his career prematurely in 1949.

Manning's Selections

Catcher: Biz Mackey, Louis Santop
Pitcher: Dick Redding, Ray Brown, Rats Henderson, Hilton Smith, Chet Brewer, Slim Jones
First Base: Mule Suttles, Ben Taylor
Second Base: Sammy T. Hughes, George Scales.
Shortstop: Dick Lundy, John Beckwith

Third Base: Oliver Marcelle
Outfield: Turkey Stearnes, Cristobal Torriente, Pete Hill, Willard Brown, Rap Dixon, Wild Bill Wright, Crush Holloway

---

FRAN O. MATTHEWS

Fran Matthews was a good, all-around first baseman, who spent nine years in the Negro Leagues, most of them with the Newark Eagles. Like many professional athletes, his career was cut short by almost three years of military service in World War II. He played with the Eagles and the Baltimore Elite Giants from 1938 through 1942, piling up a .323 batting average in 1941. On his return from the army, he played one last year with Newark before retiring. He batted .309 in his final season.

Matthews played on the same team with four future Hall of Famers— Leon Day, Ray Dandridge, Monte Irvin, and Willie Wells— as well as potential Hall of Famers Mule Suttles, Jimmy Crutchfield, Max Manning, Biz Mackey, and Dick Lundy.

Fran Matthews, who made his home in Los Angeles, California, in later years, made the following 18 selections.

MATTHEWS' SELECTIONS

Catcher: Biz Mackey
Pitcher: Ray Brown, Hilton Smith, Chet Brewer, Webster McDonald
First Base: Mule Suttles, Buck O'Neil, Ben Taylor
Second Base: Sammy T. Hughes, George Scales
Shortstop: Sam Bankhead, Bus Clarkson, Artie Wilson, Dick Lundy

Jimmie Crutchfield was an outstanding all-around outfielder for the great Pittsburgh Crawfords.

Third Base: Dewey Creacy
Outfield: Willard Brown, Jimmy Crutchfield, Wild Bill Wright

JAMES "RED" MOORE

Red Moore was a slick-fielding first baseman with a number of Negro League teams from 1936 to 1940. He also spent four years with the Atlanta Black Crackers, an independent traveling team. As James A. Riley noted, "...he was expert at handling ground balls, a master at catching bad throws and making it look easy, and he excelled at making a 3–6–3 double play." Moore is considered to be the best fielding first basemen of all time by a number of baseball experts, but his career was too short for official recognition.

Moore was slight of build (5'10", 165 pounds), with little power, but he was a decent spray hitter, whose batting average hovered around the .280 range. He played three years with the Newark Eagles and two years with the Baltimore Elite Giants, teaming with such legendary players as Mule Suttles, Ray Dandridge, Willie Wells, Dick Lundy, Leon Day, Monte Irvin, Biz Mackey, Bill Byrd, Sammy T. Hughes, and Wild Bill Wright. His roommate was Roy Campanella.

World War II essentially ended Moore's professional baseball career. He entered industry after his discharge from the army and limited his ballplaying to weekend games with the traveling team in Atlanta.

MOORE'S SELECTIONS

Catcher: Biz Mackey, Louis Santop, Double Duty Radcliffe
Pitcher: Dick Redding, Ray Brown, Max Manning, Hilton Smith, Chet Brewer, Ted Trent, Bill Byrd, Slim Jones
First Base: Mule Suttles, Buck O'Neil, George Giles
Second Base: Sammy T. Hughes, George Scales, Newt Allen
Shortstop: Sam Bankhead, Artie Wilson, Dick Lundy, Pee Wee Butts.
Third Base: Hank Thompson, Jud Wilson
Outfield: Turkey Stearnes, Willard Brown, Jimmy Crutchfield, Wild Bill Wright, Vic Harris

BUCK O'NEIL

John Jordan "Buck" O'Neil has enjoyed a lifetime career in baseball. Now 88 years old (as of November 11, 1999), he continues to be an active force in Negro baseball. He completed a distinctive 19-year playing career in the Negro Leagues in 1955, which also included eight years at the helm of the Kansas City Monarchs. He managed the Monarchs to five pennants along the way. Moving into organized baseball, he joined the Chicago Cubs as a scout and signed future Hall of Famers Ernie Banks and Lou Brock . He eventually became the first black coach with a major league team, with the Cubs in 1952. He is a member of the National Baseball Hall of Fame Veterans Committee and is one of the founding fathers, chairman of the board, and chief spokesman for the Negro Leagues Museum in Kansas City.

On the field of play, Buck O'Neil was a hard-hitting, fancy-fielding first baseman, primarily with the Kansas City Monarchs . He was a member of the Monarchs when they won four straight pennants from 1939 to 1942, and hit a lusty .353 as they swept the powerful Homestead Grays in the first World Series between the Negro National League and American League teams. He captured the 1946 batting title with an average of .353, about 55 points above his career average.

O'NEIL'S SELECTIONS

Catcher: Biz Mackey, Louis Santop
Pitcher: Andy Cooper, Hilton Smith
First Base: Mule Suttles
Second Base: Sammy T. Hughes, Newt Allen
Shortstop: Dobie Moore, Dick Lundy, John Beckwith
Third Base:
Outfield: Turkey Stearnes, Cristobal Torriente, Willard Brown, Chino Smith, Jelly Gardner, Jimmy Lyons

---

DOUBLE DUTY RADCLIFFE

Ted "Double Duty" Radcliffe is one of the legends of Negro League baseball, as well as its leading character and, at 97 years old (on July 7, 1999), its oldest surviving member. Radcliffe is definitely a Hall of Fame candidate based on his almost mythical Negro League career. He was not only an outstanding pitcher from 1928 to 1950, he was also an all-star catcher. He acquired his nickname after a doubleheader in Yankee Stadium in 1932. He caught the opening game and drove in all the runs, as Satchel Paige tossed a 4–0 shutout. Then he came back in the nightcap to pitch a

6–0 shutout of his own. The next day, in the *New York American,* Damon Runyon called him Double Duty. The name stuck.

Radcliffe appeared in six Negro League all-star games—three as a pitcher, and three as a catcher. He batted .308 with one home run and went 1–0 on the mound. According to his biographer, Kyle P. McNary, Radcliffe compiled a lifetime batting average of .303, with 10 home runs for every 550 at-bats. His pitching record was a scintillating 128–49 (.727). McNary estimated that, if all the statistics were available for Double Duty's career, he would have hit 430 career home runs and racked up a record of 502–189 on the mound.

He hit a lusty .403 in 22 games against major league all-star teams and won three decisions on the mound, without a loss. Double Duty Radcliffe's Hall of Fame selections follow. Strangely enough, he didn't vote for himself. Modesty prevailed in this survey, although in other surveys he occasionally voted for himself. Double Duty selected 17 players, plus four others who were already members of the Hall.

RADCLIFFE'S SELECTIONS

Catcher: Larry Brown
Pitcher: Satchel Paige*, Willie Foster*, Ray Brown, Hilton Smith, Dave Brown, Chet Brewer, Ted Trent, Bill Byrd, Sam Streeter
First Base: Bob Boyd, George Giles
Second Base: Newt Allen
Shortstop: Willie Wells*
Third Base: Dave Malarcher
Outfield: Turkey Stearnes*, Willard Brown, Jimmy Crutchfield, Sam Jethroe, Wild Bill Wright, Vic Harris

Note: (*) denotes a player already in the Hall of Fame.

ULYSSES A. REDD

Ulysses A. Redd was the regular shortstop for the Birmingham Black Barons in 1940 and '41. He was another one of the players whose career was interrupted by World War II. After the war, he joined the Harlem Globetrotters traveling baseball team. He finished out his Negro League career with the Chicago American Giants in 1951.

His teammates included Parnell Woods, Dan Bankhead, Willie Wells, Satchel Paige, and Theolic Smith. He presently makes his home in Baton Rouge, Louisiana.

REDD'S SELECTIONS

Catcher: Biz Mackey, Double Duty Radcliffe
Pitcher: John Donaldson, Ray Brown, Hilton Smith, Chet Brewer, Slim Jones
First Base: Mule Suttles, Buck O'Neil, Ben Taylor, Bob Boyd, George Giles, Tank Carr
Second Base: George Scales, Newt Allen
Shortstop: Sam Bankhead, Artie Wilson, John Beckwith
Third Base: Oliver Marcelle, Dewey Creacy, Dave Malarcher.
Outfield: Turkey Stearnes, Willard Brown, Jimmy Crutchfield, Sam Jethroe, Vic Harris, Charlie Blackwell

---

BOBBY ROBINSON

Bobby Robinson was an outstanding defensive third baseman in the Negro Leagues for 18 years, beginning in 1925. He was an average hitter, who had his greatest success with the Detroit Stars from 1929 to 1931. He hit a personal high of .309 in 1929. Bobby Robinson was a brickmason for thirty years after his retirement from the game, and he still enjoys the creativity of his art, at 97 years old.

ROBINSON'S SELECTIONS

Catcher: Biz Mackey, Louis Santop
Pitcher: Dick Redding, John Donaldson, Ray Brown, Ted Trent, Sam Streeter
First Base: Mule Suttles, Ben Taylor
Second Base: Sammy T. Hughes, George Scales
Shortstop: Dobie Moore, Dick Lundy
Third Base: Oliver Marcelle, Dave Malarcher
Outfield: Cristobal Torriente, Pete Hill, Spot Poles, Rap Dixon, Wild Bill Wright, Sam Bankhead

Bobby Robinson didn't select an all-time Negro League all-star team, but he did select the greatest player(s) he ever saw and also described his greatest thrill.
Greatest Player(s): "Rogan and Charleston could hit that ball, and do everything else a good ballplayer needed to do, and they could do it better than the rest I saw."

Greatest Thrill: "One day I turned in an unassisted triple play and the great manager John McGraw was in the box near our bench with some of his New York Giants players. McGraw complimented me on a great play and told me that if I was only white he would have a place for me at third base on the Giants ballclub."

TOMMY SAMPSON

Tommy Sampson was an outstanding defensive second baseman for the Birmingham Black Barons during the 1940s. He appeared in four all-star games and two World Series for the Barons. During his last World Series, in 1944, he was severely injured in a car accident, his right leg was shattered and he was on the critical list for several days.

His career was never the same after the accident. He finished his ten-year career with the New York Cubans in 1949. For most of his career he was a .300 hitter and batted .354 in 1942. He now lives in retirement in Elizabeth City, North Carolina. He selected 17 candidates.

SAMPSON'S SELECTIONS

Catcher: Biz Mackey, Double Duty Radcliffe
Pitcher: Ray Brown, Sam Streeter
First Base: Buck O'Neil, Bob Boyd, George Giles
Second Base: Sammy T. Hughes, George Scales
Shortstop: Sam Bankhead, Artie Wilson
Third Base: Hank Thompson, Jud Wilson
Outfield: Willard Brown, Jimmy Crutchfield, Sam Jethroe, Wild Bill Wright

HERBERT H. SIMPSON

Unfortunately, little is known of the specifics of Herbert Simpson's Negro League career. His career apparently spanned 10 years, from 1942 through 1951. He broke in as an outfielder with the Birmingham Black Barons in 1942. He joined the Homestead Grays as a pitcher for the 1943 season, then left the league for four years. He may have been touring with the Harlem Globetrotters. He was definitely with the Globetrotters in 1948.

His last appearance was as a pitcher with the Chicago American Giants in 1951.

He played with such outstanding players as Piper Davis, Alex Radcliffe, Double Duty Radcliffe, Sam Bankhead, Cool Papa Bell, Vic Harris, Ray Brown, Josh Gibson, Buck Leonard, and Jud Wilson. Simpson now makes his home in New Orleans, Louisana.

SIMPSON'S SELECTIONS

Catcher: Bruce Petway

Pitcher: Dick Redding, Ray Brown, Max Manning, Hilton Smith, Frank Wickware, Chet Brewer, Ted Trent

First Base: Mule Suttles, Herbert Simpson

Second Base: Sammy T. Hughes, George Scales, Newt Allen, Frank Grant

Shortstop: Bus Clarkson, Artie Wilson, Dick Lundy, John Beckwith

Third Base: Dave Malarcher

Outfield: Turkey Stearnes, Willard Brown, Jimmy Crutchfield, Heavy Johnson, Sam Jethroe, Wild Bill Wright, Fats Jenkins, Crush Holloway, Vic Harris, Herbert Simpson

THE REV. HAROLD C. TINKER, SR.

The Reverend Harold Tinker was one of the original Negro League pioneers. Born in 1905, eventually Tinker, known as Hooks in his playing days, started playing baseball with the Pittsburgh Crawfords in 1927. He held down center field for the Crawfords, which at that time was a semi-pro team. He had good speed in the outfield and generally batted in the .290 range. He also served as manager.

One of the major accomplishments of Hooks Tinker's baseball career was signing a 16-year-old third baseman to a semi-pro contract in 1928. The kids name was Josh Gibson, and he became the regular catcher for the Crawfords until he jumped to the Homestead Grays two years later. As Tinker told John Holway in *Josh and Satch,* "He was the most tremendous hitter I've ever come across in baseball — I'm barring none."

Tinker stayed with the Pittsburgh Crawfords through the 1931 season, when they became a full fledged professional team. He played alongside such legends as Dick "Cannonball" Redding, Satchel Paige, Jimmy Crutchfield, and Sam Streeter.

After leaving baseball, Harold Tinker became a preacher in Pittsburgh.

TINKER'S SELECTIONS

Catcher: Biz Mackey, Double Duty Radcliffe
Pitcher: Ray Brown, Chet Brewer, Dizzy Dismukes, Sam Streeter, Harry Kincannon, Gilbert Hill, Howard Kimbro
First Base: Mule Suttles, Buck O'Neil, Claude Johnson
Second Base: George Scales, Newt Allen, Charlie Hughes
Shortstop: Bus Clarkson, Dick Lundy, John Beckwith
Third Base: Hank Thompson, Jud Wilson, Bucky Williams
Outfield: Jelly Gardner, Jimmy Crutchfield, Sam Jethroe, Fats Jenkins, Vic Harris, Neal Harris

The Rev. Tinker added a few other comments. Josh Gibson was "one of the greatest."

"Smokey Joe Williams deserves to be in the Hall of Fame." Note: He was elected to the Hall in 1999.

"Sam Streeter also deserves to be in the Hall of Fame."

He concluded by saying, "May God bless you with your book."

JAMES "LEFTY" TURNER

James "Lefty" Turner began his professional career as the regular first baseman for the Indianapolis Crawfords in 1940. After the club folded, he moved over to the Baltimore Elite Giants in 1942, where he played out his last season as a utility infielder, batting just .100. Although his professional career was short, he played with some of the greatest players ever to set foot on a baseball diamond, including Oscar Charleston, Bus Clarkson, Jimmy Crutchfield, Bill Byrd, Roy Campanella, Sammy T. Hughes, George Scales, and Wild Bill Wright.

TURNER'S SELECTIONS

Catcher: Biz Mackey
Pitcher: Ray Brown, Andy Cooper, Hilton Smith, Bill Byrd, Dizzy Dismukes, Slim Jones
First Base: Mule Suttles, James "Lefty" Turner
Second Base: Sammy T. Hughes, George Scales

Shortstop: Dobie Moore, Sam Bankhead, Bus Clarkson, Dick Lundy
Third Base: Dewey Creacy, Jud Wilson
Outfield: Turkey Stearnes, Willard Brown, Jelly Gardner, Jimmy Crutchfield, Rap Dixon, Sam Jethroe, Wild Bill Wright, Fats Jenkins, Crush Holloway, Charlie Blackwell

James "Lefty" Turner may have had a light bat, but he was heavy on the confidence. He not only selected himself as a Hall of Fame candidate, but he chose himself as the number one first baseman.

ARMANDO VASQUEZ

Armando Vasquez was born in Güines, Cuba, on August 20, 1922. The 5'8", 160–pound handyman played all the infield and outfield positions during his five-year Negro League career, although he was primarily a first baseman. He broke in with the Indianapolis-Cincinnati Clowns in 1944, hitting .239 in 56 games. The left handed batter was a spray hitter with little power. His average never exceeded .256.

Vasquez played four years in the lower minor leagues after organized baseball became integrated. He played three years with Brandon in the independent Manitoba-Dakota League, where he batted .226, then closed out his baseball career, hitting .259 with the Thibodaux team in the Class C Evangeline League in 1954. He presently resides in New York City.

VASQUEZ'S SELECTIONS

Catcher: Biz Mackey, Louis Santop
Pitcher: Dick Redding, Ray Brown, Hilton Smith, Jose Mendez, Chet Brewer, Webster McDonald, Bill Byrd, Slim Jones
First Base: Mule Suttles, Ben Taylor, George Giles
Second Base: Sammy T. Hughes, George Scales
Shortstop: Sam Bankhead, Dick Lundy, John Beckwith
Third Base: Oliver Marcelle, Jud Wilson
Outfield: Turkey Stearnes, Cristobal Torriente, Spot Poles, Willard Brown, Chino Smith, Jimmy Lyons, Wild Bill Wright

Reviewing Armando Vasquez's selections, it is apparent that he is a true Negro League historian. There are very few of his choices that one could argue with. His knowledge of the game's pioneers, like Chino Smith, Spot Poles, and Louis Santop, is to be commended.

TWEED WEBB

Normal "Tweed" Webb was a walking encyclopedia of Negro baseball and, without a doubt, the country's foremost Negro League historian. His motto, "I've seen them all — since 1910," pretty much told the story. He had an extensive collection of data, newsclippings, and other Negro baseball memorabilia going back to 1874. Over a period of 84 years, Webb was involved with numerous Negro baseball activities. He served many years as an official Negro League scorer, was a sportswriter for the *St. Louis Argus* for 38 years, was actively involved in amateur baseball in St. Louis, and served as an advisor to the National Baseball Hall of Fame Veterans Committee on Negro League candidates.

Webb was born in 1905 and attended his first professional baseball game in 1910 when his father took him to see the St. Louis Giants battle the Indianapolis ABC's. He was a batboy for Rube Foster's Chicago American Giants in 1917. Nine years later, he played his only season of professional baseball, as shortstop for the Fort Wayne Pirates. He then returned home to St. Louis, where he became a painter. He continued to play amateur and semi-pro ball in the St. Louis area for many years.

The Negro League baseball players lost one of their most vocal supporters when Tweed Webb passed away in 1995. Before he died, however, he selected those players he felt should be considered for induction into the Hall of Fame. The players are listed in the order in which Webb placed them, with the first player listed being his first choice, the second player listed his second choice, and so on. Players who are already in the Hall of Fame are identified with an asterisk (*).

WEBB'S SELECTIONS

Catcher: Biz Mackey, Josh Gibson*, Bruce Petway

Pitcher: Satchel Paige*, Smokey Joe Williams*, Rube Foster*, John Donaldson, Bullet Joe Rogan*, Hilton Smith, Dick Redding, Nip Winters, Chet Brewer, Dizzy Dismukes, Leon Day*, Bill Byrd, Bill Foster*, Ted Trent

First Base: Ben Taylor, Buck Leonard*, Buck O'Neil

Second Base: Bingo DeMoss, Martin Dihigo*, Newt Allen, Larry Doby*, Jim Gilliam

Opposite: Wild Bill Wright was another five-point player who spent most of his career in Mexico. (Photograph courtesy James A. Riley.)

Dick Lundy, "King Richard," was one of the top three or four shortstops in Negro League history. (Photograph courtesy James A. Riley.)

Shortstop: John Henry Lloyd*, Willie Wells*, Dick Lundy, Dobie Moore

Third Base: Judy Johnson*, Dave Malarcher, Ray Dandridge*

Outfield: Oscar Charleston*, Cool Papa Bell*, Turkey Stearnes*, Cristobal Torriente, Jimmy Lyons, Monte Irvin*, Sam Jethroe, Rap Dixon, Pete Hill, Jimmy Crutchfield, Jelly Gardner

Tweed Webb rated Biz Mackey, Ben Taylor and John Donaldson among the top 13 Negro League players of all time. He had comments about other Negro League players as well.

Walter "Dobie" Moore — "Only six years in baseball. Moore was one of the best shortstops, along with Pop Lloyd, Willie Wells, and Dick Lundy. I rate Moore as one of the four best all-around shortstops in his six years with the Kansas City Monarchs. He batted .359 and helped them to win three pennants. In the 1924 Black World Series, he hit .300. Dobie had a great arm and large range at shortstop. He was a likable guy. His career was ended in 1926 when he was injured in an accidental shooting. We historians can only speculate about what he might have accomplished if he had enjoyed the luxury of a long career."

Charles "Chino" Smith — "The great outfielder and second baseman was a powerful line-drive hitter from 1925 through 1930. He played with the strong New York Lincoln Giants, Brooklyn Royal Giants, and Philadelphia Giants. He led the Negro League (in batting) two seasons with .463 and .406 averages. He was the 'Babe

Ruth' in the winter ball league in Cuba. One season (in the U.S.) he hit 24 home runs, 28 doubles. The 5'6" [player] starred at outfield and second base. He was some hitter. He died from yellow fever in Cuba in 1931. Chino and Dobie were outstanding ballplayers."

WALTER T. WILLIAMS

Walter T. Williams played for the Newark Eagles from 1937 to 1939. According to *The Negro Leagues Book* he is only listed on the roster for the 1939 season. He was a pitcher. No other information is available on his career. He presently resides in Silver Springs, Maryland.

WILLIAMS' SELECTIONS

Second Base: Tommy Sampson
Shortstop: Willie Wells
Outfield: Russell Awkard

Tommy Sampson, an outstanding defensive second baseman during his 10 year Negro League career, was also a respondent to this study.

Russell Awkard was an outstanding outfielder and a decent hitter in his two years in the Negro Leagues. His career was interrupted by World War II and, after the war, he went to work in industry, restricting his baseball to amateur games.

EARL WILSON, SR.

Earl Wilson, Sr., was a member of the Birmingham Black Barons of the Negro American League in 1938. No details of his career are available. His son, Earl Wilson, played for the Boston Red Sox and Detroit Tigers in the 1960s and compiled a major league career record of 121–109, including a 22–11 season for Detroit in 1967.

WILSON'S SELECTIONS

Catcher: Biz Mackey, Louis Santop, Double Duty Radcliffe
Pitcher: Dick Redding, John Donaldson, Ray Brown, Hilton Smith, Dave Brown, Bill Holland
First Base: Mule Suttles, Buck O'Neil

Second Base: Sammy T. Hughes, George Scales

Shortstop: Sam Bankhead, Bus Clarkson, Artie Wilson, Dick Lundy, Home Run Johnson

Third Base: Oliver Marcelle, Jud Wilson

Outfield: Turkey Stearnes, Pete Hill, Willard Brown, Jimmy Crutchfield, Sam Jethroe, Crush Holloway

Twenty-eight former Negro League veterans, who played in the leagues between 1926 and 1947 when Jackie Robinson broke into major league baseball with the Brooklyn Dodgers, selected their candidates for induction into the National Baseball Hall of Fame. All players who appeared on at least 50 percent of the ballots, are listed below, by position. Biz Mackey was the top vote-getter, with 82 percent of the vote.

Players Who Appeared on at Least 50 Percent of the Ballots

Catcher: Biz Mackey, Louis Santop

Pitcher: Hilton Smith, Ray Brown, Chet Brewer, Dick Redding

First Base: Mule Suttles

Second Base: Newt Allen, Sammy T. Hughes, George Scales

Shortstop: Dick Lundy, Artie Wilson

Outfield: Turkey Stearnes, Jimmy Crutchfield, Willard Brown, Wild Bill Wright, Sam Jethroe

Hall of Fame Candidates:
Historians' Selections

The players have spoken. They have selected the former Negro league players they feel deserve consideration for induction into the National Baseball Hall of Fame in Cooperstown, New York. This chapter will present the selections made by Negro league authors and historians. The two lists will then be compared in the next chapter, and the final Hall of Fame candidate list will be determined. It will be interesting to see how the two lists compare.

LUIS ALVELO

Luis Alvelo is one of the foremost baseball historians in Puerto Rico. He remembers the first year of the Puerto Rican Winter League (PRWL) in 1938–39. And he remembers the first great Negro league players who visited the island, players like Buck Leonard, Willard Brown, Satchel Paige, Josh Gibson, Ray Brown, Monte Irvin, and Ray Dandridge. He is an expert on the PRWL, from its inaugural season up to the present time. He has not only seen many of the Negro league legends like Martin Dihigo, Gibson, and Paige, but he has also seen many major league Hall of Famers, like Willie Mays, Roberto Clemente, Tony Perez, Robin Yount, Orlando Cepeda, Sandy Koufax, Hank Aaron, Johnny Bench, Mike Schmidt, Jim Palmer, Phil Niekro, and Steve Carlton. He has also watched the development of future Hall of Famers Roberto Alomar, Cal Ripken Jr., Wade Boggs, and Tony Gwynn. Needless to say, Alvelo probably has more impressive credentials

Ben Taylor, one of three famous ball playing brothers, held down first base on the 1900–1925 Negro league all-star team.

for evaluating Negro league Hall of Fame candidates than any other historian or author. He has, like Tweed Webb, seen them all over a period of more than 60 years.

ALVELO'S SELECTIONS

Catcher: Biz Mackey, Double Duty Radcliffe

Pitcher: Ray Brown, Hilton Smith, Jose Mendez, Chet Brewer, Bill Byrd, Slim Jones

First Base: Buck O'Neil, Ben Taylor, George Giles

Second Base: George Scales, Newt Allen

Shortstop: Sam Bankhead, Artie Wilson, Dick Lundy

Third Base: Jud Wilson, Dave Malarcher

Outfield: Cristobal Torriente, Willard Brown, Chino Smith, Jimmy Crutchfield, Rap Dixon, Sam Jethroe, Alejandro Oms, Crush Holloway, Vic Harris

Luis Alvelo had a few observations about the Negro league players.

"Willard Brown was our Babe Ruth."

"Artie Wilson was *Mr.* Shortstop."

"One of my greatest thrills was to visit Escobar Stadium and watch the ball go over the left field wall (near the beach), by Willard Brown, a long home run."

"I used to touch hands, arms and a good smile to all the ballplayers from the U.S., and local players, like Wilmer Fields, Bus Clarkson, (Bob) Thurman, Raymond Brown, and many more." "I have to thank all these excellent ballplayers who play the best baseball, and the very special Negro leaguers who visit our home fans and the hospitals and give toys to our kids at the hospitals. I remember all with great love. That's why today I am a committee member of our best Negro League Museum at Kansas City. [It's] a good way to say thanks to all these great gentlemen. God bless America."

TODD BOLTON

Todd Bolton is a long-time Negro league historian from Smithsburg, Maryland. He has researched the Negro leagues since 1978, is an active member of the Society for American Baseball Research (SABR), is a member of its Negro Leagues Committee and its Latin American Committee, is a charter member of the Negro League Baseball Museum in Kansas City, a lifetime donor to the National Baseball Hall of Fame, and a historical advisor to the Negro League Baseball Player Association. Bolton has been the recipient of many awards associated with Negro league baseball over the years, including the 1998 SABR John Coats Award and a 1999 SABR Robert Peterson Recognition Award.

He has been instrumental in creating Negro league exhibits at various locations, including Cooperstown, has served as advisor to numerous baseball projects, has contributed to many baseball books and television documentaries, and has authored numerous articles for newspapers and magazines. He also lectures on Negro league baseball to educational, civic, and professional groups.

BOLTON'S SELECTIONS

Catcher: Biz Mackey, Louis Santop
Pitcher: Dick Redding, Ray Brown, Andy Cooper, Hilton Smith, Jose Mendez, Bill Byrd
First Base: Mule Suttles, Ben Taylor
Second Base: Sammy T. Hughes, Frank Warfield
Shortstop: Sam Bankhead, Dick Lundy, John Beckwith, Horacio Martinez
Third Base: Oliver Marcelle, Jud Wilson
Outfield: Turkey Stearnes, Cristobal Torriente, Pete Hill, Bernardo Baro, Alejandro Oms, Wild Bill Wright, Fats Jenkins, Tetelo Vargas

Todd Bolton added, "Best of luck with your project. Thanks for your help in promoting the history of these great athletes."

RICHARD BOZZONE

Richard Bozzone works for the Postal Service in Tolland, Connecticut. He is a member of the Society for American Baseball Research (SABR) and a member of its Negro Leagues Committee. He is a dedicated researcher and has an extensive baseball book collection.

BOZZONE'S SELECTIONS

Catcher: Biz Mackey, Louis Santop
Pitcher: Dick Redding, Rats Henderson, Hilton Smith, Frank Wickware, Dave Brown, Jose Mendez, Slim Jones
First Base: Mule Suttles, Buck O'Neil, Ben Taylor, Bob Boyd
Second Base: George Scales, Frank Grant
Shortstop: Artie Wilson, Dick Lundy
Third Base: Oliver Marcelle, Hank Thompson, Dave Malarcher
Outfield: Turkey Stearnes, Cristobal Torriente, Pete Hill, Chino Smith, Jimmy Crutchfield, Rap Dixon, Sam Jethroe

DICK CLARK

Dick Clark is another dedicated Negro league historian and researcher. He saw his first baseball game in 1953 and developed a love for the game that has lasted for almost 50 years (his favorite player is Al Kaline). He read Robert Peterson's *Only the Ball Was White* in 1972, and that fueled his interest in the Negro leagues. He is a member of SABR and its Negro Leagues Committee. He became chairman of the committee in 1985, a position he continues to hold. He is co-editor of SABR's *The Negro Leagues Book,* along with Larry Lester. He was also part of the editing team, along with John Holway and Jim Riley, for the Negro league statistics in *The Baseball Encyclopedia* (8th ed.).

Dick has also written several articles and contributed to countless books. He collects baseball books and other magazines and reading material on baseball.

CLARK'S SELECTIONS

Catcher: Biz Mackey, Bruce Petway, Louis Santop, Double Duty Radcliffe
Pitcher: Dick Redding, John Donaldson, Ray Brown, Hilton Smith, Jose Mendez, Chet Brewer
First Base: Mule Suttles, Ben Taylor
Second Base: Sammy T. Hughes, Frank Grant

Shortstop: Sam Bankhead, Dick Lundy, John Beckwith
Third Base: Oliver Marcelle, Jud Wilson
Outfield: Turkey Stearnes, Cristobal Torriente, Spot Poles, Pete Hill, Willard Brown, Rap Dixon, Sam Jethroe, Wild Bill Wright

JEFF EASTLAND

Jeff Eastland is a businessman in Falmouth, Virginia. He belongs to SABR and is a member of its Negro Leagues Committee. Jeff is an expert on the Negro leagues and gives numerous presentations each year to school groups and hobby clubs using photos from his own collection. His objective is to educate the public in the all-important aspect of American history known as the Negro baseball leagues.

He has an extensive collection of photographs and other items relating to not only the Negro leagues but also Latin American baseball. Although Eastland is proficient in both areas, his research is an ongoing avocation. He originally became interested in Negro league baseball about 11 years ago when he bought a collection of material relating to the Homestead Grays. His subsequent study of the material converted him into an avid collector and historian.

EASTLAND'S SELECTIONS

Catcher: Biz Mackey, Bruce Petway, Louis Santop
Pitcher: Dick Redding, Ray Brown, Hilton Smith, Jose Mendez, Chet Brewer
First Base: Mule Suttles, Ben Taylor
Second Base: Sammy T. Hughes, Frank Grant
Shortstop: Sam Bankhead, Dick Lundy, John Beckwith, Grant Home Run Johnson
Third Base: Oliver Marcelle, Jud Wilson, Dave Malarcher
Outfield: Turkey Stearnes, Cristobal Torriente, Pete Hill, Spot Poles, Jimmy Lyons, Sam Jethroe, Wild Bill Wright

BOB FELLER

Bob Feller, better known in his heyday as Rapid Robert, was one of the greatest pitchers ever to toe the rubber in a major league game. He is always listed in the top 10 pitchers of all time, frequently listed in the top five, and appears first on some lists. Feller won 266 games in his 18-year major league career, but lost an estimated 95 additional victories due to military service in World War II. Feller joined the U.S. Navy at 23 years of age and didn't return to baseball until he was almost 27. He served four years in the Navy and came home with eight battle stars.

Bob Feller played baseball with and against black players most of his life. His father coached a semi-pro team in Oakview and, for tournaments, he would hire a black pitcher and catcher. Young Bob played with the Oakview team when he was 15–16 years old, and he played against many black traveling teams, like the Texas Black Spiders. During the 1930s, he barnstormed against Negro league all-star teams in the fall. He remembers many of the great Negro league players.

"[Josh] Gibson couldn't hit a curve ball, but he would hit a fastball a mile."

"[Bullet Joe] Rogan was an outstanding all-around player. He was long overdue to be elected to the Hall of Fame."

"Satchel [Paige] was one of the five or 10 best pitchers in the world. I pitched against him more than 20 times in fall barnstorming."

"[Double Duty] Radcliffe was an outstanding player."

Feller declined to select a Negro league Hall of Fame candidate team, feeling he was not qualified. Regarding my survey, he did say, however, "One thing I didn't like about your letter was your request for 27 Negro league players for the HOF. I don't believe in quotas—for Afro-Americans or whites, or anybody. I believe players should be elected to the Hall of Fame only on their merits." He voiced the sentiments of both Brent Kelley and Jim Riley regarding a quota system and, as I stated before, I agree. In fact, after giving the situation more thought, I decided to let the chips fall where they may in the final selection. The Hall of Fame candidate list will not automatically contain 27 former Negro league players. It will consist of those players who are deemed to be worthy of consideration for induction into Cooperstown by the selection committee. The final list may consist of just one player, or it may include 40 players. The thoughtful, insightful recommendations of the respondents will be the deciding factor.

JAN FINKEL

Jan Finkel is a retired English professor living with his wife on Deep Creek Lake in western Maryland. He is a member of Society for American

Baseball Research and is on their Negro Leagues Committee. Over the past seven years, he has become a vocal supporter of Hall of Fame recognition for the legendary Negro league players. He first became aware of the great number of talented Negro league players, believe it or not, through the computer game *Tony LaRussa Baseball 2*, which included, a Negro league all-star team with players like Turkey Stearnes, Mule Suttles, and Bullet Rogan in addition to major league all-star teams. His interest in the Negro league players turned into a passion, and his subsequent research revealed the gross injustice that was perpetrated by the establishment by hiding these immense talents from the American baseball public. Since then he has fought for their right to be included in the Hall of Fame. As he said, "My passion for the Negro leagues arose when I heard that the Hall's doors were closing; not to put too fine a point on it, I became outraged at the injustice of the whole thing."

Dick Redding, known affectionately as "Cannonball," was one of the top four pitchers in the Negro leagues.

Jan has presented several papers to SABR gatherings on Honus Wagner and Ty Cobb, as well as on "The Negro Leagues and the Hall of Fame."

FINKEL'S SELECTIONS

Catcher: Biz Mackey, Bruce Petway, Louis Santop
Pitcher: Dick Redding, John Donaldson, Hilton Smith, Jose Mendez
First Base: Mule Suttles, Buck O'Neil, Ben Taylor
Second Base: Sammy T. Hughes, Bill Monroe, Newt Allen
Shortstop: Dobie Moore, Dick Lundy, John Beckwith, Grant "Home Run" Johnson
Third Base: Oliver Marcelle, Jud Wilson
Outfield: Turkey Stearnes, Cristobal Torriente, Pete Hill, Willard Brown, Chino Smith, Heavy Johnson, Rap Dixon, Wild Bill Wright

THOMAS R. GARRETT

Tom Garrett is a special education specialist living in Suffolk, Virginia. He belongs to the Society for American Baseball Research (SABR), and is a member of its Negro leagues committee. His interests run from the minor leagues to the Negro leagues and include biographical research.

GARRETT'S SELECTIONS

Catcher: Biz Mackey, Bruce Petway, Louis Santop, Double Duty Radcliffe
Pitcher: Dick Redding, John Donaldson, Hilton Smith, Jose Mendez, Bill Byrd
First Base: Mule Suttles, Ben Taylor
Second Base: Sammy T. Hughes, George Scales, Frank Grant, Bingo DeMoss
Shortstop: Bus Clarkson, Dick Lundy, John Beckwith
Third Base: Alex Radcliffe
Outfield: Turkey Stearnes, Cristobal Torriente, Pete Hill, Spot Poles, Jimmy Crutchfield, Wild Bill Wright

LESLIE HEAPHY

Leslie Heaphy is an assistant professor of history at Kent State University. Her area of research is sport history, with an emphasis on the Negro leagues and women in sport. She is currently working on a book on the history of the Negro leagues. She has written a number of encyclopedia articles on players in the Negro leagues and helped with the bibliography for *The Negro Leagues Book* by Dick Clark and Larry Lester.

Leslie is a member of SABR's Negro Leagues Committee, and the chair of their Women in Baseball Committee, as well as chair for the Bob Davids Award Committee. She also belongs to the North American Society of Sport Historians (NASSH).

HEAPHY'S SELECTIONS

Catcher: Biz Mackey
Pitcher: Dick Redding, Ray Brown, Hilton Smith, Chet Brewer, Dizzy Dismukes
First Base: Mule Suttles

Second Base: Newt Allen, Frank Grant
Shortstop: Dick Lundy
Third Base: Oliver Marcelle
Outfield: Turkey Stearnes, Cristobal Torriente, Pete Hill, Willard Brown, Sam Jethroe

Heaphy also listed the names of 11 players who are already members of the Hall of Fame.

LAWRENCE D. HOGAN

Larry Hogan is a professor of history at Union County College in Cranford, New Jersey. He is a member of SABR and is on their Negro Leagues Committee. Larry is the author of *A Black News Service: Claude Barnett and the Associated Negro Press*; creator of the nationally touring exhibit, "Before You Can Say Jackie Robinson: Black Baseball in America in the Era of the Color Line"; executive producer of a video documentary with the same title; consultant to the National Baseball Hall of Fame for their Negro Leagues exhibit "Pride and Passion"; and organizer and serving as secretary/historian to the John Henry "Pop" Lloyd committee in Atlantic City, New Jersey.

HOGAN'S SELECTIONS

Catcher: Biz Mackey, Louis Santop
Pitcher: Dick Redding
First Base: Mule Suttles, Ben Taylor
Second Base: Frank Grant, Sol White
Shortstop: Dick Lundy
Third Base: Oliver Marcelle
Outfield: Turkey Stearnes, Pete Hill, Willard Brown, Wild Bill Wright, Minnie Minoso

JOHN B. HOLWAY

John Holway is one of the leading Negro league authors and historians in the country. He is a pioneer in Negro league biographical history, and an indefatigable researcher whose meticulous scrutiny of newspaper box scores (along with Dick Clark and numerous SABR volunteers) led to the development of a sizable amount of actual batting and pitching statistics for dozens of Negro league players. These statistics have permitted the various Negro league players to be evaluated on their merits for consideration for induction into the National Baseball Hall of Fame. He has recently published *The Complete Book of the Negro Leagues*, which contains the most complete batting and pitching statistics ever compiled on the great black players from the early days of baseball.

John has published numerous articles on Negro league players over the years, beginning with an article on Turkey Stearnes that appeared in the *Detroit News Sunday Magazine* on August 15, 1971. He has also written eight books on baseball, including *Blackball Stars*, winner of *Spitball* magazine's Casey Award as the best baseball book of 1989. *Blackball Stars* remains my favorite book on Negro league players, and I refer to it constantly. His other books include the acclaimed *Josh and Satch*, *Voices from the Great Black Baseball Leagues*, and *Black Diamonds*.

HOLWAY'S SELECTIONS

Catcher: Biz Mackey, Bruce Petway

Pitcher: Ray Brown, Max Manning, Andy Cooper, Hilton Smith, Leroy Matlock, Ted Trent, Nip Winters, Webster McDonald, Bill Byrd

First Base: Mule Suttles, Edgar Wesley

Second Base: Sammy T. Hughes, George Scales, Newt Allen

Shortstop: Dobie Moore, Sam Bankhead, Dick Lundy, John Beckwith

Third Base: Oliver Marcelle, Jud Wilson, Dave Malarcher

Outfield: Turkey Stearnes, Cristobal Torriente, Willard Brown, Chino Smith, Pablo "Champion" Mesa, Heavy Johnson, Vic Harris

John Holway had several other observations regarding the Hall of Fame. "Mule Suttles is the greatest player, black or white, not in the Hall." "Torriente was the best Cuban to play in the States." "Chino was great for a four-year career." "Bullet Rogan won more games than anyone and lost less than Satch (and he was 30 before he threw his first pitch)."

John also noted that Japanese legends, Sadaharu Oh, Shigeo Nagashima, and Sachio Kinugasa, also belong in the National Baseball Hall of Fame. My book *Baseball's Other All-Stars*, which discusses the greatest baseball players around the world, outside the major leagues, includes all three players. They were all members of my all-time Japan League All-Star team. And Oh and Nagashima were members of my All-World All-Star team.

LOU HUNSINGER, JR.

Lou Hunsinger, Jr., is a news reporter for the *Williamsport Sun-Gazette* in Pennsylvania. He belongs to the Society for American Baseball Research and is a member of its Negro Leagues Committee. His varied interests include the Negro leagues, the minor leagues, ballparks, nineteenth-century baseball, and women in baseball. He also has a large book collection.

Lou has written a number of articles about Negro league players, as well as about baseball in Williamsport. His article on George Stovey appeared in SABR's *National Pastime*. He also wrote the entry on Stovey for the *Biographical Dictionary of American Sports*. He is co-author of *Williamsport's Baseball Heritage*, a pictorial history of professional baseball in Williamsport from 1865 to 1976. He is president of the boosters club for the Pittsburgh Pirates Class A affiliate, the Williamsport Crosscutters, and is a member of the board of directors of the West Branch Valley chapter of the Pennsylvania Sports Hall of Fame.

HUNSINGER'S SELECTIONS

Catcher: Biz Mackey, Bruce Petway, Louis Santop
Pitcher: Dick Redding, John Donaldson, Max Manning, Hilton Smith, Jose Mendez, Chet Brewer, George Stovey
First Base: Mule Suttles, Ben Taylor
Second Base: Bill Monroe, Newt Allen, Frank Grant
Shortstop: Artie Wilson, Dick Lundy, John Beckwith
Third Base: Oliver Marcelle, Jud Wilson
Outfield: Turkey Stearnes, Cristobal Torriente, Spot Poles, Willard Brown, Pete Hill, Rap Dixon, Fats Jenkins

BRENT KELLEY

Brent Kelley is a prolific writer living in Paris, Kentucky. He is, as he says, "The author of oodles of books, mostly oral baseball histories but including two on my experiences as a veterinarian under the pen name Grant Kendall and a few young-reader contract books on basketball players and presidents." Brent has conducted literally hundreds of interviews

Turkey Stearnes, a superstar for 20 years in the Negro leagues, was finally elected to the National Baseball Hall of Fame in 2000. (Photograph courtesy John B. Holway.)

with former baseball players, from both the Negro leagues and the major leagues, in researching his subjects. His books include *They Too Wore Pinstripes, Voices from the Negro Leagues, The Early All-Stars, In the Shadow of the Babe,* and *The Negro Leagues Revisited.* He has also written at least 400 magazine and newspaper articles on many subjects, from baseball to humor to computers.

Brent is a frustrated major league wanna-be who satisfies his passionate interest in the sport through writing and collecting baseball memorabilia. His collection includes around 500 autographed photos (including Ty Cobb), 100 of which are Negro league veterans, and two autographed Negro league bats containing a total of about 75 autographs. He is a member of the Society of American Baseball Research and is on its Negro Leagues Committee.

KELLEY'S SELECTIONS

Catcher: Biz Mackey, Double Duty Radcliffe

Pitcher: Dick Redding, Hilton Smith, Chet Brewer

First Base: Mule Suttles

Second Base: Sammy T. Hughes, Frank Grant

Shortstop: Dick Lundy, John Beckwith

Third Base: Oliver Marcelle, Jud Wilson, Dave Malarcher

Outfield: Turkey Stearnes, Cristobal Torriente, Spot Poles, Willard Brown, Alejandro Oms, Wild Bill Wright

MERL F. KLEINKNECHT

Merl Kleinknecht, a retired Postal Service employee, presently resides in Galion, Ohio, with his wife. He is one of the longest service members of the Society for American Baseball Research, having joined the organization in 1971. He is a founding member of the SABR Negro Leagues Committee and served two terms as committee chairman in the seventies.

Kleinknecht is a devoted Negro league researcher, who has helped develop the playing statistics for many of the Negro league legends. His work has resulted in special recognition from the Ohio Baseball Hall of Fame and the SABR Negro Leagues Committee. He has also published many articles on the Negro leagues and its players in such journals and books as the SABR Research Journal, the Negro Leagues Baseball Museum *Discover Greatness* magazine, the *Biographical Dictionary of Sports,* the Cleveland Indians *Game Face* magazine, and Mike Shatzkin's *The Ballplayers.* He has also contributed to programs promoting the Negro leagues at the Cleveland Indians Winterfest, the Ohio Baseball Hall of Fame, and Cleveland's Western Reserve Historical Society.

KLEINKNECHT'S SELECTIONS

Catcher: Biz Mackey

Pitcher: Dick Redding, Ray Brown, Hilton Smith, Jose Mendez, Chet Brewer, Nip Winters, Webster McDonald, Sam Streeter

First Base: Mule Suttles, Ben Taylor

Second Base: Sammy T. Hughes, Bill Monroe, George Scales, Frank Grant

Shortstop: Sam Bankhead, Dick Lundy

Third Base: Jud Wilson, Dave Malarcher

Outfield: Turkey Stearnes, Cristobal Torriente, Pete Hill, Spot Poles, Willard Brown, Sam Jethroe

TED KNORR

Ted Knorr has been a Pittsburgh Pirates fan since the cradle, and was fortunate enough to be in town for the famous 1960 World Series. He also saw the 1971 and 1979 classics. He has been a SABR member since 1979 and has focused on the Negro leagues since '89. He is a member of the

SABR Negro Leagues Committee and is founder and coordinator of the
SABR Negro League Committee Research Conference, which met for the
third time in Harrisburg, Pennsylvania, in 2000.

Ted has also published articles in local and national publications on
the Harrisburg Giants of 1925, whose members included Oscar Charleston,
Rap Dixon, and the venerable Ben Taylor.

KNORR'S SELECTIONS

Catcher: Biz Mackey, Bruce Petway, Louis Santop, Double Duty Radcliffe
Pitcher: Dick Redding, John Donaldson, Max Manning, Hilton Smith,
Jose Mendez, Chet Brewer
First Base: Mule Suttles, Edgar Wesley, Buck O'Neil, Ben Taylor
Second Base: Newt Allen, Frank Grant
Shortstop: Dick Lundy, John Beckwith
Third Base: Oliver Marcelle, Jud Wilson
Outfield: Turkey Stearnes, Cristobal Torriente, Spot Poles, Willard
Brown, Heavy Johnson, Rap Dixon, Fats Jenkins

DAVID A. LAWRENCE

David A. Lawrence holds a Ph.D. in aesthetics from Stanford University and has served on the faculties of UCLA and Stanford. He has
researched and written about Negro league history for the past 16 years,
with a particular emphasis, in the past three years, on the Eastern Colored
League. David belongs to the Society for American Baseball Research and
is a member of its Negro Leagues Committee.

LAWRENCE'S SELECTIONS

Catcher: Biz Mackey, Bruce Petway, Louis Santop
Pitcher: John Donaldson, Ray Brown, Dave Brown, Jose Mendez, Nip
Winters
First Base: Mule Suttles, Edgar Wesley, Ben Taylor
Second Base: Bill Monroe, George Scales
Shortstop: Dobie Moore, Dick Lundy, Grant "Home Run" Johnson
Third Base: Oliver Marcelle, Jud Wilson
Outfield: Turkey Stearnes, Cristobal Torriente, Pete Hill, Willard Brown,
Chino Smith, Rap Dixon, Sam Jethroe, Alejandro Oms, Wild Bill Wright

LARRY LESTER

Larry Lester is one of the country's leading authorities on the Negro baseball leagues. He is co-editor, along with Dick Clark, of SABR's *The Negro Leagues Book* and has recently published another book, *The East-West Game: Black Baseball's National Showcase.* He is one of the original founders of the Negro Leagues Baseball Museum in Kansas City, Missouri, and served as their research director and treasurer for four years. He also belongs to SABR and is a member of its Negro Leagues Committee.

His writings on African Americans have appeared in numerous periodicals and books, including *The National Pastime, Biographical Dictionary of American Sports, American National Biography, The Ballplayers, World Book Encyclopedia,* and *The Dictionary of American Negro Biography.*

Larry Lester has also been a contributing researcher for many other books on black baseball, has made appearances in several films, and continues to actively campaign for worthy Negro league players for induction to the National Baseball Hall of Fame through his company NoirTech Research, Inc.

Cristobal Torriente was one of Cuba's greatest players, another superstar. (Photograph courtesy Jay Sanford.)

LESTER'S SELECTIONS

Catcher: Biz Mackey, Bruce Petway, Louis Santop
Pitcher: Dick Redding, Ray Brown, Hilton Smith, Frank Wickware, Jose Mendez, Chet Brewer, Nip Winters
First Base: Mule Suttles, Ben Taylor
Second Base: Sammy T. Hughes, Newt Allen

Shortstop: Dobie Moore, Sam Bankhead, Dick Lundy
Third Base: Oliver Marcelle, Jud Wilson
Outfield: Turkey Stearnes, Cristobal Torriente, Pete Hill, Spot Poles, Willard Brown, Sam Jethroe, Wild Bill Wright, Vic Harris

JERRY MALLOY

Jerry Malloy was a member of SABR since 1981 and was an active member of its Negro Leagues Committee. The focus of his research was on nineteenth-century black baseball and black baseball in the military. He compiled, edited, and introduced *Sol White's History of Colored Base Ball: With Other Documents on the Early Black Game, 1886–1936.* He also published several articles for SABR's journal, *The National Pastime,* including "The 25th Infantry Regiment Takes the Field." The 25th was the training ground for such Negro league legends as Bullet Rogan, Dobie Moore, and Heavy Johnson. He also provided biographies on black baseball legends Frank Grant, Moses Walker, and Sol White, for SABR's publication *Nineteenth Century Stars.* Jerry Malloy was the recipient of the 1999 Tweed Webb Lifetime Achievement Award.

MALLOY'S SELECTIONS

Catcher: Biz Mackey, Louis Santop, Double Duty Radcliffe
Pitcher: Dick Redding, Ray Brown, Hilton Smith, Jose Mendez, Bill Byrd, Slim Jones
First Base: Mule Suttles, Ben Taylor
Second Base: Bill Monroe, Newt Allen, Frank Grant
Shortstop: Dick Lundy, John Beckwith, Grant "Home Run" Johnson
Third Base: Oliver Marcelle, Jud Wilson
Outfield: Turkey Stearnes, Cristobal Torriente, Pete Hill, Spot Poles, Chino Smith, Jimmy Lyons, Rap Dixon, Wild Bill Wright

WILLIAM F. MCNEIL
(the author of this book)

I am a long-time baseball fan. My love affair with the Dodgers began back in Brooklyn, the same year Branch Rickey signed Jackie Robinson to a professional contract. I remember seeing Jackie's first game against the Boston Braves in Boston. As I remember, Boston was very friendly to Jackie, and the souvenir vendors made a fortune selling Jackie Robinson pins and other items. I also remember Jackie running wild in an exhibition game against the Class B Pawtucket Slaters in '49.

I became interested in the Negro leagues during the late 40s, as Robinson, Satchel Paige, Larry Doby, and Luke Easter flexed their muscles in the major leagues. Later, my fascination with the Negro league players was spurred on by the colorful writings of John B. Holway. He brought the Negro league legends to life again — men like Chino Smith, Dobie Moore, Turkey Stearnes, and Bullet Joe Rogan — in his book, *Blackball Stars.*

I am now a member of the Society for American Baseball Research, an obsessive researcher, and the writer of 11 books in the past 15 years. My baseball books include *The Dodgers Encyclopedia, Dodger Diary, The King of Swat, Ruth, Maris, McGwire and Sosa,* and *Baseball's Other All-Stars.* Two of them, in addition to this one, include sections on Negro league baseball. I was proud to receive Robert W. Peterson awards in both 1998 and 2000 for increasing "both the knowledge of and the public's awareness of the Negro Baseball Leagues." I hope this book will further that awareness.

McNEIL'S SELECTIONS

Catcher: Biz Mackey, Louis Santop
Pitcher: Dick Redding, John Donaldson, Ray Brown, Hilton Smith, Jose Mendez, Chet Brewer
First Base: Mule Suttles, Edgar Wesley
Second Base: Sammy T. Hughes, Bill Monroe, Newt Allen, Frank Grant
Shortstop: Dobie Moore, Bus Clarkson, Dick Lundy, John Beckwith, Grant "Home Run" Johnson
Third Base: Oliver Marcelle, Jud Wilson
Outfield: Turkey Stearnes, Cristobal Torriente, Pete Hill, Chino Smith, Alejandro Oms

---

SAMMY J. MILLER

Sammy Miller, a native of Memphis, Tennessee, currently living in the Cincinnati area, is an active member of SABR's Negro Leagues Committee. He was a man on the go during the 1990s, promoting the Negro leagues through his writing, consulting, and professional committee efforts. His article "Negro League Veteran Touches All the Bases" appeared in USA Today's *Baseball Weekly* in May 1993. He has worked for Pomegranate Publications since 1993 as a historical consultant, author/interviewer, and editor for their annual calendar, "Blackball: The Negro Baseball Leagues Calendar." He is a member of SABR and its Negro Leagues Committee, is chair of the Negro Leagues Committee Awards Committee, and editor for the committee's bi-monthly newsletter. He was a committee member for the 1998 SABR Negro League Committee National Conference, was on the Presentation Committee for the 1999 National Conference, and was a panelist at the same conference. He was a Book reviewer for *Nine: A Journal of Baseball History and Social Policy Perspectives* in 1999 and a historical consultant for the *Cincinnati Enquirer,* also in 1999.

Sammy was a recipient of a Robert Peterson Recognition Award in both 1998 and 1999. He is listed in *Marquis Who's Who in the South and Southwest,* and in the 26th edition of *International Dictionary of Biography.*

MILLER'S SELECTIONS

Catcher: Biz Mackey, Louis Santop, Larry Brown
Pitcher: Dick Redding, Ray Brown, Andy Cooper, Hilton Smith, Jose Mendez, Chet Brewer, Nip Winters, Bill Byrd
First Base: Mule Suttles, Ben Taylor
Second Base: Sammy T. Hughes, Newt Allen
Shortstop: Sam Bankhead, Dick Lundy, John Beckwith
Third Base: Oliver Marcelle, Jud Wilson, Dave Malarcher
Outfield: Turkey Stearnes, Cristobal Torriente, Pete Hill, Spot Poles, Willard Brown, Jimmy Lyons

RICK MORRIS

Rick Morris has studied the Negro leagues since 1990, when he began conducting interviews with former players. Since then Mr. Morris, a filmmaker by profession, has amassed over 20 hours of video interviews with Negro league veterans, their white major league barnstorming colleagues, noted sports journalists, and Negro league historians. He is currently working on a documentary on the integration of baseball titled *Closed Doors.* In 1998, he was a recipient of the Robert Peterson Award, presented by the Negro Leagues Chapter of SABR, for his contributions toward increasing the public's knowledge and awareness of the Negro leagues. Currently, he resides in King of Prussia, Pennsylvania, where he advocates strongly for the induction of Jud "Boojum" Wilson into the Hall of Fame.

MORRIS' SELECTIONS

Catcher: Biz Mackey, Bruce Petway, Louis Santop, Fleet Walker
Pitcher: John Donaldson, Max Manning, Chet Brewer
First Base: Mule Suttles, Ben Taylor
Second Base: Frank Grant
Shortstop: Dick Lundy, John Beckwith
Third Base: Oliver Marcelle, Jud Wilson
Outfield: Turkey Stearnes, Cristobal Torriente, Pete Hill, Spot Poles, Willard Brown, Chino Smith, Jimmy Crutchfield

ERIC NEWLAND

Eric Newland is a member of the Society for American Baseball Research and is a member of its Negro Leagues Committee. Eric is concerned about preserving the rich heritage of the Negro leagues and, as a result, has been conducting video interviews with many of the Negro league veterans. He has one of the largest collections of video interviews in the country.

NEWLAND'S SELECTIONS

Catcher: Biz Mackey, Louis Santop
Pitcher: Dick Redding, Ray Brown, Hilton Smith, Chet Brewer
First Base: Mule Suttles, Ben Taylor, George Giles
Second Base: Sammy T. Hughes, George Scales, Frank Grant
Shortstop: Dobie Moore, Artie Wilson, Dick Lundy
Third Base: Jud Wilson, Dave Malarcher
Outfield: Turkey Stearnes, Cristobal Torriente, Spot Poles, Willard Brown, Rap Dixon, Wild Bill Wright, Vic Harris

JAMES E. OVERMYER

Jim Overmyer is the author of several publications and articles on Negro league history. He wrote the popular *Queen of the Negro Leagues:*

Effa Manley and the Newark Eagles. He was a contributor to SABR's *The Negro Leagues Book,* and to *Baseball History 4.* He has presented several papers on the Negro leagues to organizations over the years, including "Cumberland Posey and the Homestead Grays," presented at the 1997 Cooperstown Symposium on Baseball and American Culture, "Baseball in the Berkshires," presented at the Lenox, Massachusetts, Historical Society, and "Something to Cheer About: The Meaning of the Negro Leagues," presented at the 1995 Cooperstown Symposium on Baseball and American Culture.

Jim is a member of the Society for American Baseball Research, a member of its Negro Leagues Committee, and a member of its Business of Baseball Committee.

OVERMYER'S SELECTIONS

Catcher: Biz Mackey, Louis Santop
Pitcher: Dick Redding, Hilton Smith, Chet Brewer
First Base: Mule Suttles
Second Base: Frank Grant
Shortstop: Grant "Home Run" Johnson
Third Base: Oliver Marcelle, Jud Wilson
Outfield: Turkey Stearnes, Cristobal Torriente

Jim Overmyer noted, "I didn't make 27 picks because I'm not really sure I could find 27 men on the list who ought to be in the Hall of Fame, which is really what I'd have to do in order to fully fill out the form."

"While there's no question that many Negro leaguers could have prospered in the white majors if given the chance (the successful transition of Irvin, Campanella, Mays, Banks, Aaron, Newcombe, Thurman, etc., pretty much proves the point), there's really no way to tell how many Negro league first-liners would have posted Hall of Fame numbers."

"Anyway, I've picked 12 guys, including our hometown hero Frank Grant, the object of my first baseball research piece several years ago. Hope this helps."

ROBERT W. PETERSON

Bob Peterson's pioneering book, *Only the Ball Was White,* introduced most of the American baseball community to the misty world of the Negro leagues—and to its legendary players. The book was first printed in 1970, when almost nobody outside the black community knew anything about ballplayers like Rube Foster, John Henry Lloyd, or Josh Gibson. As a result of the book, baseball fans not only got to know Gibson, they were also introduced to Biz Mackey, Chino Smith, Cristobal Torriente, Turkey Stearnes, and many more world-class players. Bob's book was so popular it has been reprinted several times and is once again back on the shelves at leading book stores.

Bob played semi-pro baseball in Warren, Pennsylvania, immediately after World War II. Among his team's opponents were the barnstorming Indianapolis Clowns of the Negro leagues, and one other team whose name has been lost to the ravages of time. He may well have played against Goose Tatum and Buster Haywood, and perhaps Willie Wells and Newt Allen.

Bob has been a newspaperman and a freelance writer during his career. He has written articles for the New York Times, Boy's Life, and other publications. His books include *Cages to Jump Shots: Pro Basketball's*

Jud Wilson was one of the purest hitters in baseball history. He owns the highest career batting average in both the Negro leagues and the Cuban Winter League. (Photograph courtesy John B. Holway.)

Early Years, Pigskin: The Early Years of Pro Football, and *The Boy Scouts,* a history of scouting's first 75 years in the U.S. He is a member of the Negro Leagues Committee for the Society for American Baseball Research.

PETERSON'S SELECTIONS

Catcher: Biz Mackey
Pitcher: Jose Mendez
First Base: Ben Taylor
Second Base: Bingo DeMoss
Shortstop: Dick Lundy
Third Base: Oliver Marcelle
Outfield: Turkey Stearnes, Cristobal Torriente, Spot Poles

Bob Peterson had a few other comments. "I continue to believe that 10 to 12 percent of the people in the Hall who played after 1900 and before about 1960 ought to be Negro leaguers. I know that a lot of other folks think the percentage should be higher, given the success of blacks in the majors after Jackie, but I don't know how to set a better standard than the percentage of blacks in the general population."

JAMES A. RILEY

James A. Riley was elected president of the Society for American Baseball Research in 1999. He is also a member of its Negro Leagues Committee and the regional leader for SABR's Central Florida group. He is currently the director of research for the Negro Leagues Baseball Museum.

Jim has written extensively on the history of the Negro leagues. He has authored six books including the highly acclaimed *The Biographical Encyclopedia of the Negro Baseball Leagues, Dandy, Day and the Devil, Buck Leonard: The Black Lou Gehrig, Monte Irvin: Nice Guys Finish First,* and *The All-Time All-Stars of Black Baseball.* He was an editor of the Negro leagues section to *The Baseball Encyclopedia,* and has contributed to numerous compilations of baseball books and sports publications, including the *All-Star Game Official Major League Baseball Program.* He has also appeared on several documentary television programs and lectured at many locations including the Smithsonian Institute in Washington, D.C. His selections are in order of preference.

RILEY'S SELECTIONS

Catcher: Biz Mackey, Louis Santop
Pitcher: Dick Redding, Ray Brown, Bill Byrd
First Base: Mule Suttles, Ben Taylor

Second Base: Bingo DeMoss, Newt Allen, Sammy T. Hughes
Shortstop: Dick Lundy, John Beckwith, Grant Johnson
Third Base: Jud Wilson, Oliver Marcelle
Outfield: Pete Hill, Turkey Stearnes, Cristobal Torriente, Willard Brown, Bill Wright, Spot Poles
**Cum Posey, **C. I. Taylor

**Indicates non-players.

Posey, called "The Father of the Homestead Grays" by Riley, joined the Grays as a player in 1911. He eventually became the owner of the club and built it into the most feared Negro league team in history. Posey's Grays were the first professional team, black or white, to play night games.

C. I. Taylor was a second baseman for a number of teams during the first decade of the twentieth century, but it was as a manager that he built his reputation. His most famous team was the Indianapolis ABC's, whose roster included such legendary figures as Oscar Charleston, Jimmy Lyons, Bingo DeMoss, and Dizzy Dismukes.

JAY SANFORD

Jay Sanford is a sports historian and researcher presently living in Arvada, Colorado. He belongs to the Society for American Baseball Research and is a member of its Negro Leagues Committee. He is also a member of the Colorado Historical Society's African American Council. He is a leading expert on black baseball and the Negro leagues. He has consulted on a number of Colorado Rockies events, including the Jackie Robinson celebration and the Negro league event. He also worked as a consultant on the highly acclaimed 1994 public television documentary *Baseball* by Ken Burns. His other TV credits include "They Came to Play" on KRMA and "Golden Diamonds" on KTSC-TV.

Jay has contributed to a number of baseball books, including *Lost Ball Parks, Negro Leagues,* and *Josh and Satch.* He wrote "The Denver Post Baseball Tournament" for *Heritage Magazine,* and is an archival contributor to the National Baseball Hall of Fame, the Negro Leagues Museum, the Babe Ruth Museum, and the Chicago White Sox Museum.

SANFORD'S SELECTIONS

Catcher: Biz Mackey, Louis Santop
Pitcher: Dick Redding, John Donaldson, Ray Brown, Hilton Smith, Jose Mendez, Chet Brewer, Webster McDonald, Bill Byrd, Slim Jones
First Base: Ben Taylor, George Giles

Louis Santop was one of the first great power hitters in the Negro leagues. (Photograph courtesy of NoirTech Research, Inc.)

Second Base: Sammy T. Hughes, Newt Allen, Frank Grant

Shortstop: Dobie Moore, Dick Lundy, Grant "Home Run" Johnson

Third Base: Oliver Marcelle, Jud Wilson, Bobby Robinson

Outfield: Turkey Stearnes, Cristobal Torriente, Jimmy Crutchfield, Wild Bill Wright, Vic Harris

LYLE K. WILSON

Lyle Wilson is a member of SABR and is on its Negro Leagues Committee. He has written several articles for the SABR publication *The National Pastime,* including "Willie Foster and the Washington Browns," "The Harlem Globetrotters Baseball Team," "Mr. Foster Comes to Washington," and "Andre Rogers." He has also contributed several articles on black baseball to newspapers, as well as website articles on the internet. He is the author of *Sunday Afternoons at Garfield Park, Seattle's Black Baseball Teams, 1911–1951,* published in 1997.

Lyle has an extensive Negro league baseball collection, including vintage programs of the Globetrotters baseball team as well as the Indianapolis Clowns dating back to the 40s, 50s, and 60s.

WILSON'S SELECTIONS

Catcher: Biz Mackey, Bruce Petway, Louis Santop, Double Duty Radcliffe, Quincy Trouppe

Pitcher: Dick Redding, Ray Brown, Hilton Smith, Jose Mendez, Chet Brewer

First Base: Mule Suttles, Buck O'Neil, Ben Taylor

Second Base: Sammy T. Hughes, Newt Allen, Piper Davis, Bingo DeMoss

Shortstop: Dick Lundy, John Beckwith

Third Base: Jud Wilson

Outfield: Turkey Stearnes, Cristobal Torriente, Pete Hill, Jimmy Crutchfield, Sam Jethroe, Wild Bill Wright, Fats Jenkins

Hall of Fame Candidates:
The Final Selection

The polls have been taken. The votes have been cast by both the Negro league veterans and the Negro league historians and authors. Before reviewing the results of those polls; however, and combining the results to arrive at a consensus on which players deserve to be considered for induction into the National Baseball Hall of Fame, the questions and concerns voiced by some of the respondents need to be addressed.

What great Negro league players, who are not presently members of the National Baseball Hall of Fame, deserve consideration for induction into those hallowed halls? In the preceding chapters, 28 former Negro league players plus 26 Negro league historians voted for the players they felt deserved consideration for induction into the National Baseball Hall of Fame in Cooperstown, New York. During the survey, several respondents questioned the validity of setting what they considered to be a quota. One respondent thought my logic was faulty. Another respondent failed to vote for certain players because the players didn't meet the service requirements set forth by the Hall in Cooperstown. These issues need to be discussed.

One of the rules of eligibility for induction into the National Baseball Hall of Fame in Cooperstown, New York, probably affected the vote count for several Negro league candidates. In order to be considered for the Hall of Fame, a player must have had 10-years service in the major leagues. That rule caused an indeterminate number of Negro league voters to bypass such outstanding players as Dobie Moore and Chino Smith. John Holway, for one, noted on his selection sheet that both Moore and Smith were ineligible because they didn't meet the 10-year requirement. After I informed John that, as far as this survey was concerned, the 10-year requirement was not a hard and fast rule for Negro league consideration, he said, "If eligibility for Cooperstown is not a criterion, you can add Moore and Smith." In my opinion, both those players passed the service requirement. Chino Smith played six years in the Negro leagues, plus five years in the even tougher Cuban Winter League. And, as former Negro league pitching ace Jesse "Mountain" Hubbard noted in John Holway's fine book, *Blackball Stars,* "If you can't judge a ball player in six years, you're not much of a judge."

Dobie Moore's Negro league career was limited to just seven years, but he also played two years in the Cuban Winter League and at least two years in the California Winter League against such major league talents as Jimmie Foxx, Al Simmons, Bob Meusel, and Emil "Irish" Meusel.

The Hall of Fame 10-year requirement is fallacious to begin with. As noted in chapter 2, Sandy Koufax, one of the greatest pitchers ever to toe the rubber, had only six years of world-class domination. His other six years of major league baseball were easily forgettable. Dizzy Dean is another good example. The great pitcher of the St. Louis Cardinals toiled in the major leagues for 12 years but, like Koufax, had just six outstanding years. In the other six years, he pitched a total of just 45 games and 239 innings. He

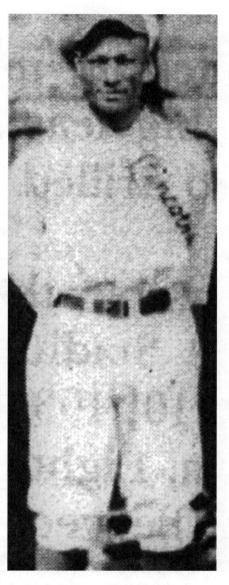

Chino Smith could challange Jud Wilson for the title of the world's greatest hitter. He hit a sizzling .434 for five years in the Negro leagues. (Photograph courtesy John B. Holway.)

pitched 96 innings in '39, 75 innings in '38, and just 54 innings in '40. In the other three years, he totaled only 14 innings! And Amos Rusie just got in under the 10-year rule by pitching three games in 1901.

Another complaint voiced about the survey was my request that the respondents vote for 27 players. Negro league experts like Brent Kelley, Bob Peterson, and Jim Overmyer said they didn't believe the voting should be on a quota basis. As Brent Kelley noted, "I don't think a quota system is even marginally valid for the selection. No one feels more strongly than I do that many outstanding Negro leaguers are not in the Hall, but each man must be evaluated on his merits, not on his color." Jim Overmyer said, "I didn't make 27 picks because I'm not really sure I could find 27 men on the list who ought to be in the Hall of Fame." And Bob Peterson said he thought "10 to 12 percent of the people in the Hall who played after 1900 and before about 1960 ought to be Negro leaguers" based on the percentage of blacks in the American population.

Their arguments are valid. There should not be a quota, at least not a random quota, such as the one utilized by the Baseball Hall of Fame. The Hall has embarrassed itself by repeatedly setting random quotas for electing Negro leaguers into the Hall. The last quota, announced in 1994, was for five Negro leaguers to be admitted into the Hall, with one player a year being elected from 1995 through 1999. Last year, they extended the quota for two more years and two more players. The number of 27 players arrived at for the survey was an estimate, not a quota. It was based on the actual number of blacks that were elected to the Hall of Fame between 1962 and 1999. That number was 16 and amounted to 29 percent of the total honorees. Making the assumption that the percentage was the same during the first half of the twentieth century as it was during the second half, then 29 percent of the 147 members elected to the Hall should have been black. That number was 43, and since 16 former Negro leaguers had been elected by the Negro Leagues Committee and the Veterans Committee between 1971 and 1999, another 27 players still need to be recognized.

Bob Peterson's concern about electing more than 10 to 12 percent of blacks to the Hall of Fame is justified, based on the percentage of blacks in the American population. However, the 29 percent number, used for this survey, is more all-encompassing. Many blacks who are presently in the major leagues are not American born. For example, since 1956, my research indicates that there have been approximately 200 major league players who were born in the Dominican Republic, an equal number from Puerto Rico, as well as a large influx of players from Venezuela, Panama, Nicaragua, Curacao, and other areas of Central and South America, and the Caribbean. By actual count, in 1999, 29 percent of the major league players were black, about 10 percent from the United States and the remainder from outside the continental limits.

In a recent SABR Latin America Committee Newsletter, Chairman Eduardo Valero reviewed the increasing participation of Latin American players in the major leagues. According to Valero, the 1999 opening-day major league rosters included 165 Latin Americans, or 19.4 percent of the total of 841 players. The minor leagues had 2,300 players in 30 organizations, not counting the Mexican League. Of the 2,300 players, 1,371 were from the Dominican Republic, 582 from Venezuela, and 122 from Puerto Rico. Most of them were black.

Brent Kelley had another concern, which he noted in his correspondence. "One of the real problems in electing blacks from years ago, of course, is that no one is around now who saw them play, at least no one with a vote. Put Duty, Bobby Robinson, Bill Lindsay, Bubba Hyde, and two or three others who are now in their 90s on the Veterans Committee, and let them vote." Brent is correct in that it would be logical and extremely valuable to have the old Negro league veterans provide the Veterans Committee with their eyewitness evaluations of the Negro league pioneers. On the other hand, it is common practice for the National Baseball Hall of Fame to elect old-time major league players without ever having seen them in action. George Davis, the great nineteenth century shortstop of the New York Giants was admitted to the Hall in 1998, 88 years after he played his last professional game. Vic Willis, whose career spanned the years from 1898 to 1910, was elected in 1995, Roger Connor (1880–1897) in 1976, Mickey Welch (1880–1892) in 1973, and Tim Keefe (1880–1893) in 1964. Unfortunately, if wrongs are to be righted and recognition given to deserving players, it is a necessary evil for the Veterans Committee to elect players they never saw in action. In my opinion, it is better to have a few players in the Hall whose skills might not have warranted their election than to leave out one truly deserving player.

Surveys and polls are far from perfect, but again, they may be the best way to determine which players are Hall of Fame material. And many of the older Negro league veterans did participate in the study, players like Double Duty Radcliffe, Red Lindsay, and the Reverend Harold Tinker. Other old timers were asked to participate, but did not respond. I have noted over the years, in polls and surveys I have read, that the participants are not especially subjective. This is true of all groups in all endeavors. It is true of baseball players as well, not only Negro league players, but also major league players. And it is true of historians and authors.

Players seem to be less subjective than historians, when it comes to evaluating the talents of their fellow players. Favoritism is evident in many of their selections. Voting often seems to be a popularity contest rather than a fair evaluation of a player's skills. This may be due to the fact that the voters had close personal relationships with many of the candidates, making it difficult for them to be completely impartial. Former players tend to favor their friends, teammates, players they played against, or players in the same league. They often ignore players from other leagues and other eras, or players with whom they did not have a friendly relationship. Also, some players, even journeymen players, have very large egos and cast votes for themselves, demeaning the entire process.

John Holway noted the same thing, but added, "Historians are biased too. Many historians have their favorite players." Cooperstown is no different, according to John. "Members of the selection committee, whether it be the Veterans Committee or the Negro Leagues Committee, use their influence to reward their old teammates. It's human nature. There are many major leaguers enshrined in Cooperstown who owe their election to an influential teammate on an advisory committee or a selection committee. The same is true with the selection of the Negro league greats. The first inductees were all easterners until someone from the West joined the committee."

In spite of all the problems associated with using a survey to determine worthy Hall of Fame candidates, it is still the best way to identify the great players. However, the final results of this study will not automatically present 27 former Negro league players for consideration for induction into the National Baseball Hall of Fame. The number 27 was an estimate only, used as a voting tool to stimulate the voters. The final number of players presented for Hall of Fame consideration will depend on the strength of the support shown each player by both the Negro league veterans and the Negro league historians. Brent Kelley said, "Your project is worthwhile and I wish you much luck, but limit selection to quality, not quantity." This study will endeavor to do that.

The survey to recommend players who should be considered for induction into the National Baseball Hall of Fame included 28 former Negro league players and 26 Negro league historians, though some did not vote. The first thing that was noticeable in the surveys was that there was more variability in the players' choices than in the historians' choices. The players cast votes for a total of 92 former players, including 21 players who were write-ins. The historians cast votes for 76 players including 14 write-ins.

In tabulating the votes from the former players, there were a total of 17 Negro league veterans who received at least 50 percent of the votes. And sos, about 5.4 percent of the nominees received 50 percent or more of the votes.

Negro League Veterans Who Received
at Least 50 Percent of the Votes from Former Players

Negro League Veteran	Number of Votes	Percentage of Votes
Biz Mackey	23	82%
Hilton Smith	22	79%
Turkey Stearnes	21	75%
Dick Lundy	21	75%
Mule Suttles	20	70%
Jimmy Crutchfield	20	70%
Willard Brown	19	68%
Wild Bill Wright	19	68%
Ray Brown	17	61%
Sammy T. Hughes	16	57%
George Scales	16	57%
Newt Allen	16	57%
Chet Brewer	15	54%
Sam Jethroe	15	54%
Dick Redding	14	50%
Louis Santop	14	50%
Artie Wilson	14	50%

Others receiving 10 or more votes included Buck O'Neil with 13, "Double Duty" Radcliffe, Sam Bankhead, and Jud Wilson with 12, Hank Thompson, and Vic Harris with 11, and Cristobal Torriente and Oliver Marcelle with 10.

The list of 17 players with 50 percent or more of the votes included two catchers, four pitchers, one first baseman, three second basemen, two shortstops, and five outfielders. No third basemen received more than 12 votes (43 percent). The reason for the absence of any third basemen is not clear. What is clear, is that the total number of votes for third basemen were the lowest of any position. Outfielders received a total of 164 votes, pitchers 146 votes, shortstops 70 votes, first basemen 61 votes, second basemen and catchers 54 votes, and third basemen just 49 votes.

Negro League Veterans Who Received
at Least 50 Percent of the Votes from Historians

Negro League Veteran	Number of Votes	Percentage of Votes
Biz Mackey	25	100%
Dick Lundy	24	96%

Negro League Veteran	Number of Votes	Percentage of Votes
Turkey Stearnes	24	96%
Cristobal Torriente	24	96%
Mule Suttles	22	88%
Hilton Smith	21	84%
Dick Redding	20	80%
Ben Taylor	20	80%
Oliver Marcelle	20	80%
Jud Wilson	20	80%
Louis Santop	19	76%
Jose Mendez	18	72%
Pete Hill	17	68%
Ray Brown	16	64%
Chet Brewer	16	64%
Frank Grant	16	64%
Willard Brown	15	60%
Sammy T. Hughes	14	56%
John Beckwith	14	56%
Spot Poles	13	52%
Wild Bill Wright	13	52%

The variation in the players' votes is apparent by the fact that only one player, Biz Mackey, received at least 80 percent of their votes. On the other hand, there were 10 players who received 80 percent or more of the historians' votes.

In comparing the two lists, it is obvious that the historians voted for many more "pioneers" than the players did. Eight of the twenty-one players selected by the historians ended their careers before 1933. Only one player selected by the players did. That was Louis Santop whose career spanned the years 1909 through 1926. The historians heavily supported such noted pioneers as Ben Taylor, Cristobal Torriente, Pete Hill, Frank Grant, Jose Mendez, Spot Poles, and Oliver Marcelle, all of whom were essentially ignored by the players.

Al Fennar, whose career covered the years 1932 to 1934, probably spoke for many of the players when he said, "I am only marking who I have played with or against. I cannot in good conscience do otherwise." As a result, the players selection list contains mostly players whose careers peaked during the 1930s and 1940s. Fifteen of the seventeen players who received 50 percent or more of the players votes retired from the game during the 1940s. Only Dick Redding (1938) and Louis Santop (1926) retired prior to 1940.

Several players who received strong support from their fellow players received little or no support from the historians. These included Jimmy Crutchfield who was chosen on 71 percent of the players' ballots but on only 24 percent of the historians' ballots, Sam Jethroe who picked up 54 percent of the players' votes and 36 percent of the historians' votes, and Artie Wilson who was selected by 50 percent of the players but only 20 percent of the historians. Crutchfield had a long career in the Negro leagues, from 1930 to 1945, and was very popular with his teammates as well as with opposing players. Jethroe and Wilson had sizzling Negro league careers, with batting averages of approximately .330 and .377 respectively. Unfortunately, their careers, particularly Wilson's, were too short for a fair evaluation of their talents. Artie Wilson played only four full years in the Negro leagues. Sam Jethroe did have a distinguished seven-year career in the

Spot Poles was called the "Ty Cobb" of the Negro leagues. (Photograph courtesy Jay Sanford.)

Negro leagues, as well as a brief but successful major league career and a long stint in AAA ball. But apparently it did not impress the voters sufficiently.

There were several surprises in the voting. Some apparent world-class players were bypassed by the voting players. Cristobal Torriente was an overwhelming favorite of the historians, racking up a monstrous 88 percent of the vote, but he elicited a lukewarm reception from the players, appearing on only 36 percent of the ballots. Jud Wilson, one of the Negro league's most dominant hitters during the 1930s, gathered 80 percent of the historians' votes, but only 43 percent of the players' votes. And John Beckwith, another explosive hitter, impressed 56 percent of the historians but only 29 percent of the players. Both Wilson and Beckwith had abrasive personalities and were known to fight with umpires, fans, and other players. It might have been their combative nature rather than their baseball ability that produced only minimal support from their peers. Certainly the voting players were familiar with both players' talents on the field, since both of them were in their prime during the 1930s. Torriente, on the other hand, whose career was essentially over by 1928, was not well known by the players doing the voting. Since he was a Cuban, he returned home after the season ended, playing in the Cuban Winter League from 1913 to 1927, so he did not cultivate many personal relationships in the United States.

Another surprise was the lack of strong support for either Sammy T. Hughes or Newt Allen. Both players were sensational Negro league stars, whose play at second base was considered a thing of beauty. Both players were exceptional defensive players, and both were good contact hitters with averages around the .300 mark. Actually Hughes, Allen, and George Scales each received 57 percent of the players' votes. Hughes also recived 56 percent of the historians' votes, but Allen garnered just 48 percent of the historians' votes, and Scales got only 28 percent.

In order to have a strong case for induction into the National Baseball Hall of Fame, the final combined poll of the players and historians had to be overwhelming for an individual player. The voting requirements for a player to be selected by the Veterans Committee for induction into the National Baseball Hall of Fame is 75 percent. The same percentage was used here for the top tier of candidates. Under that guideline, five players stood out from the rest as definite Hall of Fame candidates.

Candidate	Average	Historians' Ballots	Players' Ballots
Biz Mackey	91%	100%	82%
Hilton Smith	91%	84%	79%
Dick Lundy	85%	96%	84%
Turkey Stearnes	85%	96%	75%
Mule Suttles	79%	88%	71%

There should not be any objections to the selection of those five players. They are all worthy of residence in Cooperstown. In fact, Turkey Stearnes was elected to the Hall of Fame in 2000, and Hilton Smith in 2001.

A second tier of players was selected from those players with a combined voting percentage of 60 percent or more, a strong showing considering it was the average of both players and historians. Seven players met that requirement.

Candidate	Average	Historians' Ballots	Players' Ballots
Dick Redding	64%	80%	50%
Cristobal Torriente	64%	96%	36%

Candidate	Average	Historians' Ballots	Players' Ballots
Willard Brown	64%	71%	45%
Louis Santop	62%	76%	50%
Ray Brown	62%	64%	61%
Jud Wilson	60%	80%	43%
Wild Bill Wright	60%	52%	68%

There probably isn't much disagreement with that list either. Actually four of the players—Redding, Torriente, Santop, and Wilson—received exceptionally strong support from the historians, garnering more than 75 percent of their vote, but were slighted by the players for whatever reason. All of them, except Jud Wilson, had essentially completed their playing careers before 1930, so they were unfamiliar to most of the voting players. Jud Wilson may have cultivated an enemy or two among his contemporaries. His bat certainly didn't let him down. Ray Brown received good support from both groups, and Wild Bill Wright was favored more by the players than the historians. Willard Brown, surprisingly, was favored by the historians over the players, 71 percent to 45 percent.

After reviewing the results of the polls, it was apparent that the pioneers, the players who helped build Negro league baseball, and whose careers peaked in the nineteenth century, or during the first two decades of the twentieth century, were generally ignored by the Players Panel, most of whose careers began after 1930. They were also slighted by the Historians Panel, many of whom did not have sufficient expertise in the early game. I felt a panel of experts was needed, people whose knowledge of the early game, and the players who laid the groundwork for the great Negro leagues that followed, was without equal. This led to the formation of the Pioneers Panel, which consisted of ten historians whose research delved deeply into the early history of the black game. The panel, chosen from the 25 historian respondents, included Todd Bolton, Dick Clark, Larry Hogan, John Holway, Brent Kelley, Merl Kleinknecht, Larry Lester, Jerry Malloy, Bob Peterson, and Jim Riley. A 70 percent vote was required of the committee for a Hall of Fame induction review recommendation. Players who were subsequently selected by the Pioneer Committee, in addition to the players selected by the combined Players-Historians Panels, were:

Ben Taylor	80%
Sammy T. Hughes	80%
Oliver Marcelle	90%
Pete Hill	70%
Spot Poles	70%

Pete Hill was called by Cum Posey the most consistent hitter he ever saw.

Redding, Torriente, and Wilson also met the historians pioneer requirements, but they had been selected previously by the combined vote.

Finally, I felt one last loophole needed to be closed. I think the 10-year requirement may have prevented some players from receiving their just reward. And, it seemed to me, that other deserving players just fell through the cracks. Claiming artistic license, I selected some candidates of my own. Originally, I identified seven players I felt deserved recognition in Hall of Fame voting. They were Chino Smith, Dobie Moore, John Beckwith, John Donaldson, Grant "Home Run" Johnson, Bill Monroe, and Edgar Wesley. After due consideration, I limited my support to just three players, although I still personally believe that Donaldson, Johnson, Monroe, and Wesley are also Hall of Famers. My three selections are Chino Smith, Dobie Moore, and John Beckwith.

The reason I felt so strongly about the candidacy of these three players is that they were three of the most dominant hitters in Negro league history, a fact that cannot be ignored. The top ten major league players with the highest career batting averages, with the exception of Shoeless Joe Jackson who was banned from the game, are members in good standing in the National

Baseball Hall of Fame. And, hopefully, Jackson will join them in the near future. It is only right that the top hitters in Negro league history receive equal treatment. How do you keep a .434 hitter out of the Hall of Fame? Or a .355 hitter? Or a .352 hitter?

As for the 10-year rule, both Smith and Moore could have sat on the bench for three or four years, with mediocre results like Koufax did, to fulfill their 10-year service requirement, and their stats would still be sensational. In the end, 10 years, 7 years, or 6 years are unimportant as far as Chino and Dobie are concerned. They were two of the finest baseball players ever to don a uniform, true Hall of Famers. And John Beckwith hit the ball as far and as often as anyone in baseball history. John Holway didn't call him the "Black Bomber" for nothing.

Edgar Wesley has impressive credentials for Hall of Fame consideration, although he has been left off all the lists in this study. He only received five votes from the combined committee and just a single vote from the Historians Panel. Yet the man slugged the ball at a solid .318 clip and averaged 24 home runs per 550 at-bats. In major league terms, that would produce a .270 batting average with 30 home runs a year. And how about Tetelo Vargas who had a career average of .340 in the Negro leagues, or Valentin Dreke

John Beckwith played in the Negro leagues for 20 years, batting .352, second all-time. (Photograph courtesy NoirTech Research, Inc.)

Dobie Moore was a superstar at shortstop. He could hit, hit with power, run, field, and throw. (Photograph courtesy Robert W. Peterson collection, the National Baseball Hall of Fame Library.)

with an average of .327, or Fats Jenkins with an average of .337, or even Huck Rile who scorched the ball at a .339 clip, whacked 16 homers for every 550 at-bats, and racked up an overall 48–27 record as a pitcher. And then there's Oscar "Heavy" Johnson, the outfielder for the Kansas City Monarchs, who hit a resounding .350 with 16 home runs.

John Holway, whose 30-year research effort has helped reconstruct much of the Negro league statistical base, has identified Chino Smith as the greatest hitter in Negro league history, with an average of .434. Although he had less than 1000 at-bats in the Negro leagues, Chino also hammered Cuban Winter League pitching unmercifully, to the tune of .335. Dobie Moore led all Negro league hitters, who had more than 1700 at-bats, with a career batting average of .355. He was followed closely by Jud Wilson at .354 and John Beckwith at .352.

The four categories noted above have identified 20 former Negro league players who should be considered for induction into the Hall of Fame. That would more than double the present contingent in Cooperstown, but would still leave many outstanding players on the outside, looking in.

Those players still "on the bubble," possibly deserving consideration for entry into the National Baseball Hall of Fame but not quite getting the recognition for their efforts that other players received and lacking strong support from one or both of the selection panels include:

Candidate	Average	Historians' Ballots	Players' Ballots
Frank Grant	32%	64%	4%
Jose Mendez	40%	72%	11%
John Donaldson	23%	36%	11%
Grant "Home Run" Johnson	15%	28%	4%
Bill Monroe	13%	24%	4%
Chet Brewer	58%	64%	56%
Newt Allen	53%	48%	57%
Edgar Wesley	9%	16%	4%

One thing that militates against the final selection for Hall of Fame consideration of some players is their batting averages. Newt Allen, who is "on the bubble," had a career average in the Negro leagues of .302. Based on research presented in two of my previous works, *King of Swat* and *Baseball's Other All-Stars*, Negro league players would lose approximately 48 points off their average if they played in the major leagues. That would leave Allen with an adjusted average of .254. Sammy T. Hughes would have an adjusted average of .252, and Judy Johnson, who is already safely ensconced in Cooperstown, would have a barely visible .237 batting average. Bingo DeMoss, who was selected on four of the combined ballots, would be below the Mendoza line at .188, while Oliver Marcelle would be at .254, and Dave Malarcher would be bogged down at .219. Under those conditions, Newt Allen, Sammy T. Hughes, and Oliver Marcelle are borderline cases for entry into the Hall of Fame. Bingo DeMoss and Dave Malarcher do not have the qualifications necessary for induction. And Judy Johnson, who may have been the beneficiary of friendly faces on the selection committee of which he was also a member, didn't have the offensive firepower necessary for Hall of Fame membership.

Other players who are selected periodically for Negro league all-star teams fall into the same category. Jimmy Crutchfield, who received 71 percent of the player's votes, as noted before, was a good all-around player, often characterized as a team player, but he lacked the credentials for Hall of Fame consideration. His .280 Negro league batting average would convert to only .232 in the major leagues. Bruce Petway, a superior defensive catcher, batted only .254 in the Negro leagues and .210 in the Cuban Winter League. Jimmie Lyons, a talented outfielder with outstanding speed, batted only .297 in the Negro leagues and .288 in Cuba. First baseman George Giles, batted only .302 in the Negro leagues (adjusted to .254), certainly not high enough for Hall of Fame consideration. Buck O'Neil was in the same category. His .298 league batting average would be equivalent to just .250 in the major leagues, hardly enough for Hall of Fame consideration, unless he slugged 40 home runs a year. And Sam Bankhead, who received 20 votes from the combined panel (38 percent), batted just .297 in the Negro league averages, a figure that would convert to .249 in the majors.

Of the present 200-plus members of the Hall of Fame, only three — catcher Ray Schalk, first baseman Harmon Killebrew, and shortstop Rabbit Maranville — had career batting averages below .260. In fact, there were only seven players with averages under .270. And only two second basemen, Bobby Doerr and Nellie Fox, both at .288, had career batting averages under .300.

During 1999, the Society for American Baseball Research (SABR), conducted a survey of its members to determine the top 40 Negro leaguers of the twentieth century. The selection included managers and executives as well as players and are listed here in order of their support.

1T	Buck Leonard	20	Cristobal Torriente
1T	Satchel Paige	21	Dick Redding
3	Cool Papa Bell	22	Louis Santop
4	Oscar Charleston	26T	Buck O'Neil
5T	Rube Foster	26T	Jud Wilson
5T	Josh Gibson	28	Hilton Smith
5T	Pop Lloyd	29	Dick Lundy
8T	Martin Dihigo	30T	Larry Doby
8T	Turkey Stearnes	32	Ted "Double Duty"
8T	Willie Wells		Radcliffe
11T	Ray Dandridge	33	Ben Taylor
11T	Bullet Rogan	34	Jose Mendez
13T	Mule Suttles	35T	Newt Allen
13T	Smokey Joe Williams	35T	Sol White
15	Judy Johnson	35T	John Beckwith
16	Leon Day	38	Sam Jethroe
17	Biz Mackey	39T	Bingo DeMoss
18	Willie Foster	39T	Bruce Petway
19	Monte Irvin	39T	Quincy Trouppe

The first 12 players are now in the Hall of Fame, with the election of Turkey Stearnes. Out of the first 20 in the poll, only Mule Suttles, Biz Mackey, and Cristobal Torriente are not members of that elite group. Stearnes, Suttles, and Mackey are in the first tier selected by the player-historian poll, and Torriente is close behind. He would have been in the first tier if he had received decent support from the voting players, who only gave him 36 percent of their votes. The historians gave him an almost unanimous 96 percent victory, putting him in a tie with Stearnes and Lundy for second place in the historians' poll behind Biz Mackey.

Twenty-eight of the first thirty players in the SABR poll are generally considered to be Hall of Fame candidates by Negro league experts. Of the final 10 players listed, only John Beckwith and Ben Taylor seem to have the qualifications for Hall of Fame consideration. The other eight are either "on the bubble" or out in left field completely.

Conspicuously absent from the SABR poll are Spot Poles and Pete Hill. This is not surprising because the SABR poll had the same problems as the player-historian poll. Very few SABR members are Negro league history buffs with a good working knowledge of the black pioneers who blazed the baseball trail through segregated America that finally resulted in the formation of organized Negro leagues and eventually led to the collapse of the heinous organized baseball color barrier. Another problem associated with garnering support for Poles and Hill is a severe lack of supporting statistics. The available stats give Pete Hill just an even .300 batting average and Poles a .290 average. How these numbers compare to their actual career stats is unknown, and how they compare to major league averages of the time is also unknown. Both players have received strong support from contemporaries. Cum Posey, an early Negro league outfielder and later an owner and Negro league executive, selected Pete Hill for his all-time all-star team. He called Hill the most consistent hitter he had ever seen. And Tweed Webb placed Hill ninth on his list of great Negro league outfielders. Less is known about Spotswood Poles. Many contempories called Poles "The Black Ty Cobb" because of his scientific batting stroke and his blazing speed.

The final selection of the combined player-historian poll consists of four groups, totalling 20 players. These 20 players are qualified candidates for induction into the National Baseball Hall of Fame in Cooperstown, New York. They should be considered by the Veterans Committee.

Players Receiving at least 75 percent of the Combined Vote of the Players and Historians: Biz Mackey, Turkey Stearnes (elected to the Hall in 2000), Dick Lundy, Mule Suttles, Hilton Smith (elected to the Hall in 2001)

Players Receiving at least 60 percent of the Combined Vote of the Players and Historians: Louis Santop, Dick Redding, Ray Brown, Willard Brown, Wild Bill Wright, Jud Wilson, Cristobal Torriente

Players Selected by the Pioneers Committee: Ben Taylor, Oliver Marcelle, Sammy T. Hughes, Spot Poles, Pete Hill

Willard Brown was a long-ball hitter in the Negro leagues. In Puerto Rico, he was called "Our Babe Ruth."

Candidates Selected by the Author: Chino Smith, Dobie Moore, John Beckwith

By Position, the 20 Recommended Negro League Hall of Fame Candidates:

Catcher: Biz Mackey, Louis Santop

Pitcher: Hilton Smith, Ray Brown, Dick Redding

First Base: Mule Suttles, Ben Taylor

Second Base: Sammy T. Hughes

Shortstop: Dobie Moore, John Beckwith, Dick Lundy

Third Base: Oliver Marcelle, Jud Wilson

Outfield: Cristobal Torriente, Turkey Stearnes, Willard Brown, Wild Bill Wright, Spot Poles, Pete Hill, Chino Smith

Three borderline players also deserve further review.

Jose Mendez, who received 72 percent of the Historians Panel vote and 60 percent of the Pioneers Panel vote, was ignored by the Players Panel, probably because a sore arm essentially ended his pitching career in 1914, long before any of the Players Panel had even reached puberty. Also, Mendez, a Cuban native, returned home every winter to compete in the Cuban Winter League, so he didn't cultivate many permanent friendships in America. Chet Brewer received 58 percent of the combined vote, split almost evenly between the Historians Panel (64 percent) and the Players Panel

(56 percent). Newt Allen also received good support from both groups, but not quite enough for a recommendation. His 53 percent combined vote consisted on a 48 percent vote by the Historians Panel and 57 percent from the Players Panel.

Hall of Fame Candidates: Biographies

Twenty former Negro league players have been recommended for consideration for induction into the National Baseball Hall of Fame in Cooperstown, New York. Twelve players were selected by a combined vote of a Player's Panel and a Historians Panel. Five early Negro league pioneers were added by a special Historians Pioneer Panel. And the final three were chosen by the author. The biographies of these players follow in alphabetical order.

JOHN BECKWITH

John Beckwith, dubbed "the Black Bomber" by biographer John Holway, was one of the most devastating hitters ever to play baseball. The native of Louisville, Kentucky, broke into black baseball as a catcher with the Montgomery Gray Sox at the tender age of 14. Five years later, as a 19-year-old shortstop for the Chicago Giants, he became the first player, black or white, to hit a ball over the laundry roof behind the distant 360-foot left field fence at Cincinnati's Redland Field, home of the National League Cincinnati Reds.

Beckwith grew up in Chicago and, like most young boys, played baseball whenever he had the chance. He was always big for his age, and he soon outgrew the kids leagues in the Windy City. After breaking into the professional ranks in Montgomery, he quickly moved on to the Giants, where he spent the next seven years. He might have stayed in Chicago longer, but he had a run-in with the law and had to leave town. John was a big, moody individual, standing 6'3" tall and weighing in at a muscular 230 pounds, and he was ready to fight at the slightest affront. He battled with his teammates, with players on other teams, and with umpires, as well as with the police. As a result, the powerful slugger moved around frequently, playing with no less than 14 teams over a storied 23-year Negro league career.

Several players, including Double Duty Radcliffe, thought Beckwith's bad-attitude reputation was a bum rap. One of his teammates, Turkey Stearnes, told biographer John Holway, "John Beckwith was one of my favorite ballplayers. He'd fight in a minute, but if you didn't bother him, he didn't bother you. I never did have any trouble with him, and I played on the club right beside him."

Regardless of his personality, the mighty slugger was in a class by himself when the game began. He was versatile in the field, handling several positions competently, including catcher, shortstop, third base, and outfield. But it was with a bat in his hand that he brought *oohs* and *aahs* from the crowd. He reportedly hit the ball as a far as any man alive, including Josh Gibson and Babe Ruth. He once hit a home run in Griffith Stadium in Washington that cleared the left field fence, and struck an advertising sign 460 feet from home plate and 40 feet above the ground.

John Beckwith hit the ball far and he hit it often. In 1930 he led the Negro League West in batting with an average of .480. He also enjoyed season averages of .419 in 1921, .403 in 1924, and .402 in 1925. And he led the league in home runs twice, with 19 in 1930, and 9 the following year. Beckwith's Negro league career lasted from 1916 to 1938. When he retired, the right handed bomber left behind a Negro league career batting average of .352, third all-time for players with 1700 or more at-bats. He also averaged 31 home runs for every 550 at-bats. If he had been fortunate enough to play major league ball, it is estimated that he would have averaged about .304 with 39 home runs a year. In any one season, he could have been expected to punish the ball at a .350 clip with 50 or more home runs. According to fragmentary statistics, Big John hammered big league pitching to the tune of .317 in 24 exhibition games.

RAY BROWN

Raymond Brown was a devastating pitcher, whose sharp breaking curve ball and dancing knuckleball had batters pounding the ball into the ground all day. He was the workhorse of the Homestead Grays pitching staff for 16 years, often pitching doubleheaders, and even playing the outfield when not pitching. He was a dangerous man at the plate, rapping the ball at a .316 clip.

He pitched the Grays to nine consecutive Negro National League pennants between 1937 and 1945. They also won two World Championships in four tries. Brown joined the Grays in 1933, at the age of 25, and proceeded to go 6–1 in his first year. Two years later, he compiled a record of 12–3, then went 7–0 in 1938. He reached his peak in 1940, running up a record of 24–4 in 32 games, averaging almost eight innings per start. He followed that spectacular feat with seasons of 13–6, 12–4, 4–1, 11–3, and 4–2.

When the Negro league season ended, Raymond Brown hit the road, traveling the highway from north to south, and east to west, every year for 23 years. Satchel Paige was also a vagabond ballplayer, but where Paige usually stayed within the boundaries of the United States, Brown wore out more passports than the Bolshoi Ballet. In addition to his Negro league career, the wily right hander played ball in Mexico, Cuba, Puerto Rico, and Canada. And he was a big winner wherever he went. He went 21–4 in the Cuban Winter League in 1936, had a 12–4 record in Puerto Rico in the 1941-42 season, and was 13–4 in Mexico in 1948.

When the color line was finally broken by Jackie Robinson, Ray Brown, at 42 years of age, was too old to be invited to pitch in the major leagues. However, he did pitch in Canada for three years, and he won 11 games against 10 losses for Sherbrooke in the Class C Provincial League in 1951.

His career totals are Hall of Fame credentials. The obvious question is when?

League	Won-Lost Record	Percentage
Negro leagues	146–55	.726
Mexican League	51–36	.586
Cuban Winter League	46–20	.697
Puerto Rican Winter League	29–8	.784
Provincial League	12–10	.545
Totals	284–129	.688

WILLARD BROWN

Willard Jesse Brown was known affectionately as "Ese Hombre" (That Man) in Puerto Rico. In the U.S., he was called "Home Run" Brown. He was a terrifying hitter wherever he played. He could hit for average, and he could hit for distance. He was also an outstanding center fielder, with excellent range and a strong throwing arm. And he was a blur on the bases. He had all the attributes of a superstar. The only thing he lacked was desire.

Brown, who was born in Shreveport, Louisiana, on June 26, 1911, began his professional baseball career with the famed Kansas City Monarchs at the age of 24. His teammates included Negro league legends Ray Brown, Satchel Paige, and "Bullet Joe" Rogan. The Monarchs of the late '30s were a championship club, winning pennants in 1937, and 1939 through 1942. Home Run Brown sparked the offense, winning batting titles in 1937 (.371), 1938 (.356), and 1941 (.337). He played only two games in 1940, opting instead for the Mexican League. He led the Negro American League in home runs seven times in his career, with 8 in 143 at-bats in 1937, 6 in 104 at bats in 1938, 3 in just 89 at-bats in 1941, 7 in 181 at-bats in 1942, 6 in 113 at-bats in 1943, 13 in 230 at-bats in 1946, and 18 in 260 at-bats in 1948.

Overall, in his 15-year Negro league career, all spent with Kansas City, the 6', 195-pound bomber tattooed opposing pitchers for a .347 batting average, and an average of 20 home runs for every 550 at-bats. He had a chance to play major league ball in 1947, when his contract was purchased by the lowly St. Louis Browns of the American League. In reality, however, he didn't stand a chance of succeeding. It was only a few short weeks after Larry Doby had integrated the league, and the racial atmosphere was oppressive. He was the first black player to hit a home run in the American League, but he did it with a bat he borrowed from a white player, and the player broke the bat later so Brown wouldn't use it again. After 21 pressure-packed games, Brown gave up his major league dream and returned to the Kansas City Monarchs.

Outside the majors, Brown was a hero wherever he traveled. He played two years in Mexico, batting a cool .354 with Nuevo Laredo in 1940. His teammates included Negro leaguers Hilton Smith, Andy "Pullman" Porter, Bus Clarkson, and Lonnie Summers. He spent a few short weeks in Cuba over the winter of 1937-38, but had only 55 at-bats and a futile .145 batting average to show for it. In Puerto Rico, he was idolized. Luis Alvelo called Brown "Our Babe Ruth," and said one of his greatest thrills was attending Escobar Stadium in San Juan and seeing Brown hit a tremendous home run that carried over the left field wall and landed near the beach.

Willard Brown played baseball in the strong Puerto Rican Winter League for ten years. He led the league in hitting and in home runs three times each. He captured two triple crowns, winning his first one in 1947-48 with an average of .432, with 27 home runs and 86 RBIs, in 234 at-bats. He won his second triple crown two years later with a batting average of .353, with 16 homers and 97 RBIs in 331 at-bats. He also took the batting championship in 1946-47 with an average of .390, and the home run crown in 1948-49, with 18. When he retired, "Ese Hombre" left behind a PRWL career batting average of .350, the highest career average in PRWL history. By comparison, Roberto Clemente hit .323, Roy Campanella hit .276, and Orlando Cepeda hit .323.

It is interesting to note that Willard Brown was still terrorizing pitchers between 1946 and 1949, winning five home-run crowns and three batting titles, in two different leagues. At the same time the St. Louis Browns were anchoring the bottom of the American League, finishing last once, seventh twice (in an eight-team league), and sixth once. Pride and ignorance are terrible sins. They cost the Browns, among other things, respect in the American League. They not only lost the powerful bat of Willard Brown, they also lost the services of slugging third baseman Hank Thompson, who later went on to stardom with the New York Giants. Their replacements on the Browns, players like Eddie Pellagrini and Paul Lehner, hit in the .230 to .240 range with little power.

Willard Brown's organized-ball career did not end with his disastrous three weeks in St. Louis. In 1950, he joined Ottowa of the Class C Border League, where he pounded the league's pitchers for a .352 average. It was the highest average in the league, but he didn't have enough at-bats to qualify for the batting championship. After spending the next two years bouncing back and forth between the Negro American League, the Dominican Summer League, and the Mexican League, he returned to organized ball with Dallas of the Class AA Texas League, a notorious pitchers league. All he did there was bat a combined .307 and hit 91 home runs in 2000 at-bats, an average of 25 home runs for every 550 at-bats, over a four-year period — and he was 42 years old when he entered the league!

Willard "Home Run" Brown retired from organized ball after that season, went back to the Monarchs for one last shot in 1958 (batting .324 in 14 games), then put the bat away for good at the age of 47.

PETE HILL

Pete Hill, a powerfully built left handed hitter whose career covered the first quarter of the twentieth century, was called the most consistent hitter of his time by Cum Posey. Preston J. "Pete" Hill first saw the light of day in 1880, somewhere in the northeastern section of the country. He broke into professional baseball with the Pittsburgh Keystones in 1899. He joined Rube Foster on the Philadelphia Giants team in 1903 and followed Foster to the Chicago Union Giants in 1907. When Foster formed the Chicago American Giants four years later, Pete Hill was his first recruit.

The Chicago American Giants were the most dominant team in Negro baseball during the teens, a team built on pitching, speed, and defense. The 1917 contingent's world-class pitching staff included Cannonball Dick Redding, Frank Wickware, and Cuban Hall of Famer Luis Padron. The defense up the middle was unmatchable, with Bruce Petway, Bingo DeMoss, John Henry Lloyd, and Pete Hill. It is doubtful if there has ever been a better middle defense anywhere, even in the major leagues. The offense was led by Hill and Lloyd.

Pete Hill stood 6'1" tall, weighed a muscular 215 pounds, and had power to all fields. The left handed slugger was a line-drive hitter who hit the ball where it was pitched, and hit it with authority. John Holway credits Hill with a .300 batting average for 1555 at-bats, but those stats are from the Negro National League only, from 1920 to 1926, when Hill was in his 40s, and are not truly representative of his real hitting ability. According to Jim Riley, Hill hit .423 in 1910, .400 in 1911, .357 in 1912, and .302 in 1914, a .371 clip for four years. Richard Bak, in his book, *Turkey Stearnes and the Detroit Stars,* credited Hill with a .344 average for the Stars in 1921 and 1922, with 9 doubles, 6 triples, and 5 home runs in 215 at-bats.

Hill also played baseball in the Cuban Winter League from 1907 through 1917, hitting .307 with outstanding power. He led the league in hitting in 1910-11 with an average of .365 and also showed the way in base hits and triples. He batted .343 in 1908 and led the league in runs scored, hits, and triples. He also led the league in triples with four in 139 at-bats in 1908-09 and batted .373 in 1916-17.

The big outfielder was a five-point player who excelled in all phases of the game. He was a center fielder with exceptional range and a strong, accurate throwing arm. On the bases, he was fast and aggressive. Jim Riley said, "He was a nervy baserunner who upset pitchers and infielders like Jackie Robinson was to do a quarter decade later. He was described as a 'restless type, always in motion, jumping back and forth, trying to draw a throw from the pitcher.'"

Ben Taylor, talking to Jim Riley, paid Pete Hill the ultimate compliment when he said, "[He] will probably never have an equal as a hitter. I think he is the most dangerous man in a pinch in baseball."

SAMMY T. HUGHES

There were a number of Negro league second basemen who towered over their competition. The best of them were Martin Dihigo, George Scales, Newt Allen, Bill Monroe, Frank Grant, Bingo DeMoss—and Sammy T. Hughes. And Hughes may have been the best of the lot. A tall, rangy infielder who at 6'3" was death on line drives over the infield, and death on ground balls. He moved with the grace of a ballerina, gliding across the infield, right and left, to gobble up potential base hits from opposing batters. He was also noted for his finesse on making the double play.

Sammy T. Hughes was born in Louisville, Kentucky, on October 20, 1910. He made a name for himself playing on the sandlots of his hometown and was signed by the Louisville White Sox of the Negro National League when he was just 18. Although he played with several clubs over his 16-year professional career, he spent five years with the Baltimore Elite Giants, alongside such legends as Roy Campanella, Biz Mackey, and Wild Bill Wright. He was voted into five Negro League All-Star games during the 30s and 40s, more than any other second baseman.

But Sammy T. Hughes was more than a defensive vacuum cleaner. He was also an intelligent baserunner and a threat with the bat. According to John Holway, Hughes batted a cool .300 over his career, one of the highest batting averages recorded by any keystoner. Although he weighed a solid 190 pounds, he was not a power hitter, averaging 25 doubles, 7 triples, and 9 home runs a year. But he could handle a bat with the best of them. Usually hitting out of the second spot in the batting order, Hughes was a dangerous hit-and-run man and a talented bunter.

Hughes also starred with the Royal Giants in the California Winter League between 1934 and 1939. In addition to giving the Giants a tight inner defense, the right handed batter stroked the ball at a torrid .384 clip, with 14 home runs in 294 at-bats. His .384 average is the second highest average for players with more than 290 at-bats.

According to Robert Peterson in *Only the Ball Was White*, "Cum Posey, who had seen all the great ones since 1912, called Hughes the best second baseman in Negro baseball history."

DICK LUNDY

Dick Lundy, popularly known as "King Richard," was one of the top four shortstops in Negro league history, along with John Henry Lloyd,

Dobie Moore, and Willie Wells. He and Moore vied for the title of "Best Shortstop of the Twenties," until Moore was felled by a bullet in 1926, ending his career.

Lundy, a native of Jacksonville, Florida, began his 24-year professional baseball career as a 16-year-old infielder with his hometown team, the Duval Giants. When the Giants moved north to Atlantic City the next year, Lundy went with them. He was lured away by the Hilldale Daisies in 1917, but returned to his original team, now known as the Bacharach Giants, in 1920 where he became a fixture. After becoming manager of the team in 1926, he led the Giants to two successive Eastern Colored League championships. Later, when the East-West All-Star games were begun in 1933, Lundy was chosen for both the '33 and '34 classics.

"King Richard" was a superb defensive player, with big hands, long arms, and a graceful stride. He had tremendous range at short, and his strong throwing arm permitted him to play back on the grass and still get the runner. He had many supporters who felt he was the best of them all. Jake Stephens, another shortstop who played against Lundy for 17 years, told John Holway, "Lundy had great range. He could shoot you out from left field." Napolean "Chance" Cummings, the Giants first baseman during most of Lundy's tenure, seconded that opinion. "Lundy could go behind second base and get the ball and throw you out, go behind third and do the same thing. There's nobody in the big leagues [that] could beat Lundy playing shortstop."

What made Dick Lundy Hall of Fame material was that he was an all-around player. His defensive skills were magnificent, but so were his offensive skills. The switch-hitting Lundy stood 5'11" and weighed 180 pounds. He was a notorious fastball hitter who specialized in hitting line drives through and over the infield. Beginning in 1920, Lundy put together season averages of .344, .363, .357, .300, .360, .289, .329, .306, and .410., winning the batting championship in both '20 and '21. He also had some zip in his swing, averaging 22 doubles, 5 triples, and 13 home runs for every 550 at-bats. He captured 2 home-run titles, with 2 home-runs in 1920, and 14 in 33 games in 1924. When he retired in 1937, he left behind a career batting average of .314.

Lundy also played ball for nine years in the Cuban Winter League, making the annual trek there over the winter, between 1920 and 1930. He excelled there also, rapping the ball at a .341 clip, with 19 doubles, 6 triples, and 4 home runs a year. He hit .353 in 1924-25 and .410 in 1926-27.

It is estimated, based on his Cuban and Negro league statistics, that Lundy would have hit in the .280 range with 15 home runs a year in the major leagues.

BIZ MACKEY

Raleigh "Biz" Mackey is well known for having been Roy Campanella's mentor with the Baltimore Elite Giants after the 15-year-old Philadelphian joined the Negro league team in 1937. Mackey was a 39-year-old veteran at the time, and he taught the youngster all the tricks of the trade. After Campanella joined the Brooklyn Dodgers, Negro league veterans would say, "If you want to know what Biz Mackey was like as a catcher, just watch Campanella. Campy is a clone of Mackey."

That was high praise indeed, because the roly poly Dodger backstop had no peers behind the plate. He was an excellent handler of pitchers, often beat the runner down to first base to back up the play, was death on foul popups, and gunned down two out of every three runners who tried to steal on him.

Biz Mackey had no equal behind the plate. He may have been the greatest defensive catcher in Negro league history. And he carried a powerful bat as well. Over the course of an unforgettable 28-year career, the big switch hitter pounded the ball for a .322 average, according to John Holway's latest research.

Mackey joined the Indianapolis ABC's in 1920 when he was just 22 years old. He put his gear away for the last time in 1945 at the age of 48, racking up a .307 batting average in his farewell season. In between, the 6', 200-pounder was the class of the league behind the plate. Josh Gibson could out-hit and outslug the Texas native, but he couldn't hold his glove defensively. In fact, many Negro league experts, like Cum Posey, made Mackey the catcher on their all-time all-star teams, putting Gibson in another position.

Biz Mackey, a native of Eagle Pass, Texas, wasted no time in showing the Negro leaguers how the game should be played. Newspaper accounts of a game between the ABC's and the Kansas City Monarchs in 1920 praised his work behind the plate and noted his strong throwing arm. But he wasn't a one-dimensional player. He could also hit with the best of them. As a rookie, he hit a respectable .306. And two years later, the switch-hitting backstop pounded the ball at a blazing .352 clip, with 31 extra-base hits in just 210 at-bats. Included in the hits were an unbelievable 12 triples.

Mackey joined the Philadelphia Hilldales in 1923, where he would spend the next 13 years. And he brought his bat with him. He hit .364, .363, and .356, between 1923 and 1925. He had an off year in '26, hitting just .270, the lowest average of his career until he became a part-time player in 1934.

The jovial backstop appeared in two Negro league World Series, against the Kansas City Monarchs in 1924 and 1925. He hit just .241 in 1924, as the Hilldales lost to the Monarchs and Jose Mendez when the old veteran blanked them with a three-hitter in the 10th and final game. The next year, Mackey ripped the ball at a .360 clip, with 3 doubles, a triple and a home run, and the Hilldales got a measure of revenge, whipping the Monarchs 5–1.

Biz Mackey could play in any league. In 1924-25 he played in the Cuban Winter League and hit a solid .309. He also played at least 11 years in the California Winter League, against white teams composed of major league players, and batted .366. He visited Hawaii, and he made three barnstorming trips to the Orient, visiting the Philippines, Japan, and China. The Negro leaguers were heros in Japan, where they visited with the fans and taught the Japanese players the rudiments of the game.

In more than two dozen recorded exhibition games against major league all-star teams, the big catcher hit a sizzling .354. And he hit against the best of them, pitchers like Lefty Grove, Charlie Root, Freddie Fitzsimmons, and Bullet Joe Bush. It is estimated that he would have hit in the .270 range with 14 home runs a year in the major leagues.

Raleigh "Biz" Mackey was arguably one of the five greatest catchers in baseball history, along with Josh Gibson, Roy Campanella, Johnny Bench, and Yogi Berra. And Mackey may have been number one.

OLIVER MARCELLE

Oliver H. Marcelle was known as "The Ghost" for the way he floated across the infield in pursuit of a ground ball. According to baseball experts who saw him play, he was the greatest defensive third baseman in Negro league history. Jim Riley, in his *Biographical Encyclopedia of the Negro Leagues,* writes, "He was very fast, covered lots of territory, and possessed a quick and snappy arm. He had no equal in knocking down hard-hit balls and getting his man at first. Whether making spectacular plays to his left or his right, or fielding bunts like a master, he delighted the fans." In 1952, when the *Pittsburgh Courier* polled a panel of black baseball veterans and writers for their all-time Negro league team, Oliver Marcelle was their choice for third base.

The gifted Marcelle was born in Thibodaux, Louisiana, on June 24, 1897. After playing for a number of sandlot teams around New Orleans, he attracted the attention of the professionals and was recruited by the

Oliver "The Ghost" Marcelle was a smooth-fielding third baseman during the 1920s.

Brooklyn Royal Giants in 1918. His Negro league career lasted for a total of 17 years, seven of them with the Atlantic City Bacharach Giants, where he teamed with Dick Lundy to give the Giants an impenetrable left side of the infield.

The Ghost could not only play the field. He was also dangerous with a bat in his hands. The slightly built right handed hitter sprayed the ball to all fields, hitting mostly singles. His 166 base hits a year included just 15 doubles, 5 triples and 4 home runs. In 1921, his first full year, he hit .303. The next year, he tattooed the ball to the tune of .379 and followed that up with an average of .390. In all, Marcelle batted over .300 six times in 17 years and ended his career with a lifetime batting average of .302.

In addition to playing in the Negro leagues, Oliver Marcelle played in the Cuban Winter League from October through February. In his first year in Cuba, the 5'9", 160-pound dynamo won the batting title with an average of .393, after a spirited battle with Cuban Hall of Fame outfielder, Alejandro Oms. The Ghost went on to play nine years in Cuba, hitting .305 and averaging 14 doubles, 7 triples, and 3 home runs a year.

The Louisiana Creole was an exciting player who was adored by the fans. He was fiery, energetic, and aggressive on and off the field. In the end, his temper proved his undoing. During the winter of 1929-30, Marcelle traveled to Cuba with teammate Frank Warfield, another player with a short fuse. One night, the two friends were engaged in a craps game, when they began arguing with each other. One thing led to another and soon the game exploded into a knock-down, drag-out fight between the two. It ended suddenly when Warfield bit off a piece of Marcelle's nose.

That incident effectively ended Marcelle's playing career. The proud infielder played only four games in the Negro leagues the next year and never played another game in Cuba. He will always be remembered as a talented, intelligent player, with a fiery temperament. Off the field, he was handsome and well dressed. He was a genuine Hall of Fame third baseman.

DOBIE MOORE

Walter "Dobie" Moore was a great shortstop whose brilliant career was cut short by a tragic accident. The friendly, fun-loving Moore was born in Georgia in 1893 and joined the U.S. Army sometime around 1911. He eventually became a member of the famed 25th Infantry Division baseball team, a team that dominated the amateur sports world during the teens. The 25th included a number of players who would eventually leave the Army to play professional baseball with the Kansas City Monarchs. There was pitcher Bullet Joe Rogan, first baseman Lemuel Hawkins, second baseman Bob Fagan, and outfielders Oscar "Heavy" Johnson and Hurley McNair.

Moore was considered to be a good soldier during his 10-year military career. And he was already a sensational all-around ballplayer with a deadly bat and a trusty glove. The 25th served with honor in Hawaii from 1913 to 1918, then moved on to Fort Huachuca, Arizona, near the Mexican border. After Casey Stengel played an exhibition game against the 25th in 1919, he recommended Moore and several other players to J. L. Wilkinson, owner of the Monarchs. In 1920, Dobie Moore and Joe Rogan bought their way out of the Army and became professional baseball players.

It didn't take Dobie Moore long to be recognized in the Negro National League. In addition to playing brilliant defense, he scorched the ball at the plate, with extra-base power. After a two-year adjustment, the 5'11", 230-pound slugger hit .367 in 1922 and followed that with season averages of .358, .470, .326, and .381. In 1924, he captured the batting championship with his .470 average and also took the home-run crown with 8 in 234 at-bats. He was the Monarchs' clean-up hitter for seven years.

With Moore, Hawkins, Johnson, and McNair powering the offense, and Bullet Joe spearheading the pitching, the Monarchs raced to three league titles and one World Championship between 1924 and 1926. Rogan went 15–5, 14–2, and 12–4 over those years and was 8–4 in the World Series.

The Monarchs met the Hilldale Daisies in the '24 Classic, winning the Series 5–4, with one tie, with manager Jose Mendez blanking the Daisies 5–0 on a three-hitter in the finale. Dobie Moore hit an even .300. The following year, the Daisies defeated Kansas City 5–1, in spite of Moore's .364 onslaught. And in '26 the Monarchs lost a league playoff to the Chicago American Giants 5–4, without Moore.

Dobie Moore played winter ball in Cuba in 1923 and 1924. He hit a solid .380 the first year and led the league in both hits and triples. The next year, he hit .299. He also played in the California Winter League several years with the Los Angeles White Sox and the Colored All-Stars.

In 1926, Dobie Moore was rapping the ball at a .381 pace when his world collapsed. On May 23, the irrepressible shortstop was shot by a woman under suspicious circumstances. His leg was shattered, ending his professional baseball career. He drifted to Detroit where he disappeared into the inner city. Historian Dick Clark recently discovered box scores of semi-pro games in Detroit that showed Dobie Moore playing shortstop.

In any case, a magnificent baseball career ended abruptly. The cold statistics say that Dobie Moore had a career batting average of .355, with 32 doubles, 14 triples, and 15 home runs for every 550 at-bats. He was, according to all accounts, one of the top four shortstops in Negro league history, along with John Henry Lloyd, Willie Wells, and Dick Lundy. Chet Brewer, for one, thought Moore was the greatest Negro league shortstop ever. He said all four men were dazzling in the field, and all of them, with the exception of Wells, had strong throwing arms. But Dobie Moore could outhit all of them and was the greatest power hitter of the four, making him the best all-around shortstop in the annals of Negro league baseball.

If he had been given the chance to play in the major leagues, Dobie Moore would have peppered the ball at a .307 clip with 20 home runs a year. In some years, he would have ripped 30 or more home runs and batted in the .350 range. He was that good.

SPOT POLES

During the years that Ty Cobb was running wild in the American League, a black greyhound was causing similar distress in the Negro leagues. His name was Spot Poles, and he was a compact 5'7", 165 pound bundle of energy. He was a switch hitter who could bunt, punch the ball to any field, or wait out a base on balls. And, once on base, he terrorized opposing pitchers, much like Cobb and Jackie Robinson. In 1911, according to Robert Peterson, Poles hit a resounding .440 and swiped 41 bases in 60 games.

Spottswood Poles was born in Winchester, Virginia, on November 7, 1889. He took to baseball at an early age and progressed from one league to another until he was discovered by the professionals. He began his professional career with the Philadelphia Giants in 1909 at the age of 19, playing alongside baseball legends like John Henry Lloyd and Bruce Petway. The fleet footed Poles was installed in center field and quickly became a fixture there. His outstanding range, sure glove, and strong arm stamped him as one of the best.

After popping the ball at a .440 clip in 1911, the line-drive hitting Poles followed with averages of .398, .414, .and .487. Jim Riley reported that Poles rapped three base hits off Grover Cleveland Alexander in an exhibition game in 1913, when the 26-year-old Phillies right hander was in his prime, having just completed a 22–8 season in the National League. Poles played at least ten games against major league all-star teams over the years and tattooed their pitching to the tune of .610. Obviously, Spottswood Poles could hit the ball in any kind of competition.

Spot Poles played professional baseball for 14 years, changing teams periodically as was the practice in those days, but he spent most of his career, a total of ten years, with the New York Lincoln Giants. The early edition of the Giants was one of the greatest teams in black baseball, with Smokey Joe Williams, Cannonball Dick Redding, John Henry Lloyd, Louis Santop, Grant Johnson, and Ben Taylor. Poles was in New York until 1918, when he enlisted in the Army during World War I. He spent one year in France, where he fought in the trenches, winning five battle stars and picking up a purple heart for wounds received in battle.

Poles's exact career batting average is still a mystery. Estimates have ranged from .300 to .400, but one thing is known for certain. Many of his peers considered him to be one of the best, if not the best, players of all time. New York Giant manager John McGraw grouped Poles with John Henry Lloyd, Dick Redding, and Smokey Joe Williams as Negro league greats. Paul Robeson, the well-known black singer and actor, called Poles one of the greatest black athletes of the twentieth century. And teammate Sam Streeter claimed that Poles could outrun Cool Papa Bell, generally considered to be the fastest runner in Negro league history.

Although exact statistics are lacking in the United States, Spot Poles also played ball in the Cuban Winter League several years, and his stats are available from those years. The man known as "The Black Ty Cobb" ran wild in Cuba as well as in the U.S. In 1910-11 he pounded Cuban pitching for a .360 average and led the league in doubles. Two years later, he hit .364 and led the league in at-bats, runs scored, base hits, and triples. Overall, he compiled a career .319 average in Cuba, which would put him at or near the .300 level if he played in the major leagues.

DICK "CANNONBALL" REDDING

Cannonball Dick Redding was one of the most intimidating black pitchers during the second and third decades of the twentieth century. He was a contemporary of Smokey Joe Williams, and the two fireballers enjoyed friendly competition over the years. For three years, from 1912 through 1914, the New York Lincoln Giants had the services of both legendary pitchers. Redding was a big, rugged individual, standing 6'4" tall and tipping the scales at 210 pounds. He had overpowering speed and a deceptive back-to-the-batter windup that kept batters from digging in.

Redding was born in Atlanta, Georgia, in 1891. He began his professional baseball career with the Philadelphia Giants in 1911 at the age of 20, but jumped to the Lincoln Giants before the season was two months old. He joined forces with Williams, as noted earlier, and the pitching duo made the Giants the dominant team of the teen years. They pitched the Giants to at least two championship titles between 1911 and 1916. When the greatest pitchers in Negro league history are discussed, the top four are usually Smokey Joe Williams, Cannonball Dick Redding, Satchel Paige, and Bullet Joe Rogan. In a 1952 poll conducted by the *Pittsburgh Courier,* Williams nosed out Paige by a single vote as the greatest pitcher of all time. Rogan was third, Redding seventh. Cum Posey selected all four for his all-star team, with Williams first and Redding second. The truth is, you could probably put all four in a bag, shake it up, and whichever one you pulled out, would be the best. There was little to choose between them.

According to historian John Holway, Redding once struck out Babe Ruth three times on nine pitches. He also pitched batting practice against John McGraw's New York Giants and the Detroit Tigers, but he was so deadly that Ty Cobb refused to bat against him. That type of talent is indicative of why he was so successful in the Negro leagues. In his rookie season of 1911, he is credited with winning 17 consecutive games against tough competition.

As with most Negro league records, it is difficult to separate Redding's statistics against semi-pro teams from his statistics against the professional teams. For instance, in 1913, he reportedly ran up a record of 43–12, but that included semi-pro teams. He did, however, toss a perfect game against the Jersey City Skeeters of the Eastern League, one of the higher minor league classifications. And he also beat the New York Giants and the Boston Braves in exhibition games.

In 1914, Redding went 12–3 in league play, and in 1915 he won 23 games against only 2 losses. In the Playoff Series against Rube Foster's Chicago American Giants, he won three of four decisions, effectively shutting down Pete Hill and company.

According to Jim Riley, Dick Redding was a workhorse, and "In his prime years he often pitched doubleheaders two or three days in succession." The Cannonball was also a jovial giant who loved people and enjoyed life. Unlike many of his teammates, he was a clean-cut individual who didn't drink or party all night.

Although records are spotty, Dick Redding is credited with a record of 13–3 in 1917 and 17–12 in 1921. For his career, according to John Holway's most recent research, he won a total of 89 victories against 63 defeats in Negro league competition. The big right hander also pitched in Cuba for several seasons, but unfortunately he pitched mostly for weak teams, compiling a record of 18–23 over a five-year period. He did have one outstanding season, however, which demonstrated his true pitching capabilities. As the ace of the Fe club, the American workhorse pitched his team to the 1913 Cuban Winter League Championship, appearing in 68 percent of the team's games, racking up a 7–2 record, tossing nine complete games, and making 12 relief appearances. He was a one-man team.

LOUIS SANTOP

Louis Santop earned his nickname "Big Bertha" by hitting baseballs long distances. The original Big Bertha was a long-range German artillery piece that could hurl projectiles at enemy positions miles away. The Texas cannon duplicated that feat in baseball parks around the country.

Louis Santop Loftin was born in Tyler, Texas, on January 17, 1890. He began his baseball career with the Fort Worth Wonders in 1909, at the same time that Smokey Joe Williams was pitching for the San Antonio Black Bronchos in the same league. Both superstars left Texas the following year for careers with Negro league teams up north. Coincidentally, both players joined the New York Lincoln Giants in 1911, forming one of the most devastating batteries in the annals of professional baseball.

Santop was a powerfully built man, who towered over the other players. In the days when 5'10" was considered tall, "Top" stood over 6'4" tall and weighed a muscular 240 pounds. And he put every pound to good use. Although he was a good defensive catcher with a rifle for a throwing arm, he was best known for his long-range cannonading of opposing pitchers.

The left handed slugger quickly earned a reputation for his hitting prowess in the Negro league cities around the country, and he became the Giants' main attraction. As a result, he had to play in just about every one of the Giants' 200 games a year, in order to satisfy the crowd. Naturally, he was also paid a star's salary.

According to Jim Riley, Santop hit .470, .422, .429, and .455 for the Lincoln Giants from 1911 to 1914, while catching the blazing pitches of both Williams and Cannonball Dick Redding. He is also credited with averages of .373, .358, .364, and .389 for the years 1921–24. Top's averages prior to 1920 probably included games against semi-pro teams, but he also attacked major league pitchers in exhibition games over the years, proving he was major league material all the way. He hit against such pitching legends as Grover Cleveland Alexander, Bullet Joe Bush, and Chief Bender with great success. He hit .375 against Bender and .333 against Bush. Old Alex shut him down in four at-bats.

In spite of his size, Louis Santop was an easygoing, friendly individual who didn't use his size to intimidate other players. On the other hand, he did grow up in a tough area and often had to fight to survive. He carried that toughness into the Negro leagues with him, so it was best not to provoke him. He had enormous strength, and he could handle himself if he had to.

Santop enjoyed an 18-year career in the Negro leagues and could be counted on to hit in the high .300s every year with tremendous extra-base power. Fragmentary statistics indicate that Big Bertha would have hit in the .270 to .300 range in the major leagues, with between 32 and 40 home runs a year. And that's Hall of Fame material!

CHINO SMITH

Charles "Chino" Smith was born in Greenwood, South Carolina, in 1903, and made his way to the Negro leagues with the Philadelphia Giants in 1924. He picked up his nickname because of his Oriental eyes. During his short professional career, he played primarily for the Brooklyn Royal Giants and the New York Lincoln Giants.

Chino was a small 5'6", 168-pound bundle of dynamite. He was arguably the greatest hitter the Negro leagues ever produced. Many of his contemporaries, like pitchers Satchel Paige, Sug Cornelius, and Jesse Hubbard swore he was the best hitter they ever saw. And Larry Brown, who played with him in 1930, told John Holway that Chino was "one of the greatest hitters you ever saw. He'd hit 'em between 'em, over 'em, to the opposite field, in the trees, anywhere."

Smith always played the game hard and with a chip on his shoulder. Perhaps it was due to his small stature, where he always had to prove he was better than the bigger guys. Whatever the reason, he was a cocky little guy who strutted around like a bantam rooster and showed complete disdain for opposing pitchers. And he was a scrapper, ready to fight at the drop of a bat.

He was also one of the Negro league's best needlers. He loved to harrass opposing players before and during the game. One time in Cuba, watching New York Yankee pitcher Johnny Allen warming up, Smith told him, "Is that all you're gonna throw today? If that's all you're gonna throw, I'm gonna kill you." Another time, after being knocked down by a pitch, he got up, hit a line drive back through the box almost decapitating the pitcher, then gleefully stood on first base shouting out to the mound, "Made you duck. Made you duck." If opposing fans got on him, it just made him more determined than usual. He would stand in the batters box and watch the first two pitches go by, spitting at them as they crossed the plate. Then he would hit a line drive back through the box, sending the pitcher diving for cover.

Chino Smith had the advantage when it came to arguing with the crowd or battling the opposing pitcher. He could always back up his threats with action. And he could not only hit and drag a bunt with the best of them but, surprisingly, the little man could hit with extraordinary power. His Negro league career was short, only six years, but in that time he never hit below .326. And in 1929, he literally destroyed opposing pitchers. He scorched the ball at a .461 clip, the highest season average in Negro league history, to capture the league batting title. He also led the league with 28 doubles and 23 home runs, in just 245 at-bats. Chino also had two other .400 seasons, hitting .422 in 1927 and .429 in 1930, when he captured another batting title.

His biggest day at the plate, fittingly, came in New York's Yankee Stadium in 1930. Playing right field in the first game ever played by a black team in the "House That Ruth Built," the left handed hitter took advantage of the stadium's cozy right field stands to go three for three, with a walk, a triple, and two home runs.

Smith usually traveled to Cuba in the winter. He played in the Cuban Winter League for five years, from 1926-27 to 1930-31. He didn't have any trouble hitting in that league either, although the CWL was a tougher league than the Negro league because they not only attracted the top Negro league pitchers like Satchel Paige, Andy Cooper, and Sam Streeter, they also attracted major league pitchers like Allen, Dolf Luque, and Jesse Petty, plus the usual array of Cuban greats like Ramon Bragana, Cocaina Garcia, Jose Mendez, and Martin Dihigo.

Chino Smith hit those and other pitchers for a cool .342 in both 1926 and 1927 and followed that with averages of .333 and .338 the next two years. Tragically, the little outfielder contracted yellow fever in Cuba in the winter of 1930-31 and after struggling through eight or nine games, he collapsed. He died of the disease on January 16.

The pride of New York left some impressive statistics behind. His .434 career Negro league average is 80 points higher than the number two man, Jud Wilson. It is also 50 points higher than major league star Larry Doby, 89 points higher than Monte Irvin, and 47 points higher than Jackie Robinson. And his .335 average in Cuba, although not the highest, was the ninth best career average in the 80-year history of the league. Proving that he had no favorites, Chino Smith racked major league pitching for a .405 average in 10 exhibition games. Those kind of numbers would translate into a .350 batting average in the majors, with 15–20 home runs a year. And some years he could have been expected to challenge the magic .400 barrier, with 30 home runs.

HILTON SMITH

Hilton Smith is better known as Satchel Paige's relief man. For years, when Smith toiled for the Kansas City Monarchs, he would come into a game in the fourth or fifth inning to relieve Paige who had started. Paige was the number one drawing card in the league, and when he was scheduled to pitch, it increased the attendance by several thousand fans. So Satch would start about half the team's games to bring the crowd in, then leave after three or four innings.

Make no mistake however, Hilton Smith was one of the great pitchers in the game during the 1930s and 40s. The tall, slender right hander reportedly had the best curve ball in the league, and set it up with a rising fastball, a good sinker, and a change. He pitched both sidearm and overhand equally well and had good control.

The native of Giddings, Texas, entered professional baseball with the Monroe Monarchs in 1932 at the age of 20. Four years later, he joined

Kansas City where he spent the final 13 years of his career. He was always one of the top pitchers in the Negro American League, and he led the league in victories four times, from 1937 to 1939 when he went 10–0, 9–1, and 8–2 respectively, and in 1942 when he won eight games against only two losses. He also led the league in TRA (total run average) twice, with 3.01 in 1938 and 2.06 the following year. The Monarchs took the Western Division title five times during Smith's 13 years, capturing five league titles and one World Championship in two tries. Smith was 2–0 in World Series competition, winning one game in each series. The 6'2", 180-pound curveball artist also pitched in six All-Star games, winning one and losing two.

Like other Negro leaguers, Hilton Smith headed south when the Negro league season ended. He pitched two years in the Cuban Winter League and two years in the Mexican League. He fared just as well against the Cubans as he did against the Negro leaguers. He went 6–3 with the Marianao club in 1937-38 and 4–2 with Santa Clara the following year, pitching in a total of 23 games over the two years, with nine complete games. He pitched for Torreon in the Mexican League in 1940 and 1941, and he compiled a respectable 8–8 record for a team that went 90–97. His 26 games pitched included nine complete games. He also showed his skills against the major leaguers in exhibition games, winning six games against a single loss.

Hilton Smith was a tough act to follow. His career Negro league totals show 72 victories and just 28 losses, for a winning percentage of .720. He was elected to the National Baseball Hall of Fame in 2001.

NORMAN "TURKEY" STEARNES

Norman "Turkey" Stearnes was finally elected to the National Baseball Hall of Fame in Cooperstown, New York, on February 29, 2000. It was at least 20 years too late. One of the greatest players ever to set foot on a baseball diamond died on September 4, 1979, waiting for the call that never came.

Norman "Turkey" Stearnes was a superstar — a five-point player. He could hit, hit with power, run, field, and throw. He may have been the greatest defensive center fielder in Negro league history, although Cool Papa Bell and Oscar Charleston would probably dispute that claim.

Stearnes was born in Nashville, Tennessee, on May 8, 1901. He joined the Negro leagues in 1923 and played professional baseball for 21 years, 11 of them with the Detroit Stars. He didn't impress spectators when he first stepped into the batters box. He was a tall, slender left handed batter whose 6' frame carried just 165 pounds. And he had a strange batting stance. He stood with his right foot in the bucket and his right toe pointed straight up. But he could hit. In his rookie year of 1923 he led the Negro National League in home runs with 17 (in 57 games) and led the Detroit Stars in batting with an average of .353. In addition to his homers, the slugging center fielder rapped 15 doubles and 13 triples, for a total of 45 extra-base hits. Over a 154-game schedule, that would total 122 extra-base hits — Babe Ruth's best was 119, Lou Gehrig once had 117, Stan Musial 103, and Hank Greenberg 100; the best Ted Williams could do was 85. Turkey Stearnes was in elite company.

The Detroit slugger continued his hitting, slugging, and fielding magic year after year. He never slacked off. The Nashville native knew only one way to play the game — all out. And his personal life helped him maintain his playing skills. He was a quiet, private person, who shunned the night life that destroyed many of his teammates. He didn't drink, smoke, or chase women. But he did have a reputation for being slightly eccentric. Although he didn't talk much to his teammates, he did talk to his bat occasionally, especially when it wasn't getting him any hits. And he talked to himself in the outfield.

In spite of his unique batting stance, Stearnes could hit just about anything. He was a good fastball hitter and a good low-ball hitter. He had lightning-like wrists, and he pulled everything to dead right field. In 21 years, he hit below .316 just once, falling to .299 in 1932. With Detroit he had season averages of .364, .375, and .381, but he won his only batting championship with the Chicago American Giants in 1935, with an average of .431. His big thing was home runs. He won seven home-run crowns in 10 years, between 1923 and 1932.

Turkey Stearnes was more than a slugger, however. He had outstanding speed, and was an intelligent baserunner, who averaged 19 stolen bases a year. He also put his speed to good use in the outfield. He was the best defensive center fielder of all time, according to many of his contemporaries. He covered large expanses of ground and displayed a strong accurate throwing arm.

The Detroit superstar was at his best in postseason play. In the 1930 playoff against the St. Louis Stars, won by the Stars in seven games, he led both teams in batting, with an average of .481. Included in his hits were four doubles, one triple, and two home runs, good for ten runs batted in. Two years later, playing for Chicago, Stearnes banged out three singles and a triple as Willie Foster blanked the Nashville Elite Giants 2–0 in the seventh and final playoff game. Over his career, he hit a resounding .426 in 15 postseason games.

Stearnes also played ball in the California Winter League for at least eight years. He faced a variety of pitchers from the major leagues and the AAA minor leagues, and he punished them all, crushing the ball at a .373 pace, with 56 home runs in 754 at-bats. Against major league stars like Ferdie Schupp, Sloppy Thurston, Larry French, and Buck Newsome, he hit a solid .370 with 11 home runs in just 146 at-bats.

Norman "Turkey" Stearnes's career Negro league records show a .332 batting average, with 203 doubles (third all time), 106 triples (first), and 197 home runs (third). He averaged 32 doubles, 18 triples, and 31 home runs for every 550 at-bats. His 81 extra-base hits a year statistic is exceeded by only four people in baseball history — Josh Gibson (90), Babe Ruth (89), Hank Greenberg (83), and Lou Gehrig (82).

Turkey Stearnes would have been a .300 hitter in the major leagues, with 35 home runs a year. He probably would have had several seasons in the .330 to .350 range, with more than 50 home runs.

GEORGE "MULE" SUTTLES

George "Mule" Suttles hit 237 career home runs, the most in Negro league history and 13 more than Josh Gibson. His home-run average of 40 home runs a year is second to Gibson's 52. If Suttles had played in the major leagues, he might have averaged 51 home runs a year, putting him in the same league as Mark McGwire.

Suttles was born in Brockton, Louisiana, on March 2, 1901. He was a big kid who developed his muscular body by working in the coal mines around Birmingham. By the time he began his professional baseball career with the Birmingham Black Barons in 1923, he had grown to his full height of 6'4", and packed a solid 230 pounds on his rugged frame. Fortunately for his opponents, he didn't have a mean bone in his body. He was a gentle giant, a good-natured fellow who enjoyed life, as a well as a good joke.

With a bat in his hands, however, the Mule could always hit the ball farther than anybody, even Josh Gibson and Babe Ruth, according to his contemporaries. And, where Gibson hit line-drive home runs, Suttles's blasts were majestic, towering fly balls that looked like they would never come down. The big right handed bomber wielded a big 50-ounce bludgeon, and he generated tremendous power with it. He hit some of the longest home runs in baseball history. One of his more famous clouts came in Tropical Park in Havana, during a 1929 Cuban Winter League game.

The ball cleared the 500-foot center field fence with plenty to spare. The spot was subsequently marked with a plaque.

Mule Suttles brought excitement to the game of baseball, especially to the home fans, who would chant "kick Mule, kick" whenever he came to bat in a critical situation. And more often than not, Mule would respond by "kicking" one out of the park. He was a good low-ball hitter and a good curve ball hitter, who loved nothing better than to extend his arms and cut loose with an all-or-nothing swing. He would either miss the ball dramatically or would hit it into the next county, much like Babe Ruth was doing in the American League at the same time.

After he joined the St. Louis Stars in 1926, Suttles had a career season. He captured the batting crown with a sizzling .418 average. He also led the league in triples with 19 and in home runs with 26, in 87 games. And he swiped 11 bases, proving he could pick 'em up and lay 'em down. Mule should have been helped in his home-run derby by the dimensions of Stars Park, which had a trolley-car barn directly behind the 250-foot left field fence. Some of his home runs most assuredly did drop over the short 250-foot sign, but since he wasn't a pull hitter many of his longest hits disappeared into a cavernous 425-foot power alley in left center field, ending up as one of his 19 three-baggers.

Mule Suttles was noted for his offensive pyrotechnics, but he was not a liability on defense. His contemporaries claimed that, while he was not the most graceful first baseman, he could catch anything thrown to him. He apparently could also run down anything hit his way when he played the outfield. In the 1935 East-West All-Star game in Comiskey Park, Chicago, Suttles, in left field, raced back to the 400-foot mark to haul down a drive off the bat of Biz Mackey in the top of the 11th inning. In the bottom half of the inning, he sent the big Chicago crowd home happy by blasting a two-out, three-run, game-winning home run off the great Martin Dihigo. The Mule had kicked again.

Suttles went on to play 18 years in the Negro leagues, finishing with a career .341 batting average, the fifth-highest average in Negro league history for players with more than 2000 at-bats, according to John Holway. He also hit 237 home runs, an average of 40 homers for every 550 at-bats. And he didn't stop there. He pounded major league pitchers for a .341 average and 10 home runs in 170 plate appearances in exhibition games.

Mule Suttles also played winter ball, in either California or Cuba. He played for Cienfuegos in the Cuban Winter League in 1928-29, batting .294. The following year, he stroked the ball at a .314 clip and led the league with seven home runs. He didn't play in Cuba again until he was 38 years old and nearing the end of the trail. Although he was held to a .218 batting average, he still led the league in homers with four. His 14 home runs a year in Cuba would equate to about 33 home runs in the majors. Suttles played in the California Winter League several years, where he literally destroyed major league and high minor league pitching. Partial statistics credit him with a .378 batting average and 64 home runs in just 450 at-bats, an incredible number of homers that would equate to 77 home runs for every 550 at-bats.

Indications are that Suttles would have hit in the .270 range in the major leagues, with some seasons of .310 to .320. And his 42 home runs a year average would have reached 60 or more some years.

George "Mule" Suttles was one of the most devastating sluggers in the annals of professional baseball. Hopefully he will be rewarded with a well-deserved niche in Cooperstown in the not-too-distant future.

BEN TAYLOR

Benjamin Taylor was one the most graceful fielding first basemen in Negro league history and a dangerous hitter to boot. He was born in Anderson, South Carolina, on July 1, 1888, just as the whites-only shadow was falling across the face of organized baseball. Taylor was part of a baseball family. His brothers Charles Isham (C. I.) Taylor and James Allen (Candy Jim) Taylor both played professional baseball, and all three brothers made reputations for themselves as Negro league managers.

Ben Taylor, at 6'1" and 190 pounds, was the ideal first baseman. He batted and threw left handed. He was tall and agile, had good hands, and was particularly adept at digging out low throws. He is generally recognized as the best defensive first baseman ever to play in the Negro leagues. He could also handle a bat with the best of them. Originally a pitcher, he recorded records of 22–3 and 30–1 against all levels of competition, early in his career, according to Jim Riley. However, like Babe Ruth, he was eventually converted to an everyday player to take advantage of his deadly bat.

Ben Taylor was the first baseman for the West Baden Sprudels, managed by his brother C. I., in 1910. Over the next 20 years he played with more than 20 teams, very seldom staying more than two years with any of them. The one exception was the Indianapolis ABC's, where he spent a total of eight years over two tours of duty. With the ABC's, managed by his brother C. I., he played with such greats as Oscar Charleston, Jimmy Lyons, Dick Redding, and Bingo DeMoss. C. I. Taylor installed his kid bother into the cleanup position as soon as he arrived in Indianapolis.

In his first year, Ben hit a rousing .333. He continued to pound the ball
year after year. In 1921, he hit .421, finishing third behind Charleston and
Charles Blackwell, another dangerous long-ball threat. He did lead the league
in hits with 106 in 73 games, and doubles with 19. He also stole 14 bases.

Taylor reportedly also played several years of winter baseball in California or Cuba, but the statistics for those years have not yet been recov-
ered. One rumor said Taylor hit .500 in Cuba in the 1915-16 season, but that
has not been verified. What has been developed is his career Negro league
batting average. The slender left handed hitter was not a home-run hitter.
Instead he sent line drives to all parts of the various Negro league baseball
stadiums, compiling a .321 batting average for 20 years. During that time,
he averaged 32 doubles, 8 triples, and 6 home runs for every 550 at-bats.

After his retirement as an active player, Ben Taylor remained in the
game as a coach, manager, umpire, and instructor. Jim Riley summed it
up best. "Modest, easygoing, and soft-spoken, Taylor was a true gentleman who maintained a fair and professional demeanor, and he was an
excellent teacher of young players."

CRISTOBAL TORRIENTE

Cristobal Torriente was known in his homeland as "The Cuban Babe
Ruth." In reality, Torriente was a five-point player, but he didn't have the
Babe's power. His home-run average was more like 17 than 48. He did have
one satisfying series against the Yankee slugger, however. From October
16, 1920, until November 14, John McGraw's New York Giants played 17
exhibition games against Cuba's two finest teams, the Havana Reds and
Almendares Blues. The New Yorkers went 11–5–1 against the two teams,
but were only 5–4 against Torriente's Blues. In the five games the two players went head to head, Torriente outhit his American opponent .476 to
.375, and three home runs to one. All of Torriente's homers came in game
four, an 11–4 Almendares victory. He also added a double, good for six RBIs.

Cristobal Torriente was a superstar. Manager C. I. Taylor called him a
franchise. He was that. Standing 5'9" and weighing a compact 190 pounds,
the left-handed hitting slugger hit the ball to all fields with outstanding
power. He was a bad-ball hitter who could hit the ball off his shoetops or
above his shoulders with equal power. He starred in both the Cuban Winter League (CWL) and the American Negro league, from 1913 to 1934. In
his homeland, he had a career average of .353, the third highest average in
Cuban baseball history, behind Jud Wilson's .372 and Oscar Charleston's

.365. He won two batting titles in the CWL with a .387 batting average in 1914-15 and .360 in 1919-20, when he also led the league in doubles, triples, and home runs. He hit .402 in 1915-16, but lost the title to Eustaqio Pedroso's .413. He did however, lead the league in base hits, triples, and homers. Over his 16-year CWL career Torriente averaged 24 doubles, 16 triples, and 7 home runs a year. The seven home runs a year, accumulated primarily during the dead-ball era, would translate to 17 home runs in today's major leagues. His .353 career batting average would translate to .327 in the majors.

In the Negro leagues, Torriente was a member of Rube Foster's powerful Chicago American Giants, who captured the first three pennants in the new Negro National League, from 1920 to 1922. The southpaw slugger essentially carried the offense during those years. He captured the batting championship in both 1920 (.411) and 1923 (.412).

Torriente was a fast baserunner who could steal bases if the situation warranted it. On defense, he held down center field with the best of them. He had good range and a strong throwing arm, but primarily he was a hitter. He hit well in postseason play also, stinging the ball at a .302 clip in the 1921 playoffs against the Kansas City Monarchs. In 1926, playing for the Monarchs he hit .407 against his old teammates in a losing cause.

The Cuban strongman also played more than two dozen games against major league all-star teams in the U.S., and he handled them all easily. According to John Holway's research, he touched up the likes of 247-game winner Jack Quinn, 158-game winner Jeff Pfeffer, and 194-game winner Dolf Luque, for a .436 batting average, although they did hold him to a single home run in over 100 at-bats.

Torriente's Negro league career lasted for 20 years, during which time he averaged .336 with 33 doubles, 10 triples, and 13 home runs. Adjusting his statistics to a major league basepoint would give him a .288 career batting average with 16 home runs a year. Combining his Negro league statistics with his Cuban Winter League statistics would give him an adjusted major league average of approximately .308 with 17 home runs a year, over a long career. In his prime, he would probably have tattooed major league pitchers for season averages as high as .350–.360, with 30 home runs.

Cristobal Torriente was elected to the Cuban Baseball Hall of Fame with the first class in 1939.

JUD WILSON

Chino Smith may well have been the greatest hitter in the history of Negro league baseball. On the other hand, the greatest hitter may have been a man called Ernest Judson "Jud" Wilson. If Jud was not the best hitter, he was close to it. In fact, the statistics tend to support Wilson.

Jud Wilson was born in Remington, Virginia, on February 28, 1899. He played baseball in the Negro leagues for 24 years, after breaking in with the Baltimore Black Sox at the age of 23. He spent nine years with Baltimore, six with the Philadelphia Stars, and eight with the Homestead Grays.

Wilson, known as "Boojum" because of the sound his drives made when they hit the fence, packed a solid 185 pounds on a squat 5'8" body. He had massive shoulders and a huge chest that tapered down to a small waist and short, bowed legs. He was a terrifying hitter, driving balls all around the ballpark, usually for extra bases. He was also bad tempered. He hated all pitchers and all umpires. As teammate Jake Stephens noted in "Blackball Stars," "The minute he saw an umpire, he became a maniac." He attacked pitchers with a vengeance. Sometimes he attacked them with his batting skills, and sometimes he attacked them physically. He was a brawler who would fight at the slightest affront. Many of his teammates insisted he was a nice guy off the field, but when he put a uniform on, he became another person. He wanted to win at all costs. He was a bad loser.

He led the newly formed Eastern Colored League in batting in his sophomore year, crushing the ball to the tune of .464. He followed that barrage with season averages of .394, .397, .358, .412, .375, .346, and .371 with Baltimore. His career average in Baltimore was a stratospheric .384! After leaving Baltimore, he played two years with the Grays, hitting .362 and .370, before jumping to the Philadelphia Stars where he played for six years. All he hit in Philly was .354, .412, .309, .380, and .319. He added three more batting championships to his trophy case over the years, hitting .412 in 1927, .412 in 1934, and .380 in 1936. He also led the league in doubles, triples, and home runs, once each.

When he retired from the Negro leagues, he left behind a .354 lifetime batting average, the highest average for any player with more than 2000 at-bats (Wilson batted over 4000 times). By comparison, Chino Smith had only 694 at-bats in the Negro leagues.

Jud Wilson was primarily a hitter, but he could also handle himself in the field and on the bases. He had good speed and was an aggressive baserunner. And because of his bad temperament, the fielders usually gave him a wide berth around the bases. On defense, he played third base and first base, both acceptably. He was not flashy, and he was not graceful, but somehow he got the job done. At third base, he was noted for knocking balls down with his chest, then picking them up and throwing the runner out.

Jud Wilson made the annual trek south in the winter to play in the Cuban Winter League. He spent six pleasant winters there and almost destroyed the pitching staffs around the league. He raked opposing pitchers for averages of .430, .333, .424, .397, and .363. The pitchers finally caught up with the 36-year-old slugger in 1935, holding him to a .263 average. In all, Wilson won two batting championships in Cuba, with .430 in 1925-26 and .424 in 1927-28. He also led the league in runs scored twice, triples once, home runs once, and stolen bases once. His career batting average in Cuba was .372, which is the highest batting average in Cuban baseball history.

The fiery Virginian played in more than two dozen exhibition games against major league all-star teams and tortured the likes of Lefty Grove, Dolf Luque, and Dizzy Dean to the tune of .360. He also played in the California Winter League against major league players during the winter of 1930–31 and he hit .469 in fifteen games. And he played one year in the Puerto Rican Winter League, where he hit .404 as a 45-year-old graybeard.

Overall, Jud Wilson hit .354 in the Negro leagues, with 30 doubles, 6 triples, and 13 home runs a year. In Cuba he averaged .372 with 27 doubles, 19 triples, and 13 home runs. These numbers suggest that if he had played in the major leagues, he would have averaged .326 over a long career, with 29 doubles, 13 triples, and 19 home runs a year. In some years, during his prime, he might have pounded major league pitchers for a .365 to .375 average with 30 or more home runs.

WILD BILL WRIGHT

Burnis Wright, better known as Wild Bill Wright, was born in Milan, Tennessee, on June 6, 1914. He went on to star in both the Negro leagues and the Mexican League. He joined his first professional team, the Nashville Elite Giants, in 1932 at the age of 17. He was big, strong, and fast. He stood 6'4" and weighed a tight 220 pounds. But he was still learning his trade. During his first four years in the Negro National League (actually the team was in the Negro Southern League his first year), Wright hit .300, .244, .120, and .244. In his fifth year, now with the Washington Elite Giants, he finally unloosed his bat. During his last six years in the league, he pounded the ball for averages of .338, .410, .316, .404, .323, and .301. His Negro league career statistics show a solid .341 batting average, with 22 doubles, 12 triples, and 13 home runs for every 550 at-bats.

Wright was not only a terrific hitter, he was a complete ballplayer. He had blazing speed and was once timed at 13.2 seconds circling the bases. He was always a stolen-base threat, as well as a threat to take an extra base on a hit or to score a run on a routine play. On defense he roamed center field like a gazelle. He covered acres of ground and had a strong throwing arm.

Wright's only problem with the Negro leagues was the punishing travel schedule. It was not unusual for teams to travel 1000 miles, or more, a day, visiting three cities and playing four games. When he learned about the easier playing conditions in Mexico—very little traveling, a three-games-a-week schedule, a decent salary, plus being treated like a first-class citizen — Wild Bill headed south. He played out the remainder of his career in Mexico, from 1940 to 1951, and, when he finally retired, he opened a restaurant in Aguascalientes, a small city in the central part of the country.

Wild Bill Wright was a hero in Mexico with his tremendous talent and dedication. His first year in the league, splitting his time between Santa Rosa and Mexico City, he hit a sizzling .360, with a league-leading 30 doubles. But he was just getting warmed up. The next year, with Mexico City, he tore the cover off the ball, leading the league with a .390 batting average. He also led the league in stolen bases with 26. The following year, he led the league in batting at .366, in home runs with 13, and in runs batted in with 70, in 88 games. In all, the 6'4" switch hitter batted over .300, 12 times in 13 years. His career batting average in Mexico was .335, with 33 doubles, 10 triples, and 13 home runs for every 550 at-bats.

Wright also played in the Calfornia Winter League for several years, and he was considered, in many quarters, to be the most dangerous hitter in the league — and his teammates included Mule Suttles and Turkey Stearnes! In exhibition games against major league all-star teams in the fall, "Wild Bill" hit .371, according to author Brent Kelley. If Wright's Negro league statistics are compared with his Mexican League statistics, they are very similar. And they indicate he might have had a very successful major league career. If he had been given the opportunity to play ball at the major league level, he probably would have compiled a lifetime .294 batting average, with 28 doubles, 11 triples, 14 home runs, and 27 stolen bases a year. In some years, "Wild Bill" could have hit in .335–.345 range, with 30 home runs.

Burnis "Wild Bill" Wright was elected to the Mexican Baseball Hall of Fame in 1982.

In addition to the 20 players who were selected as candidates for election into the National Baseball Hall of Fame in Cooperstown, New York, there are a number of other players who, in the author's opinion, were world-class baseball players. Some of them may also be worthy of a place in the Hall of Fame, although they did not receive strong enough support from either the Players Panel or the Historians Panel, for consideration at this time. Perhaps, at some later date, one or more of these players may also be enshrined in Cooperstown.

NEWT ALLEN

Newt Allen, called "Colt" by his teammates because he was just a kid among men when he came up, had a Negro league career that lasted from 1922 until 1947, most of it with the famous Kansas City Monarchs. Allen was born in Austin, Texas, in 1901, but moved to Kansas City as a child. Shortly after he graduated from Lincoln High School, he was discovered by J. L. Wilkinson, owner of the Monarchs.

After one year of seasoning with Wilkinson's All-Nations team, the 22-year-old infielder was called up to the big club. He immediately established himself as one of the top second basemen in the Negro National League. He was a slick fielder with good range and a strong arm. He was particularly adept at turning the double play and often, according to teammate Plunk Drake in John Holway's *Voices from the Great Black Baseball Leagues,* "He wouldn't even look at first base on the pivot. He'd throw the ball to first under his left arm." He had the luxury of playing next to two of the greatest shortstops in Negro league history, Dobie Moore and Willie Wells. He played four years with Moore and two years with Wells, and he considered them to be about equal in talent, but he thought Wells was the smarter player. Allen even played several years at short himself after Moore's tragic accident.

Newt was also a force to be reckoned with at the plate. From his second spot in the batting order, the little 5'8", 160-pound right handed hitter could handle the bat like a magician. He could bunt for either a sacrifice or a base hit, execute the hit-and-run, or spray base hits around the outfield. Unfortunately, one of the things that prevented him from being recommended for Hall of Fame consideration was his bat. Although he sported a respectable lifetime batting average of .302 in the Negro leagues, that would convert to only .254 in the major leagues, more than 30 points below the lowest average for a HOF second baseman. Bobby Doerr and Nellie Fox, both at .288, are the only second baseman presently in Cooperstown with batting averages below the magic .300 mark.

Allen did occasionally put together some impressive offensive seasons. In 1925, his third full season with the Monarchs, he broke the .300 barrier for the first time, hitting .308 in 82 games. He also hit .334 in 1927, .330 in 1929, .345 in 1930, .326 in 1932, .363 in 1937, and .323 in 1940.

Over the course of his career, the Texas native helped the Monarchs capture nine league pennants, and two World Championships. In the 1924 World Series against the Hilldale Daisies, Allen hit .282 as the Monarchs took the Series, 5–4, with the venerable Jose Mendez blanking the Daisies 5–0 in the finale. The next year, he rapped the ball at a .417 pace in a league playoff series against the St. Louis Stars, then hit .259 in a losing World Series against Hilldale. In 1942, he hit .267 in the World Series, as the Monarchs swept the Homestead Grays four straight. He also played in four East-West All-Star games, 1936–38 and '41.

Like most Negro leaguers, Newt Allen often played baseball year-round. He played with Almendares in the Cuban Winter League in 1924 and 1937, batting a combined .278. He also played winter ball in Mexico, Puerto Rico, Venezuela and California. He spent six years on the west coast, hitting .324.

Newt Allen was one of the top four or five second basemen in Negro league history. Perhaps it will be enough to get him into Cooperstown one day.

CHET BREWER

Chester Arthur Brewer had a long and storied professional baseball career, one that carried him to many of the countries in the western hemisphere. The native of Leavenworth, Kansas, began his career with the Kansas City Monarchs in 1925 as a fuzzy-cheeked 18 year old. It took him just one year to establish himself as a world-class pitcher. He racked up a record of 12–1 in 1926.

The tall lanky right hander was primarily a finesse pitcher who had good control and a mean streak reminiscent of Don Drysdale or Bob Gibson. Nobody dug in against Brewer unless they were prepared to take one in the ribs. He had a moving fastball, a sharp breaking drop, a good curve, a screwball, his famous emory ball, and that mean streak!

Brewer's best year with the Monarchs was 1929 when he won 17 games against just 3 losses. He also went 10–3 for the Cleveland Buckeyes in '43 and 12–6 for the same team in '47. One of his more famous games was a 12-inning pitching duel against Smokey Joe Williams of the Homestead

Grays. The game, which was played under the lights in Muehlebach Stadium in Kansas City, ended when the Grays pushed over the only run of the game, on a walk to Charleston and a single by Chaney White. Chet Brewer fanned 19 Grays during the game, including 10 in a row at one stretch. Smokey Joe set 20 Monarchs down on strikes.

All in all, over a period of 24 years, the 6'4", 176-pound hurler won 104 Negro league games against 69 losses, for a .601 winning percentage, according to *The Negro Leagues Book.*

Brewer, like many of his compatriots, often traveled south to Mexico, following the greenbacks. Playing for Tampico in 1938, he compiled a record of 17–5. He was 12–7 the following year and finished his Mexican career in 1944, winning only 3 of 15 decisions for the last-place Mexico City Reds.

He spent two winters playing ball in Panama, and the second year he pitched the Panama team to their only Caribbean World Series. He played one year in Cuba, going 2–2 for Havana in 1930-31, and one year in Puerto Rico, showing a 7–6 record for Caguas in 1947-48. He was also involved in the famous Dominican Summer League in 1937 that pitted teams of four presidential candidates against one another. He won two games against three losses for Aguilas, losing the final game of the season to Satchel Paige's pennant-winning Santo Domingo Dragones 4–3, on Sam Bankhead's dramatic seventh-inning home run. Earlier in the season, he had beaten Satch 4–2 with a strong no-hitter.

The tall control artist finally made it into organized baseball in 1952, at the advanced baseball age of 45. He went 6–5 for Riverside and 1–4 for Visalia in the California League, before putting the glove away for good. Over the years, he had shown he could match pitches with the best of them by going 5–0 against major league opposition in exhibition games. In one game in 1930, pitching against sluggers like Jimmie Foxx, Pinky Higgins, and Heinie Manush, Brewer tossed a neat 11–0 shutout.

Chet Brewer was a world-class pitcher, who would have been a star in the major leagues. His career spanned 28 years, including 20 years in the Negro leagues. It is quite likely that Brewer would have won more than 200 games in the big leagues, with 300 victories a distinct possibility.

JOHN DONALDSON

John Donaldson was one of the top southpaw pitchers of the early twentieth century. He and Rube Foster could match pitches with the major league's best left handers, including Rube Waddell and Eddie Plank. The

6', 185-pounder, was a power pitcher who relied on a sharp-breaking curve ball to send discouraged batters back to the dugout with their bats on their shoulders. He was, according to Jim Riley, "a poised left hander with pinpoint control." Like many of the black pitchers of the first half of the twentieth century, he had four or five dependable pitches, including the aforementioned curve, a drop, a good fastball, and a deadly change-up.

Donaldson, who was born in Glasgow, Missouri, on February 20, 1892, began his professional career with J. L. Wilkinson's All-Nations team in 1913. The team, which included both whites and blacks as well as a Chinese player, a Hawaiian, and a girl, toured the country, playing against all types of opposition: professional, semi-pro, and amateur. Obviously much too talented for the opposition, Donaldson hardly ever lost a game and averaged 20 strikeouts for every nine innings. He once tossed three straight no-hitters.

When the Negro National League was formed in 1920, Donaldson was signed by the Kansas City Monarchs. He pitched for the Monarchs for seven years between 1920 and 1934, choosing to tour with independent teams from 1924 to 1930.

Donaldson played baseball 12 months a year for more than two decades. During the winter, he often played ball in the Florida Hotel League. Some years he traveled to Cuba and other years he played in the California Winter League. In 1916-17 he starred for the Los Angeles White Sox in California. In addition to his pitching skills, Donaldson was also a good hitter and a strong defensive player. He often played shortstop or the outfield when not pitching. Riley noted that he hit a solid .320 for the Monarchs in 1921. He often batted in the third slot in the batting order, but often hit leadoff to take advantage of his speed.

Unfortunately for Donaldson, his statistics are scant. Most of his career was spent outside the organized Negro leagues, so box scores are difficult to locate. His records in Cuba are still missing, and the statistics from the Florida Hotel League and the California Winter League have yet to be compiled. However, baseball expert John McGraw considered John Donaldson to be one of the finest pitchers of his generation. He was tall, graceful, and cool under fire. He didn't drink, or smoke, or carouse. He was a winner.

VALENTIN DREKE

Valentin Dreke was a racehorse out of Union De Reyes, Cuba, who thrilled baseball fans in both the United States and his home country for

11 years, from 1918 to 1928. He began his American career with the Cuban Stars in 1918. When the Negro National League was formed in 1920, the Stars became one of the founding teams. Dreke played alongside other Cuban legends like Eustaquio Pedroso, Bernardo Baro, and Jose Hernandez. And he was the best of the lot. He tormented Negro league pitchers with season averages of .353, .378, .429, .319, .416, and .327. His nine-year Negro league career produced an excellent .327 batting average, with 22 doubles, 7 triples, and 4 home runs a year. In addition to his average, Dreke could also handle the bat with the best of them. As the Cuban's leadoff man, the 5'8", 160-pound Cuban Flash was adept at getting on base and stealing his way into scoring position. Batting left handed, he could spray the ball to all fields, beat out drag bunts, or coax a walk at a critical time. He was also a dangerous player in the outfield, running down long hits and throwing out baserunners with a strong, accurate throwing arm.

In his home country, Dreke starred for the Almendares Blues during the 20s. As in the states, he controlled the game with his knack for reaching base and his blazing speed on the bases. He didn't have a lot of power, averaging only 18 doubles, 2 triples, and 1 home run a year, which compared favorably to his Negro league averages, but he had a good on-base percentage. And once on base, he was even money to score, averaging over 100 runs scored a year.

Valentin Dreke retired from the Cuban Winter League after the 1928 season, leaving behind a .307 batting average. He was elected to the Cuban Baseball Hall of Fame in 1945.

FRANK GRANT

Ulysses F. "Frank" Grant, a native of Pittsfield, Massachusetts, may have been the best second baseman in professional baseball in the nineteenth century, black or white. The major leagues had Hall of Famer Bid McPhee and Fred Dunlap, but the minor leagues and the Negro leagues had Grant. McPhee was an outstanding defensive wizard for the Cincinnati Reds, whose single season fielding average, set in 1897, lasted almost 30 years. He was also a solid hitter with some pop in his bat. Dunlap, known as "Sure Shot" because of his magic glove, was also dangerous at the plate. In 1884, he led the Union Association in home runs with 13 in just 449 at-bats and in hitting with an average of .412. His 160 runs scored in 101 games was the record for many years.

As good as McPhee and Dunlap were, however, Frank Grant was

better. He was their equal in the field, in spite of having to confront racism every day. Some white players tried to spike him every time they slid into second base. He finally started wearing wooden shin guards to protect his legs. At the plate, the 5'8", 155-pound right handed slugger had no peers. His six-year minor league career batting average of .337 was 45 points higher than Dunlap's and 66 points higher than McPhee's. He broke into professional baseball with the Meriden club in the Eastern League in 1886, hitting .316. He moved on to Buffalo in the International League before the season was half over and rapped the ball at a .344 clip for the New York team. The following year, Grant hit .353 in 105 games with 26 doubles, 10 triples, and a league-leading 11 home runs. He continued his cannonading in '88, hitting 11 more home runs and compiling a .346 batting average.

Unfortunately for Grant and the other black players in organized baseball, the color barrier began to close after the '88 season. Buffalo refused to sign their star player in 1889, and he was forced to look for work elsewhere. He played with three teams in four different minor leagues over the next three years, then was driven out of organized ball for good. His minor league stats suggested that he could have hit in the .303 range in the major leagues and would have been one of the top home-run hitters, along with Dan Brothers and Sam Thompson. His nine home runs a year average would equate to approximately 29 in the live-ball era.

Frank Grant finished his baseball career with several Negro league teams, finally retiring in 1903.

CLARENCE "FATS" JENKINS

Clarence "Fats" Jenkins may be the greatest secret in Negro league history. When the great black outfielders are discussed, the names of Cool Papa Bell, Oscar Charleston, and Turkey Stearnes are thrown around with abandon. But the name Fats Jenkins is seldom heard. And the truth is, Fats Jenkins was also a world-class outfielder who enjoyed a successful 21-year career in the Negro leagues.

Like most Negro leaguers, Jenkins moved around from team to team, wherever the money was best. He spent most of his time, however — seven years— with the New York Black Yankees. Jenkins was a short, stocky left handed hitter, who stood just 5'7" in his stocking feet and topped the scales at 180 pounds. He was an intelligent player who, realizing he was not a power hitter, concentrated on getting on base and taking advantage of his outstanding speed. His extra-base contributions were minimal, totaling only 24 extra base hits a year, 16 of them doubles, but he perfected the technique of hitting the ball where it was pitched and just trying to drop it into an open spot in the outfield.

His technique was extremely successful, as he finished his career in the upper echelon of Negro league hitters. According to John Holway, only seven hitters, four Hall of Famers and three potential Hall of Famers, finished with higher batting averages than Jenkins's .337. Batting in the leadoff position, he was particularly adept at beating out Baltimore chops and bunts to the infield. It was then that he could turn his 90-foot hits into doubles and triples with his flying feet. He was regarded as an outstanding base stealer who made life miserable for opposing pitchers.

Fats Jenkins was born in New York City on January 19, 1898. He began his professional baseball career with his hometown Lincoln Giants in 1920 and quickly established himself as an exciting hitter, baserunner, and outfielder. He covered large expanses of ground in the outfield and kept baserunners honest with an accurate throwing arm. He had his greatest season with the bat in 1927 when he pounded the ball at a sizzling .398 clip for the Harrisburg Giants. He also showed averages of .379 and .365 with the Bacharach Giants.

In addition to baseball, Jenkins also played professional basketball with the Renaissance team, one of the most popular black touring teams in the country.

OSCAR "HEAVY" JOHNSON

Oscar "Heavy" Johnson came out of the U.S. Army's famous 25th Infantry Regiment in 1922, joining former Army teammates Dobie Moore, Bullet Rogan, Hurley McNair, and Lemuel Hawkins on the Kansas City Monarchs. He was 26 years old. He went on to star in the Negro leagues for 11 years.

Heavy Johnson was a big man, standing 6' and weighing a bulky 250 pounds. He played outfield most of his career, but he also caught occasionally and even played some second base. It was with a bat in his hands, however, that he is best remembered. In his rookie season, the right handed bomber slugged the ball at a .389 pace. The next year, he hit .380, with 18 home runs in just 46 games. According to John Holway, over the course of a 12-year career, Johnson compiled a .350 batting average with 17 home runs a year.

In addition to his Negro league career, the Atchison, Kansas, native played in Cuba one year and hit a resounding .345. If he had had the opportunity to play major league ball, he could have been expected to hit around .302 with 21 home runs a year.

DAVE MALARCHER

David Julius Malarcher, better known as "Gentleman Dave," was unique among the rough, tough men who gravitated toward the Negro leagues in the early decades of the twentieth century—a college man who neither smoked, drank, or chased after women. Malarcher was a well-conditioned athlete who played the game with considerable skill and enthusiasm.

The 5'7", 150-pound infielder was born in Whitehall, Louisiana, on October 18, 1894. He attended Dillard University in New Orleans before leaving to join the Indianapolis ABC's in 1916. He quickly developed into the finest-fielding third baseman in the game and is still recognized as one of the top four third baseman of all time, along with Dandridge, Judy Johnson, and Oliver Marcelle.

Although slight of build, the speedy switch hitter could handle a bat with the best of them. He was an expert bunter and a dangerous hit-and-run man. He was also a patient hitter who was adept at drawing bases on balls. Once on base, he was a constant threat to steal.

Dave Malarcher was a Hall of Fame defensive third baseman, but the fragmentary batting statistics that have been uncovered to date give him only a .267 batting average which, converted to a major league level, would be just slightly above the Mendoza line at .220. That low average would put him in the same class with players like Mark Belanger, whose fielding skills were unsurpassed in major league history but whose .228 batting average prevented him from receiving the honors he so richly deserved. According to Jim Riley, Malarcher had seasons where he hit .309, .344, and .330, but those were few and far between. In other seasons he could do no better than .240, .227, and .235.

Dave Malarcher played 19 years in the Negro leagues, 9 of them with the Chicago American Giants. During his time with the Giants, the team won five league championships, including the first three in Negro National League history, 1920 to 1923. After Malarcher assumed the position of player-manager, the Giants captured the only two World Series they played in, defeating the Bacharach Giants 5–3 in both 1926 and 1927. Malarcher led the team in stolen bases in both series.

After his retirement from professional baseball in 1934, the man from Louisiana operated a successful real estate business. He was also a talented poet who had several of his works published.

JOSE MENDEZ

Jose Mendez, one of the brightest stars of Cuban baseball from 1908 to 1927, was born in Cardenas, Matanzas, Cuba, on March 19, 1887. He began his professional career as a fireballing right handed pitcher with the Almendares Blues of the Cuban League in 1908. He went undefeated his first year, running up a record of 9–0, and followed that with seasons of 15–6, 7–0, 11–2, 9–5, 1–4, 10–0, and 2–0.

The young 20-year-old pitcher quickly became the hero of the Cuban baseball world and was known affectionately as "el Diamante Negro" or "the Black Diamond." His star burned even brighter after he stifled the major league teams that visited his homeland for exhibition series over the years. In 1908, the young 5'8", 160-pound Pedro Martinez clone blanked the Cincinnati Reds 1–0 on a one-hitter, with nine strikeouts. Two weeks later, according to Cuban baseball historian Jorge Figueredo, Mendez tossed seven shutout innings against those same Reds and followed that up with another shutout victory, this time a five-hit, eight-strikeout, 3–0 gem.

In subsequent years, he defeated pitchers like Eddie Plank (twice) and Pittsburgh's 25-game winner Howie Camnitz. He also saved a game against the New York Giants's legendary ace, Christy Mathewson, by blanking John McGraw's boys on one hit over four innings. In 1912, he outpitched Mathewson 4–3 in 10 innings and edged the Dodgers's great southpaw Nap Rucker, 2–1.

Overall, Jose Mendez compiled a record of 72–26 in the Cuban League, a dazzling .735 winning percentage. He played shortstop, third base, and the outfield when not pitching.

Mendez also played baseball in the Negro leagues during the summer, from 1908 to 1926. He gained his greatest fame as playing manager of the Kansas City Monarchs from 1920 to 1926. Hampered by a sore arm, Mendez pitched infrequently but could still rise to the occasion when necessary. He went 20–4 on the mound during his tenure in Kansas City. In postseason play he was even better. While leading the Monarchs to three successive league titles and two World Championships between 1923 and 1925, Mendez set an example in courage for everyone to follow. In the ninth and final game of the '24 classic, with the Series tied at four games apiece and his pitching staff depleted, the 37-year-old Black Diamond took the mound to face Hilldale's talented submarine pitcher, Scrip Lee. The aging veteran matched goose eggs with Lee for seven innings, before his team exploded for five runs in the bottom of the eighth. He finished with a 5–0, three-hit shutout and a World Championship. It was his finest hour.

Jose Mendez died of broncopneumonia just four years later, at the age of 41. He was elected to the Cuban Baseball Hall of Fame in 1939. His plaque should also be hanging in Cooperstown.

TED "DOUBLE DUTY" RADCLIFFE

Theodore Roosevelt Radcliffe was one of the most unforgettable characters ever to play in the Negro leagues. He was also one of the most talented and one of the most versatile. The patriarch of black baseball, the league's oldest living veteran, first saw the light of day in Mobile, Alabama, on July 7, 1902. He began his professional career with the Detroit Stars in 1928, two years after Satchel Paige. He played his last game in 1951, ending a memorable 24-year career.

He began his career as a catcher, hitting .265 for the Stars and pounding eight home runs in just 253 at-bats. Playing alongside legends like Turkey Stearnes and Cristobal Torriente, Radcliffe improved his average to .310 the next year, popping 12 extra-base hits in 126 at-bats. The 5'10", 190-pound receiver jumped to Gilkerson's Union Giants in 1929, beginning a nomadic existence that saw him play for dozens of teams during his career. He also began pitching in '29, running up a record of 9–0 in his first year on the mound.

In 1932, playing with the Pittsburgh Crawfords, Radcliffe caught Satchel Paige in the opener of a doubleheader in Yankee Stadium, hitting a home run to spark Satch's 5–0 victory. In the nightcap, the cocky 30 year old pitched his own shutout, winning 6–0. The next day, in the New York newspaper, sportswriter Damon Runyon referred to him as "Double Duty." He is still known as Double Duty, or just "Duty."

The rugged right handed hitter put together some good seasons at the bat during his 24-year career. He hit .300 in 1930, .362 in '34, and .368 in '37. According to his biographer, Kyle P. McNary, Duty had a .303 career batting average with 10 home runs for every 550 at-bats. On the mound, he finished with 128 victories against 48 losses, a .727 winning percentage. McNary estimated that if all the statistics were available, Radcliffe would have accumulated over 4000 base hits and 430 home runs. His pitching totals would have included 502 victories against just 189 losses. Of course, these estimates compiled by McNary include Radcliffe's record against all kinds of opposition, semi-pro and amateur as well as professional.

Double Duty Radcliffe was a raconteur nonpareil. He could talk for hours, recounting the most outrageous tales ever heard. Naturally most of them concerned his unmatched baseball skills. When not talking baseball, he was talking about his many romantic conquests. He considered himself to be a ladies man and was always on the prowl for female companionship. He didn't smoke or drink, saving his energies for more rewarding pursuits.

Separating the wheat from the chaff is not easy in Radcliffe's case, but what facts are known support his candidacy for the National Baseball Hall of Fame in Cooperstown, New York. As Jim Riley reported, Duty played for three of the greatest teams in Negro league history, and he contributed to their success. Playing with the St. Louis Stars in 1930, the big right hander batted .283 and went 10–2 on the mound. The next year, with the Homestead Grays, he hit .298 and had a pitching record of 9–5. And in '32, as a member of the famed Pittsburgh Crawfords, Double Duty batted .325 and had a won-lost record of 19–8.

Ted Radcliffe was voted into six East-West All-Star games, showing the respect fans had for him. He batted .308 in all-star competition and won his only decision on the mound. The partial statistics that have been uncovered by John Holway show Double Duty with a batting average of .280 and 10 home runs a year. His pitching slate shows a record of 52–32 for a winning percentage of .619.

Radcliffe frequently pitched in other countries during the winter months. In 1938 and 1939, he pitched for the Almendares Blues in the Cuban Winter League, going 5–8 in '38 and 7–3 the following year. In 1940, he pitched for the powerful Vera Cruz Blues in the Mexican League. Playing under manager Martin Dihigo and alongside teammates Josh Gibson, Cool Papa Bell, Ray Dandridge, and Willie Wells, Radcliffe was 5–6 for the pennant-winning Blues. He also pitched in Puerto Rico, South America, and Canada. And in exhibition games against major league opposition, he hit a resounding .403 in 22 games and went 3–0 on the mound.

EDWARD "HUCK" RILE

Edward Rile was one of the biggest men ever to play baseball in the Negro leagues. Born in Columbus, Ohio, around 1901, the powerful switch

Double Duty Radcliffe was an all-star on the mound or behind the plate. He could do it all.

hitter grew to 6'6" and weighed a muscular 230 pounds by the time he broke into professional baseball with the Indianapolis ABC's in 1920.

Originally a pitcher, the big right hander put together season marks of 2–1, 3–0, 4–5, 14–8, 5–1, 2–5, and 4–1 on the mound, according to Jim Riley. By 1926, Rile was alternating between the mound and first base to take advantage of his mighty bat. He enjoyed his greatest success with the Detroit Stars from 1927 to 1930. Joining Turkey Stearnes and Cristobel Torriente, the colossus helped give the Stars a powerful offensive attack. As Richard Bak recorded in his fine book, *Turkey Stearnes and the Detroit Stars,* Rile slugged the ball at a .406 clip in '27, with 23 doubles, 6 triples, and 10 home runs in just 234 at-bats. He also paced the pitching staff, going 14–6 for the third-place Stars and producing one of the greatest all-around seasons by an individual in Negro league history.

The following three years he concentrated on hitting, limiting his pitching to 10 games, with four wins and two losses, over the three-year period. But at bat, he continued to pound the ball. He hit .372 in 1928, leading the league in base hits with 111 and in doubles with 27. He also hit eight home runs and stole seven bases. In '29 he slumped to .299 but still hit 10 home runs. And the following year, as the Stars captured the National League pennant, Huck Rile hit .323 with 17 doubles, 9 triples, and 8 home runs in 226 at-bats. His four-year stats in Detroit, as presented by Bak, are very impressive. He accumulated 354 base hits in 1009 at-bats, for a .351 batting average. He hit 79 doubles, 19 triples, and 36 home runs, giving him a .574 slugging average. He also stole 18 bases and went 18–8 on the mound.

The slugging first sacker jumped to the Brooklyn Royal Giants in 1931, playing out the rest of his 17-year career there. According to John Holway, Huck Rile compiled a career .339 batting average from statistics uncovered to date, with an average of 16 home runs for every 550 at-bats. Jim Riley's log credits Rile with a 48–27 slate as a pitcher.

GEORGE SCALES

George Walter Scales was one of the greatest second basemen ever to play Negro league baseball. He is frequently selected by Negro league veterans and baseball historians as the all-time Negro league second baseman.

Scales was born in Talladega, Alabama, on August 16, 1900. He attended Talladega College for a while, but professional baseball beckoned and he joined the Montgomery Grey Sox in 1919, moving up to the Negro National League St. Louis Giants in 1921. He played in the Negro leagues for 28 years, spending seven years with the New York Lincoln Giants and nine years with the Baltimore Elite Giants.

George Scales played all the infield positions as well as the outfield, but at 5'11" and 195 pounds, he was a little on the chubby side (his nickname was Tubby) and lacked the speed and range to be a good shortstop or outfielder, so he settled in at second base where his natural talents made him an all-star. He was an intelligent player who depended on good positioning to compensate for his lack of range. He was an outstanding double-play man with a strong throwing arm.

Scales was not only a good defensive second baseman, he could also handle a bat. In fact, he was considered to be one of the best curve-ball hitters in the league. He was a line-drive hitter who had decent extra-base power. During his stay with the Lincoln Giants, according to Jim Riley, he put together seasons of .429, .367, .361, .222, .446, .338, and .387.

Moving on to the New York Black Yankees in 1932, George Scales began a managerial career that lasted until 1952. He was known as a tough manager who drove his players hard, but he was considered to be one of the best in the business.

In addition to his Negro league career, Scales also played baseball all over the western hemisphere. In 1937, he played in the infamous Dominican Republic summer league, batting .295 for the Estrellas Orientales team. He also played three years in the Cuban Winter League from 1927 to 1930. He hit .282 and .321 for the Almendares Blues and .290 for the Havana Reds.

George Scales had a long and distinguished career in Puerto Rico. He made his first visit to the island country for an exhibition series in 1926 as a member of the Lincoln Giants. He returned many times over the next 34 years as both a player and a manager. His playing statistics are unavailable, but his managerial record is unsurpassed in Puerto Rican Winter League (PRWL) history. He was Manager of the Year six times between

1941 and 1951. His Ponce team won five league titles in six years. His 46–47 team rallied from a 3–0 deficit to capture the playoff with Caguas. His 50–51 Santurce Crabbers, with Willard Brown and Bob Thurman, went on to win the Caribbean World Series. According to Puerto Rican baseball historian Luis Alvelo, George Scales was the greatest manager in PRWL history.

Scales's Negro league statistics showed a career average of .309, with 35 doubles, 7 triples, and 14 home runs a year. In Cuba, he averaged .299 for three years, with 18 doubles, 12 triples and 5 home runs for every 550 at-bats. If he had played major league baseball, he could have been expected to hit in the mid .260s, with about 19 home runs a year. In some years he could have hit over .300 with 30 home runs.

He became a stockbroker after retirement.

TETELO VARGAS

Juan Estando "Tetelo" Vargas was one of the fastest players in the Negro leagues, as well as one of its better hitters. Known as the "Dominican Deer," he was a fleet center fielder with exceptional range and a strong, accurate throwing arm.

Tetelo Vargas was born in Santo Domingo, Dominican Republic, on April 6, 1906. He began playing baseball at an early age, eventually moving into the Negro leagues in the United States with the Cuban Stars in 1927. He was brilliant on defense but even more impressive on offense. He was tall and skinny, packing a scant 160 pounds on his 5'10" frame, but he was an excellent hitter who sprayed singles all over the field and who was adept at beating out bunts. And on the bases, he could fly. One of the top base stealers in the Negro leagues, he was a blur going from first to third on a base hit.

He starred in the Negro leagues for 18 years, compiling a .340 batting average, 19th all time. He averaged 20 doubles, two triples, and one home run for every 550 at-bats.

The right handed hitter played ball all over western hemisphere for 30 years, with way-stops in the United States, Puerto Rico, the Dominican Republic, Cuba, Canada, Colombia, and Venezuela. He averaged .320 in Puerto Rico, with five home runs for every 550 at-bats. In 1944, he became the oldest batting champion in Puerto Rican Winter League (PRWL) history, pounding the ball at a .410 clip in 55 games, at the age of 38. He also led the league in runs scored four times, triples twice, and stolen bases twice. Luis Alvelo noted he had "speed and a hot bat always." Milito Navarro, one of Puerto Rica's greatest players, noted in Tom Van Hyning's book on the PRWL, "Tetelo was reliable and produced in the clutch. I saw him score from first on a single. Another time, he made it home from second on a long fly ball to right field. He was one of my idols in baseball — a very complete ballplayer."

Tetelo Vargas played in the summer and winter leagues in his homeland between 1951 and 1956. He won the Dominican Summer League batting title with Estrellas Orientales at the advanced baseball age of 47, batting .355 in 49 games. His five-year average in the league was .322 with 29 doubles, 6 triples, and 2 home runs. He fanned just 26 times for every 550 at-bats, with 61 bases on balls. His stolen-base totals are unavailable. He is a member of the Baseball Hall of Fame in both the Dominican Republic and Puerto Rico.

Based on his statistics in other leagues, Tetelo Vargas might have hit about .293 in the major leagues, with some seasons in the .330 to .340 range. He would also have been a dangerous stolen-base threat and a world class-defensive center fielder.

EDGAR WESLEY

Edgar Wesley was one of the many slugging first basemen to play in the Negro leagues over the first half of the twentieth century. The big 6', 200-pound left handed hitter was one of the most dangerous men at the plate in his prime. He played in the Negro leagues from 1918 to 1931, primarily with the Detroit Stars.

After the Detroit Stars became members of the Negro National League, Wesley was one of their stars. He led the league with 10 home runs in just 158 at-bats in 1920, while hitting .285, and followed that up with averages of .336 and .344 the next two years. When Turkey Stearnes joined the team in 1923, the two bombers put on quite a show. They tied for the league lead in home runs with 17 apiece, with Stearnes hitting the ball at a .353 clip and Wesley tattooing opposing pitchers to the tune of .339.

Wesley jumped to the Harrisburg Giants in 1924 but returned to the Stars the next three years, leading the league in batting (.424) and home runs (18) in 1925 and hitting .300 with 15 homers in 1926. He didn't play much in 1927. Overall, Wesley's Detroit career statistics, according to Richard Bak, showed a .338 batting average, with 26 doubles, 6 triples, and 37 home runs for every 550 at-bats.

John Holway's career statistics for Edgar Wesley were slightly more conservative. They show a .318 batting average with 24 home runs a year. Macmillan's *Encyclopedia* credits Wesley with a .324 batting average, with 28 doubles, 7 triples, and 28 home runs a year.

It is obvious that Edgar Wesley was a force to be reckoned with at the plate. He would have been a dangerous hitter in the major leagues, probably averaging in the range of .280 with 37 home runs a year. In some years, the big left handed slugger could have hit as high as .330 with 55 or more home runs.

Edgar Wesley was also a competent defensive first baseman and a fast, intelligent baserunner. And he was a good role model off the field, quiet and well behaved.

All-Time Negro League All-Star Team: Players' Selections

Panels of Negro league veterans and baseball historians have selected those Negro league players they feel deserve consideration for admission into the National Baseball Hall of Fame in Cooperstown, New York. They selected a total of 20 players as candidates for the Hall of Fame. One of the players, Turkey Stearnes, was subsequently elected to the Hall in 2000. Hilton Smith was admitted in 2001. Eighteen players remain to be recognized. Also, there were three additional players "on the bubble," who should be considered.

In addition to the Hall of Fame survey, a second survey was conducted asking the panels to select their all-time Negro league All-Star team. A total of 59 responses were received, approximately 35 percent of those polled. The respondents were also asked to chose the greatest player in Negro league history, the greatest manager, and to describe their greatest thrill in baseball.

HERBERT BARNHILL

Herbert Barnhill, the tough little backstop for the Chicago American Giants during the war years of 1944 to 1946, selected these players.

Catcher: Double Duty Radcliffe
Pitcher: Hilton Smith
First Base: Buck O'Neil

Sammy T. Hughes is regarded by many baseball experts as the greatest second baseman in Negro League history. (Photograph courtesy James A. Riley.)

Second Base: Sammy T. Hughes
Shortstop: Sam Bankhead
Third Base Jud Wilson
Outfield: Jimmie Crutchfield, Willard Brown, Sam Jethroe

Herbert Barnhill did not vote for the greatest player in the Negro leagues, nor did he relate his greatest thrill in the game.

Four of the players Barnhill selected for the all-star team were teammates in Kansas City and Chicago—Willard Brown, Hilton Smith, Buck O'Neil, and Jimmie Crutchfield. Interestingly, he bypassed two other teammates who are established Hall of Famers, Satchel Paige and Willie Wells.

JAMES "COOL PAPA" BELL

James "Cool Papa" Bell is a member of the National Baseball Hall of Fame, having been elected to that prestigious group in 1974. Bell starred in the Negro leagues for 25 years, from 1922 through 1946, compiling a .328 batting average in over 4,700 at-bats. He was reportedly the fastest man in the Negro leagues, often scoring from first base on a single and from second base on an infield out. Satchel Paige claimed that Bell could turn off the light switch in his hotel room and be in bed before the light went out.

Not content with playing only in the Negro leagues, Bell also strutted his wares all over the western hemisphere 12 months a year. He played winter baseball in Cuba and in the California Winter League (a pre–Jackie Robinson integrated professional circuit that included many major leaguers such as Babe Herman, Johnny Frederick, and Bob and Irish Meusel). He also passed some summers in Mexico and the Dominican Republic. And the pride of Starkville, Mississippi, hit the ball wherever he played. He hit .292 in Cuba, .366 in California, a blazing .367 in Mexico, and .318 in the Dominican Republic.

Cool Papa Bell selected his all-star team in the book *The All-Stars* by Nick Acocella and Donald Dewey.

Catcher: Biz Mackey
Pitcher: Ted Trent, Willie Foster
First Base: Oscar Charleston
Second Base: Sammy T. Hughes
Shortstop: Willie Wells
Third Base: Judy Johnson
Outfield: Monte Irvin, Turkey Stearnes, Rap Dixon
Greatest player: Bell was quoted as saying, "Norman Stearnes, the Detroit center fielder, was the greatest ballplayer I ever saw. Trent died young, but there was a stretch of about six years where no white all-star team beat him."

CHARLIE BIOT

Charlie Biot was an outfielder for the Newark Eagles, New York Black Yankees, and Baltimore Elite Giants from 1939 to 1941. At 6'3" and a solid 180-pounds, he was an outstanding defensive outfielder who had wide range and a dependable glove. He was also a .300 hitter who once hit a game-winning ninth-inning home run off Ace Adams of the New York Giants in an exhibition game. His career ended prematurely when he entered the U.S. Army during World War II.

Charlie Biot died in East Orange, New Jersey, on March 3, 2000, at the age of 82. He made these selections several years ago.

Catcher: Roy Campanella
Pitcher: (RH) Jimmy Hill, Leon Day
First Base: Buck Leonard
Second Base: Sam Bankhead
Shortstop: Willie Wells
Third Base: Ray Dandridge
Outfield: Wild Bill Wright, Henry Kimbro, Jimmie Crutchfield
Utility: Martin Dihigo
Manager: Tex Burnett

Charlie Biot was a teammate of Leon Day, Willie Wells, and Roy Campanella, but he also played with Hall of Famer Monte Irvin, as well as Biz Mackey and Mule Suttles.

Greatest player: Martin Dihigo. "Dihigo was a Cuban ballplayer. He could catch, also pitch, and play everywhere else as good as anybody, including Satchel Paige and Cannonball Redding."

Greatest thrill: "I was playing with the Baltimore Elite Giants in Bugle Field and went behind the lights to catch Buck Leonard's fly ball in Baltimore. I also caught a ball off Goose Curry's bat in Sulphur Dell Field in Nashville, Tennessee. I went back two times and the third time spinning around caught the ball for the third out. I only missed one fly ball in the three years I played — 1939, 1940, and 1941. I was a center fielder those three years."

MARLIN CARTER

Marlin Carter, called Mel or Pee Wee, was a native of Haslam, Texas. He enjoyed a long and productive Negro league career from 1932 to 1948. He played all infield positions except first base but was primarily a third baseman. During his career, he played with five different teams but is best remembered as a member of the Memphis Red Sox.

The diminutive Carter, who tipped the scales at 159 pounds soaking wet, was a popular player, both with his teammates and with the fans. He often batted first or second in the lineup, to take advantage of his keen batting eye as well as his skillful bat-handling techniques. He was adept at drawing bases on balls, and he could lay down a bunt or execute a hit-and-run when needed.

Marlin Carter had his best season with the bat in 1936, when he scorched the ball at a .387 clip for the Cincinnati Tigers. The peppery little infielder died in his adopted hometown of Memphis on December 20, 1993. He was seven days short of 81.

His all-time all-star selections follow. The selections include both Negro league players and major league players, because that was the initial intent of the survey. The major league–Negro league concept eventually had to be replaced with a Negro league–only all-star team because there were not enough Negro league players who actually played against the major leaguers in exhibition games.

Catcher: Josh Gibson, Johnnie Bench
Pitcher: (RH) Satchel Paige, Bob Feller, (LH) Willie Foster
First Base: Stan Musial, Buck Leonard
Second Base: Rhyne Sandberg, Davey Lopes
Shortstop: Ernie Banks, Phil Rizzuto

Third Base: Brooks Robinson, Judy Johnson

Outfield: (LF) Hank Aaron, Billy Williams, (CF):James "Cool Papa" Bell, Willie Mays, (RF):Frank Robinson, Roberto Clemente.

Manager: Sparky Anderson

Marlin Carter noted, "I only voted for players I played with or played against or saw play."

BILL "READY" CASH

William Walker Cash, better known as Ready Cash to baseball enthusiasts, played with the Philadelphia Stars in the Negro National League from 1943 to 1950, compiling a .261 career batting average. He entered organized baseball with Granby, Quebec, Canada, of the Provincial League in 1951 and pounded 16 home runs for Granby in 105 games to go along with a .296 batting average. Unfortunately, integration came too late for the stocky catcher to make a push for the big time, and he retired from the game after the 1952 season.

Frank Grant was one of the best all-around second baseman, black or white, in the nineteenth century. (Photograph courtesy Jay Sanford.)

He has stayed active in the sport as a member of the SABR Negro Leagues Committee. Cash made the following his all-star team selections.

Catcher: Biz Mackey, Josh Gibson
Pitcher: (RH) Hilton Smith, (LH) Barney Brown
First Base: Buck Leonard
Second Base: Bonnie Serrell
Shortstop: Pop Lloyd
Third Base: Raymond Dandridge
Outfield: Art Pennington, Gene Benson, Cool Papa Bell
Manager: Oscar Charleston

Surprisingly, only two of Cash's selections, Gene Benson and Barney Brown, were teammates. Cash played alongside Satchel Paige a couple of years, but old Satch couldn't beat out Hilton Smith on Cash's team. Charleston managed the Philadelphia Stars from 1948 to 1950.

Greatest player: "Josh Gibson because he was the greatest hitter that I (ever saw), and other players that I have been involved with say the same thing."

Greatest thrill: "I had so many, but one of the greatest thrills I had was in the 1949 East-West All-Star Game in Comiskey Park in Chicago. The East team was a 4–1 underdog, and we won the game 4–0. We had the commissioner and Hank Greenberg in attendance with 51,000 people in attendance."

Note: Bill Cash cracked a double in four trips to the plate.

JOHNNIE COWAN

Johnnie Cowan played Negro league baseball for eight years, from 1942 through 1950. He was primarily a second baseman, but also played third base and outfield. He was a top defensive player with a strong arm and was noted as a good pivot man on the double play. His teammates included Jimmie Crutchfield, George Scales, Chet Brewer, Sam Jethroe, and Willie Wells.

At the time the survey was conducted, Cowan was ill, but he still returned his ballot with the note, "I can't give you any information. I am not feeling well. Mr. Johnnie Cowan." The spunky infielder passed away on October 24, 1993, in his hometown of Birmingham, Alabama, at the age of 80.

PIPER DAVIS

Lorenzo "Piper" Davis was born in Piper, Alabama, on July 3, 1917. He joined the Birmingham Black Barons of the Negro American League in 1942 and played with them for nine years. He was an outstanding second baseman, as well as an offensive threat. His .322 career batting average included season averages of .360, .353, .378, and .383. When integration came, he jumped into organized baseball and although he never had the opportunity to play in the major leagues, he enjoyed a successful seven-year career in the AAA Pacific Coast League, batting .287 in 687 games.

Piper Davis didn't participate in the survey, remarking, "I am sorry that I can't name you an all-star team. I didn't play against or see all the Negro stars. I only played against Feller's team one time in the winter. Sorry.

Yours in Sports,
Lorenzo "Piper" Davis.

P.S. We had two leagues when I played in the Negro league, the American West and the Eastern. I played in Newark, against two teams in New York, the Black Yankees and the Cubans, and against the Philadelphia Stars. I played in the West where Chicago, Kansas City, Memphis Red Sox, and Birmingham Black Barons played."

ROSS DAVIS

Ross Davis was a pitcher for eight years in the Negro National League from 1940 to 1947, with two years out for military service in World War II. The resident of Long Beach, California, made the following all-star selections.

Catcher: Roy Campanella
Pitcher: Satchel Paige, Hilton Smith
First Base: Archie Ware
Second Base: Sammy T. Hughes
Shortstop: Thomas "Pee Wee" Butts
Third Base: Parnell Woods
Outfield: Sam Jethroe, Dave Pope, Al Smith
Utility: Jerry Benjamin

A few comments should be made regarding some of Davis's selections since they are unique. Archie Ware, an 11-year veteran of the Negro leagues, played first base for several teams but spent most of his career with the Cleveland Buckeyes. He was a flashy-fielding first baseman according to Jim Riley, with a respectable .295 batting average. He had his two best seasons with the bat in 1947 and 1948 when he put together two successive .349 years. He was the starting first baseman on the West all-star team from 1944 to 1946.

Parnell Woods was a good-hitting third baseman from 1933 to 1949, starring with such teams as the Birmingham Black Barons and the Cleveland Buckeyes. He was a scrappy 170-pound infielder who put together a .315 career batting average, with individual averages of .343, .343, and .335. He was selected for the East-West all-star game four times. Although he was too old to think about a major league career, the 37-year-old infielder joined Oakland in the Pacific Coast League in 1949 and hit a respectable .275.

Dave Pope was a 5'10", 170 pound speedster, who jumped from the Negro leagues to organized ball in 1948 and proceeded to lead two leagues in triples. He ran out 18 triples in 120 games for Wilkes Barre in the Eastern League in 1950, hit another 13 triples the next year for the same team, then led the American Association with 14 triples in 1953. Pope went on to play major league ball with Cleveland and Baltimore for three years.

Al Smith, another graduate of the Negro leagues, played in the major leagues for 12 years, rapping 1,458 base hits in 5,357 at-bats, for a .272 batting average. A popular photo shows a fan in the left field bleachers accidentally spilling a container of beer on Al's head in the 1959 World Series.

Jerry Benjamin enjoyed a 17-year career in the Negro leagues, from 1932 to 1948. He is best known as the center fielder on the powerful Homestead Grays "dynasty" team from 1935 to 1948. The Grays captured nine successive league titles from 1937 to 1945. Benjamin was a steady .300 hitter, a speedy baserunner, and a dependable defensive outfielder.

Greatest player: "Buck Leonard: Flawless fielder; short, quick batting strokes, with power."

Greatest thrill: "Decoration Day (1940). I pitched a no-hitter (actually it was 6⅔ innings of a seven-inning game. The reporters got it wrong. Bubber Hubert relieved me in the seventh). Anyway, I was 2 for 2, with a single, double, and a stolen base. This was against the Newark Eagles. On that team was Biz [Mackey], Mule [Suttles], [Monte] Irvin, and I believe Willie Wells. Campanella was my catcher."

LEON DAY

Leon Day was one of the top Negro league pitchers of his day. He starred for the Baltimore Elite Giants eight years, beginning in 1936. He also played for several other teams in a career that spanned 17 seasons. John Holway's research credits Day with a career record of 68 and 40, for a winning percentage of .694, sixth all-time in the Negro leagues.

The 5'9", 170-pound fireballer led the league in pitching in 1939 with a record of 12–4. He appeared in a record seven East-West All-Star Games, posting a 1–0 record. In one game, he fanned five batters in 2⅓ innings of shutout ball. Day lost two years to military service in World War II but, on his return, he showed he hadn't lost a step when he tossed a no-hitter at the Philadelphia Stars on opening day, 1946.

In addition to his Negro league career, the rugged right hander also played ball in Mexico and Venezuela. Pitching for Caracas in the Venezuelan League in 1940, he rolled up a record of 12–1. The same year he went 6–0 with Vera Cruz in the Mexican League for a season total of 18–1.

Late in his career, Leon Day entered organized baseball with Winnepeg in the Man-Dak League, winning 4–2. He went 1–1 for Toronto in the International League, 13–9 with Scranton of the Eastern League, and 5–5 with Edmonton of the Western International League before retiring in 1954 at the age of 37.

Like most Negro league pitchers, Day could also handle a bat and frequently played the outfield or second base when he wasn't pitching. He left a career batting average of .299 in the Negro leagues and .295 in organized baseball. His best year with the bat was 1947 when he pummeled Mexican League pitchers to the tune of .359 in 56 games.

Leon Day's all-star selections follow. Day selected an all-time all-star team composed of the best Negro leaguers and major leaguers. He chose only two major league players for his 20-man squad, Cal Ripken, Jr., and Brooks Robinson, both from his hometown Baltimore Orioles.

#1 choice
Catcher: Biz Mackey
Pitcher: (RH) Satchel Paige, (LH) Slim Jones
First Base: Buck Leonard
Second Base: Larry Doby
Shortstop: Willie Wells
Third Base: Ray Dandridge, Brooks Robinson
Outfield: Rap Dixon, Cool Papa Bell, Martin Dihigo
Utility: Sam Bankhead
Manager: Ben Taylor

#2 choice
Catcher: Leon Ruffin
Pitcher: (RH) Leon Day, (LH) Barney Brown
First Base:
Second Base: Dick Seay
Shortstop: Cal Ripken, Jr.
Third Base: Brooks Robinson
Outfield: Monte Irvin, Jimmie Crutchfield
Utility:
Manager:
Greatest player: "It's impossible for me to say. I saw so many"
Greatest thrill: "My greatest thrill was being able to play in the Negro

leagues, playing with and against some of the greatest ballplayers who ever lived. And I pitched a no-hitter in 1946 against the Philadelphia Stars.

P.S. Don't forget my address when your book comes out."

Sadly, Leon Day didn't live to see my book published, but he did live long enough to see himself elected into the National Baseball Hall of Fame in Cooperstown, New York. The modest pitcher died on March 13, 1995, just one week after learning he would be joining Satchel Paige, Josh Gibson, and other legends of the Negro leagues in the Hall of Fame.

LOU DIALS

Oland Cecil Dials, better known as Lou, was born on January 10, 1904. He grew up to be an outstanding Negro league outfielder, playing with a number of teams between 1925 and 1936. He debuted with the Chicago American Giants in '25, spending six years with the team over two tours of duty. He also played with the Birmingham Black Barons, Homestead Grays, and Hilldale Daisies, among others.

Lou Dials was a smooth-swinging left handed hitter, standing 5'10" and weighing a solid 185 pounds. He was a fair hitter with good power. According to Richard Bak, in his book on the Detroit Stars, Dials played for the team in 1930 and 1931, compiling a batting average of .266 with 13 doubles, 7 triples, and 7 home runs in 214 at-bats. On the basis of a 550 at-bat season, Dial's power numbers would convert to 33 doubles, 18 triples, and 18 home runs, a very impressive showing.

Dials also played baseball in Mexico and in the California Winter League, against all-star teams of major and minor league players. Some of the major leaguers who played in the league over the years included Bob Meusel, Babe Herman, Jimmie Foxx, Tony Lazzeri, and Casey Stengel.

Lou Dials chose a combined major league–Negro league all-star team.

Catcher: Biz Mackey (Negro league)
Pitcher: (RH) Bullet Rogan (Negro league), (LH) Lefty Grove
First Base: Lou Gehrig
Second Base: Eddie Collins
Shortstop: Honus Wagner
Third Base: Buck Weaver (Black Sox)
Outfield: Oscar Charleston (Negro league), Babe Ruth, Ty Cobb
Utility: Martin Dihigo (Negro league)
Manager: John McGraw

Greatest player: "Martin Dihigo was the best all-around player in the world. He could play all positions. He was a good pitcher, a good hitter, and a good manager."

Greatest thrill: "My greatest thrill in baseball was hitting a home run in the ninth inning to beat the Mexican League All-Stars, 3–2. The game was played in Wrigley Field in Los Angeles in September 1938."

Note: The Mexican team were the Mexican champions. They had pummeled a Pacific Coast League all-star team on November 6, 1938, by scores of 11–3 and 4–0. They played the Colored All-Stars in a double-header the following week. The two teams split the doubleheader, with the Mexican champions taking the opener by a count of 3–1, and the All-Stars capturing the nightcap 4–0, beating the legendary Ramon Bragana. The following week, the two teams split again. Manager Lou Dials walloped a 10th inning home run to win the opener, 3–2, before 7,500 fans in Wrigley Field. The Mexicans took the five-inning nightcap 4–1.

MAHLON DUCKETT

Mahlon Duckett enjoyed an 11-year career in the Negro leagues, from 1940 through 1950. During his tenure with the Philadelphia Stars and the Homestead Grays, he played with some of the greatest players in Negro league history, including Sam Bankhead, Buck Leonard, Jackie Robinson, Oscar Charleston, and Chet Brewer. His all-time all-star team selections follow.

Catcher: Josh Gibson, Roy Campanella

Pitcher: (RH) Satchel Paige, Hilton Smith, (LH) Barney Brown, Roy Partlow

First Base: Buck Leonard, Mule Suttles

Second Base: Larry Doby, Sammy T. Hughes

Shortstop: Willie Wells, Dick Lundy

Third Base: Ray Dandridge, Judy Johnson

Outfield: Turkey Stearnes, Wild Bill Wright, Gene Benson, Willard Brown, Oscar Charleston, Red Parnell

Manager: Oscar Charleston

Greatest player: "Josh Gibson, the catcher for the Homestead Grays. Josh could do it all. He was a great receiver, great throwing arm, could not only hit for power, but had a remarkable batting average. And he had speed. Josh is my choice for the greatest."

Greatest thrill: "One of my greatest thrills was in 1941. At the age of

18 years, I hit a game-winning home run off the great Satchel Paige. It happened in Yankee Stadium before about 45 or 50 thousand fans."

BERNARD FERNANDEZ

Bernard Fernandez, a native of Cuba, played in the Negro leagues from 1938 to 1949. His combined major league–Negro league all-star selections follow.

Catcher: Biz Mackey, Josh Gibson
Pitcher: (RH) Satchel Paige, Bob Gibson, (LH) John Stanley, Louis Tiant
First Base: Buck O'Neil
Second Base: Junior Gilliam
Shortstop: Jackie Robinson
Third Base: Hank Thompson
Outfield: James Cool Papa Bell, Louis Santop, Oscar Charleston
Utility: Double Duty Radcliffe
Greatest player: "Jackie Robinson. He was an all around player. He could do it all."
Greatest thrill: "My greatest thrill in baseball was pitching in the Yankee Stadium."

RODOLFO FERNANDEZ

Rodolfo Fernandez was one of the top pitchers in professional baseball, outside organized baseball, during the 1930s. He pitched for 12 years in the Negro leagues, with the Cuban Stars and the New York Cubans. He also pitched in the Cuban Winter League, the Dominican Republic, Venezuela, and Mexico.

Fernandez selected the following for his all-time Negro league all-star team.

Catcher: Joshua Gibson
Pitcher: (RH) Satchel Paige, (LH) Luis Tiant (father)
First Base: Buck Leonard
Second Base: Newt Allen
Shortstop: Willie Wells

Third Base: Raymond Dandridge
Outfield: Oscar Charleston, Bill Wright, Martin Dihigo
Utility: Sammy Bankhead
Manager: George Scales

Rodolfo added, "I'm sorry I didn't give you too many players, because I tried to give you my all-stars from the Negroes I saw when I played in the Negro leagues."

Greatest player: "Roy Campanella, Jackie Robinson, Joe DiMaggio, Willie Mays, Stan Musial, Carl Furillo, Ted Williams, Yogi Berra, Baby Ruth, Lou Gehrig, Tony Lazzeri, Frank Crosetti, Al Simmons, Earl Averill, Jimmy Foxx, Bob Feller, Lefty Grove, and too many others."

STANLEY GLENN

Stanley Rudolph Glenn was born in Wachatreague, Virginia, on September 19, 1926. He grew into a strapping 6'3" 200-pound catcher, who played in the Negro leagues for seven years, from 1944 through 1950.

Glenn was an excellent defensive catcher with a strong throwing arm, but his weak bat prevented him from achieving stardom in the professional ranks. When integration came, the right handed hitter tried his hand at organized baseball, with modest success. His last year as a professional was his best year with the bat. He hit a respectable .275 for Quebec in the Provincial League, with 16 home runs in just 375 at-bats.

Stanley Glenn selected a combined Negro league–major league all-star team.

Newt Allen was a great all-around second baseman for more than 20 years.

Catcher: Josh Gibson
Pitcher: (RH) Satchel Paige, (LH) Sandy Koufax
First Base: Buck Leonard
Second Base: Jackie Robinson
Shortstop: Thomas Butts
Third Base: Raymond Dandridge
Outfield: Oscar Charleston, Willie Mays, Ted Williams
Utility: Junior Gilliam
Manager: Oscar Charleston
Greatest player: "Willie Mays. Check the stats with anyone. You'll see his being colorful naturally."
Greatest thrill: "My greatest thrill in baseball was catching any pitcher, especially Paige."

WILLIE GRACE

Willie Grace, a nine-year veteran of the Negro leagues, played with some outstanding baseball players during his tenure as a professional, including Chet Brewer, Sam Jethroe, Jimmie Crutchfield, Quincy Trouppe, and Al Smith.

Grace selected the following Negro league all-star team.

Catcher: Biz Mackey
Pitcher: (RH) Hilton Smith, (LH) Verdell Mathis
First Base: Mule Suttles
Second Base: Newt Allen
Shortstop: Artie Wilson
Third Base: Hank Thompson
Outfield: Willard Brown, Neil Robinson, Sam Jethroe
Utility: Chippy Britt
Manager: Jim Taylor

Chippy Britt, Grace's selection as a utility player, made a career out of being versatile. Over a long and productive 25-year Negro league career from 1920 through 1944, Britt pitched and played all the other positions on a team. According to Jim Riley, Britt caught for the 1924-25 Baltimore Black Sox, hitting .315 and .345, as well as going 5–4 on the mound.

Greatest player: Willie Mays.
Greatest thrill: None listed.

COWAN HYDE

Cowan "Bubba" Hyde was another long-term Negro league veteran, playing for such teams as the Birmingham Black Barons and the Chicago American Giants from 1927 through 1950. His longest tenure was with the Memphis Red Sox. His two tours of duty in Tennessee lasted a total of 15 years. He also entered organized baseball in 1950 as a 42-year-old graybeard and played four years in the northern leagues before retiring in 1953.

Bubba Hyde was a slight 150-pound speedster who roamed the outfield like a frightened fawn. He was also an exceptional hitter and base stealer. Batting in the first or second slots in the batting order, the little right handed hitter was a consistent .300 batter, who was frequently given the green light to run whenever he got on base. He entered organized baseball in 1950, playing four years in the lower minor leagues. He compiled an even .300 batting average in Canada, even though he was 45 years old when he bowed out.

Bubba Hyde selected a combined Negro league–major league all-star team.

Catcher: Roy Campanella
Pitcher: (RH) Johnny Sain, (LH) Bill Foster
First Base: Buck Leonard
Second Base: Newt Allen
Shortstop: Willie Wells Sr.
Third Base: Ken Keltner
Outfield: Ted Williams, Willie Mays, Turkey Stearnes
Utility: Felton Snow
Manager: Dave Malarcher
Greatest player: "Willie Wells. Because of his all-around ability."
Greatest thrill: "Playing in the all-star games."

MONTE IRVIN

Monte Irvin is best known to American baseball fans as the outstanding left fielder of the 1954 World Champion New York Giants and its 1951 predecessor. But long before major league stardom came to the baseball legend, he was a slugging center fielder for the Newark Eagles of the Negro National League.

Dave Malarcher was a great defensive third baseman for the Chicago American Giants during the 1920s. (Photograph courtesy Robert W. Peterson Collection, National Baseball Hall of Fame Library.)

The Hall of Fame outfielder has selected three different all-star teams—a major league all-star team, a Negro league all-star team, and a combined Negro league–major league all-star team.

Monte Irvin's All-Time Major League All-Star Team:

Catcher: Mickey Cochrane, Bill Dickey, Yogi Berra

Pitcher: (RH) Walter Johnson, Christy Matthewson, Nolan Ryan, (LH) Lefty Grove, Carl Hubbell, Warren Spahn

First Base: Lou Gehrig, Stan Musial

Second Base: Rogers Hornsby, Charlie Gehringer

Shortstop: H.Wagner, Pee Wee Reese

Third Base: Mike Schmidt, Brooks Robinson

Outfield: Joe DiMaggio, Mickey Mantle, Babe Ruth, Joe Jackson, Ty Cobb, Ted Williams

Utility: Al Kaline

Manager: John McGraw, Leo Durocher, Earl Weaver

Greatest player: "Before the war, Joe DiMaggio was the greatest I had seen—was a natural leader and could do the five things a superstar has to do."

Monte Irvin's All-Time Negro League All-Star Team:

Catcher: Josh Gibson, Roy Campanella, Biz Mackey

Pitcher: (RH) Satchel Paige, Bullet Rogan, Joe Williams, Leon Day, (LH) Slim Jones, Willie Foster

First Base: Buck Leonard, George Giles

Second Base: Sammy T. Hughes, Newt Allen, Jackie Robinson

Shortstop: Willie Wells, John Henry Lloyd, Dick Lundy
Third Base: Ray Dandridge, Oliver Marcelle
Outfield: Willie Mays, Cristobal Torriente, Oscar Charleston, Turkey Stearnes, Cool Papa Bell, Bill Wright
Utility: Martin Dihigo, Raymond Brown
Manager: Rube Foster, C. I. Taylor
Greatest player: "Josh Gibson could hit, run, throw, field, and hit for power. He was dominant in every phase of the game and had boyish charisma. He's a legend very few people had the pleasure to see perform."

Monte Irvin's combined Negro league–major league all-star team:

Catcher: Josh Gibson, Bill Dickey
Pitcher: (RH) Satchel Paige, Walter Johnson, Bob Gibson, (LH) Lefty Grove, Sandy Koufax
First base: Buck Leonard, Lou Gehrig, Stan Musial
Second Base: Charlie Gehringer, Jackie Robinson, Rogers Hornsby
Shortstop: John Henry Lloyd, Hans Wagner
Third Base: Mike Schmidt, Ray Dandridge
Outfield: Willie Mays, Ted Williams, Oscar Charleston, Joe Dimaggio, Mickey Mantle, Babe Ruth
Utility: Martin Dihigo, Hank Aaron
Manager: Earl Weaver, Leo Durocher, John McGraw
Greatest player: "Joe DiMaggio before the war (World War II). Willie Mays from 1949 until today."

JOSH JOHNSON

Josh Johnson, a rugged catcher for the Homestead Grays from the mid 30s till the early 40s selected the following combined Negro league–major league all-time, all-star team.

Catcher: Josh Gibson
Pitcher: (RH) Satchel Paige, (LH) Verdell Mathis
First Base: Buck Leonard
Second Base: Willie Wells
Shortstop: Honus Wagner
Third Base: Brooks Robinson
Outfield: Willie Mays, Stan Musial, Ted Williams

Utility: Jackie Robinson
Manager: Oscar Charleston

Johnson also selected an alternate team

Catcher: Roy Campanella
Pitcher: (RH) Ray Brown, (LH) Roy Partlow
First Base: George Giles
Second Base: Sammy Hughes
Shortstop: Dick Lundy
Third base: Ray Dandridge
Outfield: Cool Papa Bell, Duke Snider, Martin Dihigo
Utility: Sam Bankhead
Manager: Candy Jim Taylor
Greatest player: "Martin Dihigo—because he could play most any position, equally as well."

BUCK LEONARD

Walter "Buck" Leonard passed away from complications of a stroke on November 27, 1998, in Rocky Mount, North Carolina, his lifetime hometown. He was 91.

Leonard was a legend in Negro league baseball for 17 years. He teamed with Josh Gibson on the Homestead Grays for nine years, powering them to nine successive Negro National League titles from 1937 through 1945. The slugging duo was known as the "Thunder Twins" to Negro league fans and a sure poison to opposing pitchers. According to Negro league historian John Holway, Leonard compiled a .335 lifetime batting average with the Grays, with 15 home runs a year.

The powerful left handed hitter also hit a solid .326 for three years in Mexico, .284 in Cuba, and .390 in Puerto Rico. He joined Portsmouth in the Piedmont League in 1953 at the age of 45, hitting .333 in 10 games, then retired to business in Rocky Mount.

Buck Leonard's combined Negro league–major league all-star team follows.

Catcher: Roy Campanella
Pitcher: (RH) Satchel Paige, (LH) Sandy Koufax
First Base: Walter "Buck" Leonard
Second Base: Bucky Harris
Shortstop: Cal Ripken

Third Base: Judy Johnson
Outfield: Willie Mays, Babe Ruth, Wild Bill Wright
Manager: Billy Martin

Previously, in Acocella's and Dewey's book, Leonard had selected the following all-time Negro league team.

Catcher: Josh Gibson
Pitcher: (RH) Satchel Paige, (LH) Slim Jones
First Base: Johnny Washington
Second Base: Sammy Hughes
Shortstop: Willie Wells
Third Base: Ray Dandridge
Outfield: Fats Jenkins, Cool Papa Bell, Bill Wright

JOHN MILES

John Miles was born in San Antonio, Texas, on August 11, 1922. He began his professional baseball career with the Chicago American Giants in 1946. The big 6'3", 228-pound right handed slugger picked

Fats Jenkins, a speedy outfielder and a .300 hitter, was recommended for Hall of Fame consideration by many former players. (Photograph courtesy the Robert W. Peterson Collection, National Baseball Hall of Fame Library.)

up his nickname Mule by smashing two home runs in one game. According to Jim Riley, Miles's manager, Candy Jim Taylor told him, "You hit that ball like a mule kicks."

Miles stayed with the Giants for three years. He was a decent outfielder with a strong throwing arm and, although he showed good power at the plate, his low batting average kept him hidden in the bottom part of the batting order.

Miles had some distinguished teammates, including Chet Brewer, Sug Cornelius, Quincy Trouppe, Jim Pendleton, and Theolic Smith. He selected his all-time all-star team, including many of the players already recognized throughout this survey.

Catcher: Josh Gibson
Pitcher: (RH) Leroy Satchel Paige, (LH) Eugene Collins
First Base: Buck Leonard
Second Base: Jackie Robinson
Shortstop: Ernie Banks
Third Base: Hank Thompson
Outfield: Hank Aaron, Willie Mays, Cool Papa Bell
Utility: Monte Irvin
Manager: Jim "Candy" Taylor
Greatest player: "Catcher Josh Gibson. He was the hardest hitter I had ever seen — also had a very good arm — Satchel Paige was the greatest pitcher. He had the greatest fastball in any league."

JAMES "RED" MOORE

Red Moore was a member of the Newark Eagles during the time they boasted their "million-dollar" infield of Mule Suttles, Dick Seay, Willie Wells, and Ray Dandridge. Occasionally he joined the legendary inner defense at first base, with Suttles moving to the outfield. In 1937 the gold glove first baseman posted a solid .280 batting average for the second-place Eagles, who trailed only the powerful Homestead Grays in the Negro National League.

Moore's selections for the greatest Negro league players of all time follows.

Catcher: Roy Campanella
Pitcher: (RH) Satchel Paige, (LH) Slim Jones
First Base: Buck Leonard
Second Base: Newt Allen
Shortstop: Willie Wells
Third Base: Ray Dandridge
Outfield: Turkey Stearnes, Cool Papa Bell, Wild Bill Wright
Utility: Sam Bankhead
Manager: Oscar Charleston
Greatest player: "I have seen a lot of great baseball players. They were great at certain positions. I couldn't truthfully name one baseball player as the greatest."

Greatest thrill: "My greatest thrill in baseball was being able to play in the Negro baseball leagues. I was involved in many spectacular plays around first base."

BUCK O'NEIL

John Jordan O'Neil, Jr., was an outstanding professional baseball player for 19 years. Now, as he approaches his 90th birthday (on November 13, 2001), he is the Negro leagues' most visible and enthusiastic supporter.

Buck O'Neil selected two all-time all-star teams: a Negro league team, and a combined Negro league–major league all-star team.

O'Neil's All-Time Negro League All-Star Team:

Catcher: Josh Gibson
Pitcher: (RH) Satchel Paige, (LH) Willie Foster
First Base: Buck Leonard
Second Base: Newt Allen
Shortstop: Willie Wells
Third Base: Ray Dandridge
Outfield: Oscar Charleston, Turkey Stearnes, Cool Papa Bell
Utility: Martin Dihigo
Manager: Rube Foster
Greatest Negro league player: "Oscar Charleston — the closest player to Charleston was Willie Mays."
Greatest thrill: "Being good enough to compete in the Negro leagues — which fielded some of the greatest players ever."

O'Neil's combined All-Time All-Star Team:

Catcher: Josh Gibson
Pitcher: (RH) Satchel Paige, (LH) Lefty Grove
First Base: Buck Leonard
Second Base: Jackie Robinson
Shortstop: Willie Wells
Third Base: Brooks Robinson
Outfield: Hank Aaron, Willie Mays, Babe Ruth
Utility: Martin Dihigo
Manager: Rube Foster
Greatest player: "Willie Mays — excellent defensively and offensively — could do it all excellently."

ART "SUPERMAN" PENNINGTON

Art "Superman" Pennington was a talented all-around ballplayer whose career spanned both the Negro leagues and organized baseball. The

5'11", 185-pound right handed hitter toiled in the Negro leagues for ten years, compiling a fine .323 batting average with 15 home runs a year. His best year was 1945 when he stung the ball at a .359 clip and led the Negro American League in doubles with 16, in 68 games.

Superman also enjoyed three years in Mexico where he hit an even .300. When integration arrived, the Missouri native joined Portland in the Pacific Coast League, batting .208. At Salem in the Western International League Pennington hit a more representative .308. Three years later, he returned to organized ball, pounding Three-I league pitching for a .349 average with 17 doubles, 10 triples, and 20 home runs in 116 games. He hit over .300 the following two years, eventually closing out a memorable career in 1959 at the age of 36.

Art Pennington selected his all-time all-star team.

Catcher: Josh Gibson, Bill Cash, Ted Radcliffe
Pitcher: (RH) Satchel Paige, Hilton Smith, Raymond Brown, (LH) Verdel Mathis, Barney Brown
First Base: Bob Boyd, Buck O'Neil, Luke Easter
Second Base: Bonnie Serrell, Willie Wells, Billy Horn, Piper Davis
Shortstop: Artie Wilson, Bus Clarkson, Jesse Williams
Third Base: Ray Dandridge, Parnell Woods
Outfield: Sam Jethroe, Duckie Davenport, Willard Brown, Neil Robinson, Sam Bankhead Art "Superman" Pennington, Bill Wright, Sam Hill
Utility: Gentry Jessup, Booker McDaniels, Jimmie Crutchfield
Manager: Candy Jim Taylor
Greatest player: "Satchel Paige, Bonnie Serrell, Ray Dandridge, Josh Gibson, Frank Duncan, Larry Brown, Bill Cash, Ted Radcliffe, Booker McDaniels— They were all great."

At one point I sent Art one proposed combined Negro league-major league all-star team for his comments. He replied: "Your first team should be Josh Gibson and Campanella, not Bill Dickey. And you should have Art "Superman" Pennington for utility. I could play with the best of them. Some of the players that you named I do not know of them — for shortstop you should name Willie Wells. I know most of these players are older than I — but I could play. Believe me."

Art Pennington was an excellent professional baseball player, in the Negro leagues, Mexico, the Pacific Coast League, the Western International League and several other strong leagues, for 20 years. He had many weapons as a utility player and was therefore able to play more than one position well. Confidence may have been his greatest asset.

ANDY "PULLMAN" PORTER

Andrew Porter was born in Little Rock, Arkansas, on March 11, 1911. He became a professional baseball player in 1932 when he joined the Louisville Black Caps, but he spent his most productive years with the Baltimore Elite Giants, over two tours of duty, in 1938-39 and 1942–46.

Porter was a tall right handed power pitcher, packing 190 pounds on a sleek 6'4" frame. He had a blazing fast ball, and complemented it with a deceptive slider. But he also had streaks of wildness from time to time that kept batters on the defensive. His Negro league career covered 17 years, and his incomplete statistics show a fine 37–16 won-lost record. His best year was in 1942 with Baltimore when his 8–0 record helped the Giants capture the Negro National League pennant. His teammates on that club included Roy Campanella, Bill Byrd, Sammy T. Hughes, George Scales, and Wild Bill Wright.

The much-traveled Porter also pitched in Cuba and Mexico during the thirties and forties. He spent two winters in Cuba, compiling a 9–9 record. In Mexico, he had three busy years, from 1939 to 1941. He went 10–7 in '39, then jumped to 21–14 the next year, when he led the Mexican League in games pitched (42), innings pitched (296), bases on balls (125), and strikeouts (232). In '41 his 11–16 record led the league in losses, innings pitched (235), and strikeouts (133).

Pullman Porter selected his greatest Negro league all-star team.

Catcher: Raleigh Mackey
Pitcher: (RH) Leroy Paige, (LH) Willie Foster
First Base: B. Leonard
Second Base: Samuel Hughes
Shortstop: Willie Wells
Third Base: Raymond Dandridge
Outfield: James Bell, Oscar Charleston, Burnis Wright
Utility: Martin Dihigo

DOUBLE DUTY RADCLIFFE

Theodore Roosevelt "Double Duty" Radcliffe is the Negro league's patriarch. On July 7, 2002, Double Duty will reach the magic 100 mark. The Chicago resident selected the following all-time Negro league all-star team.

Catcher: Josh Gibson, Larry Brown, Leon Ruffin
Pitcher: (RH) Satchel Paige, (LH) Willie Foster
First Base: Buck Leonard, George Giles
Second Base: Newt Allen, Sammy Hughes
Shortstop: Willie Wells, Art Wilson
Third Base: Alex Radcliffe, Ray Dandridge
Outfield: Cool Papa Bell, Turkey Stearnes, Willard Brown
Utility: Sam Bankhead
Manager: Ted "Double Duty" Radcliffe
Greatest player: "Turkey Stearnes and Willie Wells. Willie Wells because he could do it all. No weaknesses."
Greatest thrill: "I hit a home run in the 1944 East-West All-Star Game to win the game, and my mother met me at the dugout. That did it."

Research indicates that Double Duty has been selecting all-star teams for more than half a century. I recently ran across this letter from him with his all-star selections in a copy of the *Chicago Defender,* dated January 14, 1933.

Player	Position	Club
J. Bell	center field	Monarchs
F. Jenkins	right field	New York Yanks
J. Wilson	third base	Crawfords
G. Scales	second base	New York Yanks
Stearnes	left field	Chicago
Giles	first base	Monarchs
Lundy	shortstop	Black Sox
Mackey	catcher	Hilldale
Paige	pitcher	Crawfords
Foster	pitcher	Chicago
DeMoss	manager	

Radcliffe went on to say: "I have read with interest the picks of the various baseball players, fans, and critics of what they term the best players in the game, and for the first time in my life I am joining the parade. Naming the nine best players from a field that contains hundreds is a difficult task, but having seen practically all of the major clubs, East and West, in action, mine should be as good as any others. Fact is the whole thing is a matter of opinion. The above nine is, in my opinion, the best ball club that could be assembled from the two sections. Every man can run, hit, throw, and has brains."

ULYSSES A. REDD

Ulysses A. Redd, the regular shortstop for the Birmingham Black Barons before World War II short-circuited his professional baseball career, selected the following Negro league all-star team.

Catcher: Double Duty Radcliffe
Pitcher: (RH) Ray Brown, (LH) Verdell Mathis
First Base: Mule Suttles
Second Base: Newt Allen
Shortstop: Sam Bankhead
Third Base: Oliver Marcelle
Outfield: Turkey Stearnes, Willard Brown, Jimmie Crutchfield
Utility: Sammy T. Hughes
Manager: Biz Mackey
Greatest player: "This is tough for me. I've seen a lot of great players. I must go with Willie 'Chico' Wells. The reason is simple. I had the honor of playing with him in Canada. I learned a lot from him."
Greatest thrill: "My greatest thrill was to go to spring training with the Birmingham Black Barons in 1940 and making the team with so many of us in camp."

TOMMY SAMPSON

Tommy Sampson, a teammate of Ulysses A. Redd on the Birmingham Black Barons in the early 1940s, selected the following all-time Negro league All-Star team.

Catcher: Biz Mackey
Pitcher: (RH) Ray Brown, (LH) Sam Streeter
First Base: Buck O'Neil
Second Base: Sammy T. Hughes
Shortstop: Sam Bankhead
Third Base: Hank Thompson
Outfield: Jimmie Crutchfield, Wild Bill Wright, Vic Harris
Manager: Jim Taylor
Greatest player: "I say Josh Gibson and Satchel Paige and Willie Mays."
Greatest thrill: "The 1943 East-West Game." Note: Tommy Sampson

was voted to play in the 1943 East-West All-Star Game in Chicago. He played second base for the West, got one hit in three at-bats, and drove in the first run in the Wests 2–1 victory. Sampson also played in three other all-star games—1940–42.

HERBERT H. SIMPSON

Herbert Simpson, a teammate of Sampson's, was a pitcher and an outfielder during the 1940s. He selected the following all-star team.

Catcher: Bruce Petway, Double Duty Radcliffe
Pitcher: (RH) Ray Brown, Max Manning, (LH) Bill Holland, Ted Trent
First Base: Buck Leonard, Mule Suttles
Second Base: Newt Allen, Sammy T. Hughes
Shortstop: Artie Wilson, Bus Clarkson
Third Base: Dave Malarcher, Hank Thompson
Outfield: Turkey Stearnes, Willard Brown, Jimmie Crutchfield, Vic Harris, Wild Bill Wright, Sam Jethroe
Utility: Chet Brewer, Biz Mackey
Manager: Vic Harris

It should be noted that Simpson's choices for left handed pitcher did not throw with their left hand. Many of the Negro league veterans ignored the request for left handed pitchers.
Greatest player: "Josh Gibson, Willie Wells, Bus Clarkson, John Beckwith, Hilton Smith, Frank Wickware, Newt Allen, George Scales, Jesse Williams, Jelly Gardner, Fats Jenkins, Satchel Paige."
Greatest thrill: "I had a two base hit off Satchel Paige here in New Orleans and my mother, father, sister, uncles, and friends all saw and enjoyed it. A double off Satchel. In another game, the pitcher walked Luke Easter to pitch to me and I doubled."

HILTON SMITH

Hilton Smith was born in Giddings, Texas, on February 27, 1912. He became a professional baseball player in 1932, at the age of 20, when he joined the Monroe (Louisiana) Monarchs of the Negro Southern League.

He earned his reputation as a great pitcher after he became a member of the Kansas City Monarchs. During his 13 years in Kansas City, Hilton was known as Satchel's relief pitcher. Paige was a huge drawing card, and everyone wanted to see him pitch, so he would pitch the first three or four innings of a game, then Smith would come on to finish up. As a result, Paige had a modest won-lost record because he seldom pitched the required five innings necessary to be the winning pitcher. Hilton Smith, on the other hand, was the beneficiary of the baseball rules. In fact, his .720 winning percentage, based on a 72–28 record, is the third highest in Negro league history, behind Leroy Matlock and Ray Brown.

The 6'2", 180-pound right hander relied on the league's best curve ball to stifle the opposition. He also threw a moving fastball, a slider, and a change of pace. In addition, he walked less than 1.6 batters a game and yielded only 6.7 hits for every nine innings, a winning combination. He put together some outstanding seasons for the Monarchs, going 9–1 in 1938, 8–2 in 1939, and a league-leading 10–0 the following year. He led the league in wins again in '42 with eight, against three losses. In '46 he went 8–2, and in '47 he was 7–3.

Hilton Smith also pitched in Cuba two years, compiling a gaudy 10–5 record for Marinao and Santa Clara. He selected a combined Negro league–major league all-star team.

Catcher: Josh Gibson
Pitcher: (RH) Lon Warneke, Bob Feller, Bob Lemon, Ray Brown, Satchel Paige
First Base: Buck Leonard
Second Base: Martin Dihigo
Shortstop: Willie Wells
Third Base: Ken Keltner
Outfield: Sam Chapman, Charlie Keller

LONNIE SUMMERS

Lonnie Summers, a native of Davis, Oklahoma, played in the Negro leagues for 12 years, from 1938 to 1949, with 4 years out for military service during World War II. The big, 6', 210-pound right handed hitting slugger was a perennial .300 hitter in the Negro American League, with decent power. He played all the infield-outfield positions early in his career before settling down as a catcher.

Summers divided his time between the Negro leagues and the

Jose Mendez, one of Cuba's greatest pitchers, played and managed in the Negro leagues for almost 20 years. (Photograph courtesy Robert W. Peterson Collection, National Baseball Hall of Fame Library.)

Mexican league. He played south of the border six years, primarily with Tampico. He compiled a .294 batting average in the Mexican League. In 1952, the 36-year-old baseball veteran entered organized baseball, with San Diego in the AAA Pacific Coast League. He finished out his career with Yakima in the Northwest League, hitting .312 with 14 home runs in 119 games in 1954. He played three games two years later, then called it a day at the age of 40.

Summers's son, Jesus Sommers, was one of Mexico's foremost sluggers, batting .291 and rapping out 3,004 base hits over a monumental 27-year career.

Lonnie Summers selected his all-star team.

Catcher: Biz Mackey
Pitcher: (RH) Satchel Paige, (LH) Slim Jones
First Base: Jim West
Second Base: Sammy T. Hughes
Shortstop: Willie Wells
Third Base: Ray Dandridge
Outfield: Wild Bill Wright, Willie Mays, Hank Aaron
Utility: Felton Snow
Manager: Candy Jim Taylor
Greatest player: "Josh Gibson."

Jim West, Summers's all-star selection at first base, may not be known to many people. West was a fancy-fielding first baseman for several teams over a productive 18-year career. According to Jim Riley, West batted .422 for the Nashville Elite Giants in 1934. He also hit .403 in 1936 and .378 the following year. In 1938, after the team moved to Baltimore, Shifty Jim pounded the ball at a .403 clip and in 1944 he hit .350. The 6'2", 218-pound switch hitter ended his career with a .308 average.

JAMES TURNER

James "Lefty" Turner had a short Negro league career, but he wasn't short on confidence, as shown by his selection of himself for the all-time Negro league first baseman in his selections for an all-star team.

Catcher: Double Duty Radcliffe
Pitcher: (RH) Satchel Paige, (LH) Bill Byrd
First Base: James "Lefty" Turner
Second Base: Sammy T. Hughes
Shortstop: Sam Bankhead
Third Base: Jud Wilson
Outfield: Turkey Stearnes, Fats Jenkins, Jimmie Crutchfield
Manager: John Henry "Pop" Lloyd
Greatest player: "Josh Gibson. Because he did 'everything' so well. Josh did everything that a ballplayer could do."
Greatest thrill: "My greatest thrill in baseball was playing in Yankee Stadium in New York as the Pittsburgh Crawford's first baseman."

ARMANDO VASQUEZ

Armando Vasquez, a native of Cuba now residing in New York City, made the following all-time Negro league all-star selections.

Catcher: Josh Gibson
Pitcher: (RH) Satchel Paige, (LH) Ray Brown
First Base: Buck Leonard
Second Base: George Scales
Shortstop: Willie Wells
Third Base: Ray Dandridge
Outfield: Cristobal Torriente, Cool Papa Bell, Oscar Charleston
Utility: Martin Dihigo, Leon Day
Manager: Rube Foster
Greatest player: "Martin Dihigo."

EDSALL WALKER

Edsall Walker was born in Catskill, New York, on September 13, 1913. He grew up playing all sports but gradually gravitated towards baseball, his first love. He joined the Homestead Grays as a pitcher in 1936 and was immediately dubbed "The Catskill Wild Man" because of his lack of control. Over the years, he developed into an outstanding pitcher with a blazing fastball and just enough control to keep the batters off balance, yet get them out.

He played for the Grays during their "dynasty" years, when they captured nine consecutive Negro National League pennants. Walker, who was called "Big," because of his size (6', 215 pounds), and also to differentiate him from a teammate who was called "Little Walker," played on eight pennant winners, missing only the 1942 season when he worked in a shipyard during World War II.

Big Walker had an added advantage. He was a southpaw who complemented the Grays right handed contingent of Ray Brown and Tom "Big Train" Parker. The Catskill Wild Man led the 1938 championship team, with an 8–1 record. Two years later he went 10–5 and in 1943 had an 8–3 record.

Edsall Walker played Negro league ball for 10 years, then retired to Albany, New York, at the young age of 32. His Negro league all-star team consists of the following players.

Catcher: Josh Gibson
Pitcher: (RH) Leon Day, Satchel Paige, (LH) Barney Brown
First Base: Buck Leonard
Second Base: Sammy Hughes
Shortstop: Willie Wells
Third Base: Ray Dandridge
Outfield: Cool Papa Bell, Wild Bill Wright, Vic Harris, Willie Mays
Utility: Sammy Bankhead, Ray Brown
Manager: Oscar Charleston
Greatest player: "Cool Papa Bell. He could hit, run, and throw, and steal bases. He could go from first to third on a bunt. Josh Gibson. He could hit, run, and throw. Also he was big and strong."
Greatest thrill: "Playing on nine straight pennant winners for the Grays 36–45. Three Hall of Famers on the team at one time."

NORMAL "TWEED" WEBB

Normal "Tweed" Webb played only one year of professional baseball. He was the shortstop for the Fort Wayne Pirates in 1927, but returned to his hometown of St. Louis the following year to enter business. He remained active in baseball, playing semi-pro ball around the area, and acting in various official administrative capacities over a period of 70 years. He also became the foremost historian of Negro league baseball, with his motto of "I've seen 'em all."

He selected two all-time all-star teams, a Negro league all-star team and a combined Negro league-major league all-star team.

Tweed Webb's Negro League All-Star Team:

Catcher: Biz Mackey
Pitcher: (RH) Smokey Joe Williams, (LH) Satchel Paige (chose Paige over any left hander)
First Base: Ben Taylor
Second Base: Bingo DeMoss
Shortstop: John Henry "Pop" Lloyd
Third Base: Judy Johnson
Outfield: Oscar Charleston, Cool Papa Bell, Turkey Stearnes
Utility: Pete Hill
Manager: Rube Foster

Second Team
Josh Gibson, Rube Foster, John Donaldson, Buck Leonard, Martin Dihigo, Willie Wells, Dave Malarcher, Cristobal Torriente, Jimmie Lyons, Monte Irvin

Tweed Webb's combined Negro league–major league all-star team:

Catcher: Roy Campanella
Pitcher: (RH) Smokey Joe Williams, (LH) Sandy Koufax
First Base: Ben Taylor
Second Base: Jackie Robinson
Shortstop: John Henry "Pop" Lloyd
Third Base: Brooks Robinson
Outfield: Babe Ruth, Mickey Mantle, Willie Mays
Utility: Hank Aaron
Manager: Rube Foster
Greatest player: "Willie Mays! Considered by many the greatest player of all times. Mays was the prototype of the complete player. He hit for average and power, ran the bases with intelligence and speed, played a spectacular center field, and possessed a great arm."
Greatest thrill: "In 1974 I experienced what I call my greatest thrill in baseball, the first black to be elected to the St. Louis Amateur Baseball Hall of Fame. However, my greatest thrill occurred on August 12, 1974. I had

the honor of seeing my best friend, Cool Papa Bell, get enshrined at Cooperstown, New York."

EARL WILSON, SR.

Earl Wilson, Sr., pitcher for the 1938 Birmingham Black Barons, selected the following all-time Negro league all-star team.

Catcher: Josh Gibson
Pitcher: (RH) Leroy Satchel Paige, (LH) John Donaldson
First Base: Buck Leonard
Second Base: Lorenzo "Piper" Davis
Shortstop: Willie Wells
Third Base: Ray Dandridge
Outfield: Cool Papa Bell, Willard Brown, Pete Hill
Utility: Artie Wilson
Manager: Biz Mackey
Greatest player: "Pepper Bassett. He was a good all-around baseball player, with a good sense of humor."

John Donaldson, an early pitching star, is considered by many baseball experts to be the top left handed pitcher in Negro league history. (Photograph courtesy James A. Riley.)

Greatest thrill: "My greatest thrill was being able to play baseball with so many of the greatest Negro players in the world. I was young and I enjoyed it all."

Thirty-five Negro league veterans, all of whom played professional ball in the great black leagues prior to the time that Jackie Robinson broke the color barrier, have made their selections for the all-time Negro league all-star team. These men played Negro league baseball at a time when the black leagues were still at full strength, with future Hall of Famers, like Monte Irvin, Satchel Paige, Larry Doby, Cool Papa Bell, and Roy Campanella, still wearing their uniforms. Most of the respondents witnessed these players in their prime. They also saw a young and powerful Josh Gibson during his glory years and watched legends like John Henry Lloyd, Jud Wilson, Oscar Charleston, Bullet Joe Rogan, and Smokey Joe Williams finish out their careers.

There is a considerable amount of variation in the selections, as you might imagine when you ask 35 people to vote on anything. In many cases, people voted for teammates and friends. And, as we have seen, the more outrageous of them even vote for themselves. But, in the end, the best players usually come to the top, as the weight of such a substantial numbers of voters is more important than friendships. The final tally is listed below. Unlike the vote for Hall of Fame candidates, the top two players at each position are listed, as well as the top seven pitchers.

Players' Votes for All-Time Negro League All-Star Team

Position	Player	Votes
Catcher:	Josh Gibson	17
	Biz Mackey	11
Pitcher:	Satchel Paige	22
	Ray Brown	11
	Hilton Smith	9
	Willie Foster	8
	Leon Day	6
	Barney Brown	5
	Slim Jones	5
First Base:	Buck Leonard	21
	Buck O'Neil	5
Second Base:	Sammy T. Hughes	16
	Newt Allen	9
Shortstop:	Willie Wells	19
	Dick Lundy	5
	Artie Wilson	5
Third Base:	Ray Dandridge	19
	Hank Thompson	5
Outfield:	Cool Papa Bell	15
	Turkey Stearnes	12
	Wild Bill Wright	12
	Oscar Charleston	11
	Willie Mays	9
	Willard Brown	8
	Jimmy Crutchfield	8
Utility:	Martin Dihigo	9
	Sammy Bankhead	8
Manager:	Oscar Charleston	6
	Candy Jim Taylor	6

One glaring problem with the selections of the Negro league veterans is the lack of votes for the great pioneers of the first three decades of the twentieth century. The veterans voted only for players of their generation, which is normal. And, although they saw some of the legends playing the game, players like John Henry Lloyd and Smokey Joe Williams, they saw them and remembered them as they were in their '40s, only shadows of their former selves.

Veterans' Choices for Greatest
Player in Negro League History

Player	Votes
Josh Gibson	8
Martin Dihigo	4
Willie Mays	3
Willie Wells	3

Veterans' Choices for Greatest Negro League Manager

Manager	Votes
Oscar Charleston	8
Candy Jim Taylor	6
Rube Foster	4

It will be interesting to see how the historians poll compares to the Negro league veterans poll.

All-Time Negro League All-Star Team: Historians' Selections

A total of 24 historians and authors participated in the survey. They, as a group, are the most knowledgeable Negro baseball league historians ever assembled. They have researched the area of black baseball, in some cases for decades, have interviewed literally hundreds of Negro league veterans, and have poured through thousands of newspapers on microfilm in the dusty basements of dozens of libraries nationwide to uncover the vast wealth of batting and pitching statistics that have lain hidden for most of the twentieth century.

These are their choices for the all-time Negro league all-star team.

TODD BOLTON

Todd Bolton, a member of SABR's Negro Leagues Committee and an active participant in many projects to increase the public's awareness of Negro league baseball, made the following selections.

First Choice
Catcher: Josh Gibson
Pitcher: Jose Mendez
First Base: Ben Taylor
Second Base: Bingo DeMoss
Shortstop: John Henry "Pop" Lloyd
Third Base: Judy Johnson

Outfield: James "Cool Papa" Bell, Cristobal Torriente, Alejandro Oms
Manager: Rube Foster
Owner: Cum Posey

Second Choice
Catcher: Biz Mackey
Pitcher: Smokey Joe Williams
First Base: Buck Leonard
Second Base: Frank Warfield
Shortstop: Horacio Martinez
Third Base: Oliver Marcelle
Outfield: Monte Irvin, Martin Dihigo, Oscar Charleston
Manager: C. I. Taylor
Owner: Alejandro Pompez

RICHARD BOZZONE

Richard Bozzone, a member of SABR's Negro Leagues Committee, selected the following all-time Negro league all-star team.

First choice
Catcher: Josh Gibson
Pitcher: (RH) Satchel Paige, (LH) Bill Foster, Leon Day
First Base: Buck Leonard
Second Base: Bingo DeMoss
Shortstop: Willie Wells
Third Base: Ray Dandridge
Outfield: Cool Papa Bell, Monte Irvin, Oscar Charleston
Utility: Hank Thompson
Manager: Rube Foster

Second choice
Catcher: Biz Mackey
Pitcher: Smokey Joe Williams
First Base: Ben Taylor
Second Base: Martin Dihigo
Shortstop: John Henry Lloyd
Third Base: Judy Johnson
Outfield: Turkey Stearnes, Cristobal Torriente, Pete Hill

Utility: Willard Brown

Manager: Vic Harris

Greatest player: "Buck Leonard — greatest all-around left handed batter in Negro league baseball. At the age of 41, in 1948, he hit .395, coming off a .410 batting average the year before."

DICK CLARK

Dick Clark, a Negro league historian for almost 30 years and present chairman of the Negro Leagues Committee of SABR, selected two all-star teams — a Negro league all-star team and a combined Negro league-major league all-star team.

Dick Clark's All-Time Negro League All-Star Team.

Catcher: Josh Gibson, Biz Mackey

Pitcher: (RH) Wilbur Rogan, Satchel Paige, (LH) Willie Foster, Dave Brown

First Base: Buck Leonard, Ben Taylor

Second Base: Sammy T. Hughes, Newt Allen

Shortstop: John Henry Lloyd, Willie Wells

Josh Gibson, the Negro league's greatest home run hitter, was predicted to average over 60 home runs a year if he played in the major leagues. (Photograph courtesy John B. Holway.)

Third Base: Ray Dandridge, Jud Wilson

Outfield: Oscar Charleston, Cool Papa Bell, Turkey Stearnes, Cristobal Torriente, Pete Hill, Willard Brown

Utility: Martin Dihigo, Monte Irvin

DH: Mule Suttles, Spot Poles

Greatest Player: "Oscar Charleston. There are a lot of players that could fit this title. Charleston was a terrific center fielder like Tris Speaker on defense but with more power. A terrific competitor (top five all time). After slowing down he changed to first base and remained a superior hitter. A long-time manager, top-flight hitter, 40 years in the game. Plus, whenever Negro league teams played major league teams prior to Landis's edict to stop, it was always Charleston plus a couple others (from a group of players) who would be selected to be added to a team's roster for the game(s). He would have been something to see when he was young. A combo of Cobb and Ruth."

Dick Clark's Combined Negro League– Major League All-Star Team

	1st choice	2nd choice	3rd choice	4th choice
Catcher:	Gibson	J. Bench	Cochrane	Mackey
Pitcher: (RH)	W. Johnson	Joe Williams	Paige	Alexander
(LH)	Grove	W. Foster	Spahn	Koufax
First Base:	Gehrig	Foxx	Leonard	Greenberg
Second Base:	Gehringer	J. Morgan	Lajoie	Hornsby
Shortstop:	Wagner	Lloyd	W. Wells	Banks
Third Base:	Schmidt	Mathews	Dandridge	J. Wilson
Outfield:	T. Williams	M. Irvin	T. Stearnes	Simmons
	Charleston	Mays	Cobb	Speaker
	Ruth	Aaron	Torriente	Kaline
Utility:	Dihigo	J. Rogan	Musial	J. Robinson
				L. Day
Manager:	R. Foster	McGraw	McKechnie	C. I. Taylor

Greatest player: "I've been watching games since 1952, and the greatest player I've seen in person was Al Kaline."

JEFF EASTLAND

Jeff Eastland, a Negro league expert and a member of SABR's Negro Leagues Committee, selected the following all-time Negro league all-star team.

Catcher: Josh Gibson, Roy Campanella
Pitcher: (RH) Smokey Joe Williams, Satchel Paige, (LH) W. Foster
First Base: Buck Leonard, Mule Suttles
Second Base: Martin Dihigo, Frank Grant

Shortstop: John Henry Lloyd, Willie Wells
Third Base: Ray Dandridge, Judy Johnson
Outfield: Oscar Charleston, Monte Irvin, Cool Papa Bell, C. Torriente, Turkey Stearnes, Pete Hill
Utility: Jud Wilson
Manager: Rube Foster
Greatest player: "Oscar Charleston."

JAN FINKEL

Jan Finkel, a member of SABR's Negro Leagues Committee, submitted the following choices for his all-time Negro league all-star team.

Catcher: Josh Gibson, Biz Mackey
Pitcher: (RH) Bullet Rogan, Smokey Joe Willams, (LH) Bill Foster, John Donaldson
First Base: Buck Leonard, Ben Taylor, Mule Suttles
Second Base: Sammy T. Hughes, Newt Allen
Shortstop: John Henry Lloyd, Willie Wells
Third Base: Ray Dandridge, Judy Johnson, Oliver Marcelle
Outfield: Oscar Charleston, Monte Irvin, Cool Papa Bell, Pete Hill, Turkey Stearnes, Cristobal Torriente
Utility: Martin Dihigo, John Beckwith
Manager: Rube Foster, Buck O'Neil
Greatest player: "Josh Gibson. He may have been the greatest hitter anywhere, and he played the toughest position quite well. Martin Dihigo. He was the most versatile player of all time. I thought of putting him at second base (above) but decided not to restrict him. I'd find a way to play him every day. I think Turkey Stearnes is the greatest player not in the Hall of Fame. Period."

As noted previously, Turkey Stearnes was finally elected to the Hall of Fame in 2000, after the survey was completed.

TOM GARRETT

Tom Garrett is a member of SABR and its Negro Leagues Committee. His selections for the all-time Negro league all-star team follow.

Catcher: Josh Gibson, Biz Mackey
Pitcher: (RH) Smokey Joe Williams, Satchel Paige, (LH) Willie Foster
First Base: Buck Leonard, Mule Suttles
Second Base: Martin Dihigo, Bingo Demoss
Shortstop: Pop Lloyd, Willie Wells
Third Base: Ray Dandridge, Judy Johnson
Outfield: Oscar Charleston, Bill Wright, Turkey Stearnes, Jimmy
Crutchfield, Cool Papa Bell, Pete Hill
Utility: Dick Lundy
Manager: Rube Foster, C. I. Taylor
Greatest player: "My selection for the greatest player in the Negro
leagues is Buck Leonard. [He had] consistency, [he was in] 11 all-star games
[he was a] great fielder and hitter [and he was a] team leader."

LESLIE HEAPHY

Leslie Heaphy, assistant professor of history at Kent State University,
and a Negro league researcher, selected the following all-time Negro league
all-star team.

Catcher: Josh Gibson, Biz Mackey
Pitcher: (RH) Hilton Smith, Satchel Paige, (LH) Willie Foster
First Base: Mule Suttles, Buck Leonard
Second Base: Frank Grant, Newt Allen
Shortstop: John H. Lloyd, Willie Wells
Third Base: Oliver Marcelle, Ray Dandridge
Outfield: Martin Dihigo, Turkey Stearnes, Oscar Charleston, Cristo-
bal Torriente, James Bell, Willard Brown
Utility: Pete Hill
Manager: Rube Foster, C. I. Taylor
Greatest player: "Cool Papa Bell is my favorite from reading and
watching documentaries— exciting to watch; great outfielder."

JOHN HOLWAY

John Holway, probably the most dedicated researcher and the most
prolific author in the area of Negro league baseball, has selected the following all-time Negro league all-star team.

Willie Foster was the Negro leagues' greatest southpaw pitcher during the 1920s and 30s. (Photograph courtesy John B. Holway.)

Catcher: Mackey, Duncan
Pitcher: (RH) Rogan, R. Brown, Paige, Williams, W. Bell, (LH) B. Foster, N. Winters
First Base: Suttles, Leonard
Second Base: DeMoss, Hughes
Shortstop: Lloyd, Wells
Third Base: Dandridge, Wilson
Outfield: Charleston, Irvin, Stearnes, Bell, Torriente, W. Brown
Utility: Gibson, Beckwith
Manager: R. Foster, Harris
Greatest player: "Gibson. Power, average, skill position (good arm, handler of pitchers)."

LOU HUNSINGER, JR.

Lou Hunsinger, a news reporter and Negro league historian, selected the following all-time Negro league all-star team.

Catcher: Josh Gibson
Pitcher: (RH) Smokey Joe Williams, (LH) Cristobal Torriente
First Base: Buck Leonard
Second Base: Bill Monroe
Shortstop: Willie Wells
Third Base: Judy Johnson
Outfield: Oscar Charleston, Rap Dixon, Martin Dihigo
Utility: Newt Allen
Manager: Rube Foster
Greatest player: "Martin Dihigo. He could do it all as a dazzling outfielder to an overpowering pitcher."

FRANK KEETZ

Frank Keetz is a retired teacher and a member of SABR. He is also a Negro league historian and the author of *The Mohawk Colored Giants of Schenectady.* He chose a combined Negro league–major league all-star team:

Catcher: Johnny Bench
Pitcher: (RH) Satchel Paige, (LH) Warren Spahn
First Base: Buck Leonard
Second Base: Rogers Hornsby
Shortstop: Honus Wagner
Third Base: Mike Schmidt
Outfield: Babe Ruth, Willie Mays, Hank Aaron
Utility: Pete Rose
Manager: Walter Alston
Greatest player: "Allie Reynolds (with Cleveland. He sure impressed me!)"

BRENT KELLEY

Brent Kelley is one of the Negro league's greatest assets. He has interviewed dozens (maybe a hundred or more) of Negro league veterans over the years and has published their reminiscences in several popular books. His all-time Negro league all-star team follows.

Catcher: Josh Gibson, Biz Mackey (Eggie Clarke was the best defensively)

Pitcher: (RH) Satchel Paige, Hilton Smith, Dick Redding, Joe Williams, Bullet Rogan (if you don't like one of these, put in Sam Jones), (LH) Willie Foster, Verdell Mathis

First Base: Buck Leonard, Ben Taylor (Bob Boyd is greatly under-rated)

Second Base: Bingo DeMoss, Piper Davis

Shortstop: Pop Lloyd, Willie Wells (Dick Lundy was a very close third)

Third Base: Oliver Marcelle, Jud Wilson

Outfield: Oscar Charleston, Jud Wilson, Cool Papa Bell, Pete Hill, Cristobal Torriente, Bill Wright

Utility: Martin Dihigo, John Beckwith (Duty is hard to leave out)

Manager: Rube Foster, Vic Harris

Greatest player: "The greatest: Wow. This is really tough. I'll take Charleston by an eyelash over Gibson. Obviously I've never seen any of these guys play (except Sam Jones and Piper Davis), but in interviewing more than 100 former players, and in reading of the exploits of the old-timers, the feeling I get is that Gibson was the best hitter in the world, any color (although I can't imagine anyone being better than Cobb), but Charleston was probably a more complete player who may well have been Josh's equal as a pure hitter."

MERL F. KLEINKNECHT

Merl Kleinknecht, one of the founding members of SABR's Negro Leagues Committee, selected the following all-time Negro league all-star team.

Catcher: Josh Gibson, Biz Mackey

Pitcher: (RH) Satchel Paige, Bullet Rogan, (LH) Willie Foster, Nip Winters

First Base: Buck Leonard, Mule Suttles

Second Base: Sam Hughes, George Scales

Shortstop: Pop Lloyd, Willie Wells

Third base: Ray Dandridge, Judy Johnson

Outfield: Oscar Charleston, Cristobal Torriente, Cool Papa Bell, Pete Hill, Turkey Stearnes, Sam Jethroe

Utility: Martin Dihigo, Monte Irvin

Manager: Rube Foster, Vic Harris

Greatest player: "Josh Gibson. Great hitter for power and average and outstanding catcher."

TED KNORR

Ted Knorr, a long-standing member of SABR and a member of the Negro Leagues Committee, selected the following all-time Negro league all-star team.

Catcher: Gibson, Mackey
Pitcher: (RH) PaigeWilliams, (LH) W. Foster, Donaldson
First Base: Leonard, Ben Taylor
Second Base: Newt Allen, Frank Grant
Shortstop: Lloyd, Wells
Third Base: Marcelle, Jud Wilson
Outfield: Charleston, Dixon, Bell, Jenkins, Torriente, Poles
Utility: Dihigo, Rogan
Manager: Rube Foster, Charleston

DAVID A. LAWRENCE

David A. Lawrence, Negro league historian, selected the following players for his all-time Negro league all-star team.

Catcher: Gibson, Mackey
Pitcher: (RH) Paige, R. Foster, (LH) W. Foster, Donaldson
First Base: J. Wilson, Wesley (not Leonard)
Second Base: Monroe, Scales
Shortstop: J. H. Lloyd, W. Moore
Third Base: Marcelle, W. J. Johnson
Outfield: Stearnes, B. Wright, Charleston, Hill (not J. T. Bell), Torriente, C. Smith
Utility: Dihigo, Rogan
Manager: R. Foster, Malarcher
Greatest player: "The greatest I personally saw was Mays. The greatest Negro leaguer of all time was probably Charleston."

LARRY LESTER

Larry Lester, co-editor of *The Negro Leagues Book,* and a leading authority on the Negro leagues and its players, selected the following all-star team.

First choice
Catcher: Josh Gibson
Pitcher: Satchel Paige, Smokey Joe Williams, Wilbur "Bullet" Rogan, Hilton Smith, Ray Brown, Leon Day, Willie Foster
First Base: Buck Leonard
Second Base: Newt Allen
Shortstop: Pop Lloyd
Third Base: Jud Wilson
Outfield: Turkey Stearnes, Cool Papa Bell, Oscar Charleston
Utility: Sam Bankhead, Martin Dihigo
Manager: Rube Foster, Sol White

Second choice
Catcher: Biz Mackey
Pitcher:
First Base: Ben Taylor
Second Base: Bingo DeMoss
Shortstop: Willie Wells
Third Base: Judy Johnson
Outfield: Willard Brown, Mule Suttles, Pete Hill
Utility:
Manager:
Greatest player: "A no brainer. Bullet Rogan. Rogan was the ace of any pitching staff. No relief pitcher need apply. A high average hitter who had power, and showed speed on the bases. Perhaps the only player, besides Martin Dihigo, capable of leading the league in most wins, lowest ERA, most strikeouts, most home runs, most RBIs, highest batting average, all in the same season. A dual triple-crown threat. It's criminal to think Bullet Rogan is not the greatest player of all time."

WILLIAM F. MCNEIL

I selected two all-star teams— an all-time Negro league all-star team and an all-time all-star team of players I saw play (obviously mostly major leaguers).

W. F. McNeil's all-time Negro league all-star team:

Catcher: Josh Gibson, Biz Mackey
Pitcher: (RH) Smokey Joe Williams, Bullet Joe Rogan, Satchel Paige, (LH) Willie Foster, Barney Brown

First Base: Buck Leonard, Mule Suttles
Second Base: Sammy T. Hughes, Martin Dihigo
Shortstop: John Henry Lloyd, Dobie Moore
Third Base: Ray Dandridge, Oliver Marcelle
Outfield: Turkey Stearnes, Cristobal Torriente, Oscar Charleston, Willard Brown, Chino Smith, Cool Papa Bell
Utility: Jud Wilson, John Beckwith
Manager: Rube Foster
Greatest player: Josh Gibson. From all I have heard and read, he was the greatest home run hitter of all time — including major league players. He hit more home runs in fewer at-bats than any man who ever lived. If he was hitting against the lively ball that Mark McGwire is hitting against, and against the AAA pitchers that McGwire sees, he might hit 80 or 90 home runs. I asked no less an expert than Roy Campanella who the best hitter he ever saw was, and he told me, "That's an easy question. Josh Gibson. I played against him eight or nine years in the Negro leagues. Josh played for the Pittsburgh Crawfords, and one year he hit 84 home runs. He was the greatest home run hitter that ever was. Satchel Paige pitched for the same team for many years, and they were probably the greatest catcher-pitcher combination in baseball history. It's too bad the color barrier wasn't broken till 1946. Most white folks never got to see Paige and Gibson in their prime, and that's a shame. They were in a class by themselves."

Defensively, Gibson was an outstanding receiver. Walter Johnson, one of the greatest pitchers that ever lived, said Gibson was the best catcher he ever saw, even better than Bill Dickey and Mickey Cochrane. Gibson called an excellent game, had a cannon for an arm, and was a steel wall when blocking the plate.

W. F. McNeil's all-time team personally seen:

Catcher: Roy Campanella
Pitcher: (RH) Bob Gibson, (LH) Sandy Koufax
First Base: Stan Musial
Second Base: Jackie Robinson
Shortstop: Pee Wee Reese
Third Base: Brooks Robinson
Outfield: Willie Mays, Joe DiMaggio, Ted Williams
Manager: Leo Durocher

The greatest player I ever saw was Jackie Robinson. He was the only player who could dominate an entire game. He was solid on defense. He could hit for average and for power. And he was an outstanding bunter.

But, when he was on base, he was at his best. He terrified pitchers. One time, after being knocked down by Sad Sam Jones and drawing a base on balls, he told Jones he was going to make him swallow his toothpick. Then he proceeded to steal second, third, and home to win the game. There was a saying at the time that went, "If the game lasts long enough Robinson will win it." I saw him play against the Boston Braves farm team, the Pawtucket Slaters, and what he did to those outfielders was a sin. He drove them crazy, running wild on the bases. There will never be another Jackie Robinson."

SAMMY MILLER

Sammy Miller is one of the most active Negro league supporters, with his writing, consulting, and committee activities. Miller's selections for an all-time Negro league all-star team follow.

Catcher: Josh Gibson, Biz Mackey
Pitcher: (RH) Joe Williams, Bullet Rogan, (LH) Willie Foster, Andy Cooper
First Base: Buck Leonard, Mule Suttles
Second Base: Bingo DeMoss, Newt Allen
Shortstop: Pop Lloyd, Pee Wee Butts
Third Base: Ray Dandridge, Jud Wilson
Outfield: Willard Brown, Turkey Stearnes, Oscar Charleston, Monte Irvin, Cristobal Torriente, Spots Poles
Utility: Martin Dihigo, Sam Bankhead
Manager: Rube Foster, C. I. Taylor
Greatest player: "Oscar Charleston. Throughout his career, he was compared (and rightly so) to both Ruth and Cobb. He could do everything they could do and on an equal level. If you were to put Ruth and Cobb together you would have the greatest player of all time, and his name would be Oscar Charleston."

RICK MORRIS

Rick Morris is another prolific Negro league historian-interviewer, having transferred the memories of dozens of former players to videotape. Rick selected only five players for his all-star team.

Catcher: Petway
First Base: Buck Leonard
Shortstop: Pop Lloyd
Third Base: Jud Wilson
Outfield: Fuzzy Walton
Manager: Buck O'Neil

Note: Fuzzy Walton, a name that might be unknown to most readers, was an outfielder with the Baltimore Black Sox and the Pittsburgh Crawfords during the 1930s.

Greatest player: "Boojum — highest average in Cuba, everywhere major leaguers had a chance to prove their superiority."

ERIC NEWLAND

Eric Newland is a member of SABR and a member of its Negro Leagues Committee. His all-time Negro league all-star team follows.

Catcher: Josh Gibson, Biz Mackey
Pitcher: (RH) Satchel Paige, Leon Day, (LH) Bill Foster, John Donaldson
First Base: Buck Leonard, Piper Davis
Second Base: Bingo DeMoss, Sammy T. Hughes
Shortstop: Willie Wells, John Henry Lloyd
Third Base: Ray Dandridge, Judy Johnson
Outfield: Cool Papa Bell, Turkey Stearnes, Cristobal Torriente, Wild Bill Wright, Oscar Charleston
Utility: Martin Dihigo
Manager: Rube Foster

Greatest player: "Mickey Mantle (sorry about that). If you grew up in Westchester County, New York, growing up a Yankee fan — his stature, strength, speed, switch hitting — [he was] a larger than life hero for a preteen."

Greatest thrill: "My greatest thrill was being with my father going to the World Series one cool October evening [and] sitting in the upper deck directly behind home plate [for] game 6 of the 1977 World Series at Yankee Stadium.

"What a view to watch Reggie Jackson blast three consecutive home runs— Reggie's powerful swing, a blast (line drive) into the right field seats quicker than the blink of an eye it was gone. Reggie's third one was his most prodigious home run — into the autumn sky, launched high, and seemingly the white ball disappearing into the night sky, only to re-enter the earth's orbit. The contrast of the night sky, the black center field bleachers — as Robert Peterson said, 'Only the ball was white.'"

JIM OVERMYER

Jim Overmyer, Negro league historian and author of *Queen of the Negro Leagues: Effa Manley and the Newark Eagles*, offered his all-star selections.

Catcher: Josh Gibson, Biz Mackey

Pitcher: (RH) Joe Williams, Satchel Paige, Joe Rogan, Leon Day, Dick Redding, (LH) Bill Foster, John Donaldson

First Base: Buck Leonard, Ben Taylor

Second Base: Ray Dandridge, Bingo DeMoss

Shortstop: Pop Lloyd, Willie Wells

Third Base: Judy Johnson, Oliver Marcelle

Outfield: Monte Irvin, Pete Hill, Oscar Charleston, Cool Papa Bell, Cristobal Torriente, Chino Smith

Utility: Martin Dihigo, John Beckwith

Manager: Rube Foster, Vic Harris

Greatest player: "My choice for all-time best player is Oscar Charleston. He combined the best position attributes — he hit for average and power and had a lot of speed in his younger days. He was a premier center fielder (note his selection in 1952 ahead of Bell), who became a premier first baseman when he slowed down in his 30s."

Jim Overmyer noted, "Well, all-time all-star teams are as subjective as it gets, but fun nevertheless. Here's mine, although I must disclose that most of it is based on the 1952 Pittsburgh *Courier* all-time team, with a few adjustments to accommodate all Hall of Famers and a few other favorites."

ROBERT W. PETERSON

Bob Peterson responded with the following note.

"This kind of survey is not my cup of tea. Of the 60-odd players for whom I have bio sketches in OTBWW [*Only the Ball Was White*], I actually saw only four or five play, and I was very young when I did. So I don't feel comfortable making choices. Sorry. Bob."

JIM RILEY

Jim Riley, noted Negro league historian and author of the monumental publication *The Biographical Encyclopedia of the Negro Baseball Leagues,* has submitted the following all-star selections.

1st Team
Catcher: Josh Gibson
Pitcher: Satchel Paige, Joe Williams, Willie Foster, Bullet Rogan
First Base: Buck Leonard
Second Base: Bingo DeMoss
Shortstop: John Henry Lloyd
Third Base: Ray Dandridge
Outfield: Oscar Charleston, Cool Papa Bell, Pete Hill
Utility: Martin Dihigo

2nd Team
Catcher: Biz Mackey
Pitcher: Leon Day, Dick Redding, Hilton Smith
First Base: Mule Suttles
Second Base: Newt Allen
Shortstop: Willie Wells
Third Base: Jud Wilson
Outfield: Turkey Stearnes, Cristobal Torriente, Monte Irvin
Utility: John Beckwith

"Note: If there was no utility player category, Dihigo would be placed on the first team at second base. Also, the pitchers are listed in order of preference under first team and then continuing with the second team."

JAY SANFORD

Jay Sanford is a member of SABR as well as a member of the Colorado Historical Society. He selected the following players for his all-time Negro league all-star team.

Catcher: Josh Gibson, Biz Mackey

Pitcher: (RH) (2) Smokey Joe Williams, (3) Satchel Paige, (5) Chet Brewer, (6) Dick Redding, (LH) (1) John Donaldson, (4) Bill Foster, (7) Dave Brown

First Base: Buck Leonard, George Giles

Second Base: Newt Allen, Sammy T. Hughes

Shortstop: John Henry Lloyd, Willie Wells

Willie Wells, known as "The Devil" in Mexico, was one of the top three shortstops in Negro league history. Many consider him to be first. (Photograph courtesy John B. Holway.)

Third Base: Oliver Marcelle, Judy Johnson

Outfield: Monte Irvin, Chris Torriente, Oscar Charleston, Cool Papa Bell, Turkey Stearnes, Bill Wright

Utility: Bullet Rogan, Martin Dihigo

Manager: (brothers)C. I. Taylor, Candy Jim Taylor

Jay Sanford noted, "It was difficult to leave Dobie Moore and Dick Lundy off of this team. Also Jose Mendez!"

"My pitchers should be ranked by the number I placed in front of their names."

Greatest player: "Willie Mays. I would arrive at Forbes Field two hours before game time to watch Willie take infield practice and see how he would interact with the other players. He loved to be at the ballpark. As a player I could not see where he had any weakness. He did it all better than anyone."

Negro leagues greatest player: "Oscar Charleston: A great hitter, hit with power, and was at his best with men on base. Excellent speed and had a great glove in the outfield and at first base. Most of all, he performed at a high level for many years. Here in Denver, at age 40, Oscar went two for five against the Rogers Hornsby's All-Stars. The Negro National League Stars won the doubleheader. Charleston drove in the winning run with a sacrifice fly in the nightcap. *The Denver Post* called him 'The greatest Negro hitter of all-time.'"

Greatest thrill: [Note: Jay Sanford selected three thrills. I chose the one that directly involved Negro leaguers.]

"Satchel Paige and a team he called the Cuban All-Stars came to my hometown (DuBois, Pennsylvania.) and played our strong semi-pro team. Satch pitched the first three innings facing our nine starters and struck out every man. For the remainder of the game, Satchel worked his way along the fenceline signing autographs and visiting with the fans. I became a researcher of black baseball and the Negro leagues that day. I was either 13 or 14 years old."

EDUARDO VALERO

Eduardo Valero is one of Puerto Rico's foremost baseball historians. He has over 45 years experience as a sports journalist for radio, television, newspapers, magazines, and news agencies. He was assistant sports editor of *El Nuevo Día,* sports editor of *El Imparcial,* and feature writer of *El Vocero de Puerto Rico.*

As a sportscaster, he has covered such events as the Centro American-Caribbean, Pan American, and Olympic Games. He has covered World Boxing Championship fights, World and Caribbean Baseball Series, and international World Basketball Tournaments.

He is a member of the Puerto Rico Sports Hall of Fame and the Puerto Rico Baseball Hall of Fame. He is member of the Society for American Baseball Research (SABR) and is presently Chairman of its Latin American Committee. He knew many of the greatest Negro league players personally, including Josh Gibson, Satchel Paige, Raymond Brown, and Leon Day. He is well qualified to select an all-time Negro league all-star team.

Catcher: Josh Gibson, Louis Santop
Pitcher: (RH) Satchel Paige, Leon Day, (LH) Barney Brown, Manuel "Cocaina" Garcia
First Base: Buck Leonard, Oscar Charleston
Second Base: Dick Seay, Marvin Williams
Shortstop: Willie Wells, Buster Clarkson
Third Base: Ray Dandridge, Judy Johnson
Outfield: Cool Papa Bell, Juan E. Vargas, Willard Brown, Frank Coimbre, Monte Irvin, Alejandro Oms
Utility: Martin Dihigo, Raymond Brown
Manager: George Scales, Vic Harris
Greatest player: "Joshua Gibson was the greatest player I ever saw, both as a hitter and as a catcher. I don't have any doubt that he could have been the home run record holder in a season as well as lifetime (in the

major leagues). However, I do consider Raymond Brown to be the most complete player. A magnificent pitcher, an outstanding center fielder, and a great hitter. That's why I'm including him and another friend, Leon Day, who had the same features, including being an infielder. Both were inducted in the Puerto Rican Hall of Fame. I believe that Raymond Brown should be elected to the Baseball Hall of Fame (in Cooperstown) in the near future."

Greatest thrill: "My greatest thrill in baseball was watching the pitching duels between Satchel Paige, Impo Barnhill, and Leon Day in the Puerto Rican Winter League"

Judy Johnson was one of the top two all-around third baseman during the 1920s and 30s. (Photograph courtesy Todd Bolton.)

LYLE K. WILSON

Lyle Wilson is a member of SABR's Negro Leagues Committee. His selections for an all-time Negro league all-star team follow.

Catcher: Josh Gibson
Pitcher: (RH) Satchel Paige, (LH) Willie Foster
First Base: Buck Leonard
Second Base: Newt Allen
Shortstop: John Henry "Pop" Lloyd
Third Base: Ray Dandridge
Outfield: Oscar Charleston, Cool Papa Bell, Turkey Stearnes
Utility: Martin Dihigo
Manager: Rube Foster
Greatest player: "Satchel Paige would be the greatest I saw personally. From all I have read, Pop Lloyd was probably the greatest ever — irrespective of color."

Twenty-four Negro league historians cast their votes for the all-time Negro league all-star team, the greatest Negro league player, and the greatest Negro league manager. The results are presented below. The number of votes received by each player follows his name.

Historians' Votes for All-Time Negro League All-Star Team

Position	Player	Votes
Catcher:	Josh Gibson	19
	Biz Mackey	16
Pitcher:	Satchel Paige	15
	Willie Foster	16
	Smokey Joe Williams	14
	Bullet Joe Rogan	11
	John Donaldson	7
	Leon Day	4
	Nip Winters	3
First Base:	Buck Leonard	19
	Mule Suttles	9
Second Base:	Newt Allen	8
	Bingo DeMoss	8
Shortstop:	John Henry Lloyd	18
	Willie Wells	14
Third Base:	Judy Johnson	13
	Ray Dandridge	12
Outfield:	Oscar Charleston	19
	Cristobal Torriente	17
	Cool Papa Bell	15
	Turkey Stearnes	15
	Monte Irvin	11
	Pete Hill	8
Utility:	Martin Dihigo	15
	John Beckwith	5
Manager:	Rube Foster	14
	C. I. Taylor	5

The historians' choices for the greatest player in Negro league history were:

Oscar Charleston	7
Josh Gibson	5
Buck Leonard	2

The historians' choices for the greatest Negro league manager were:

Rube Foster	14
C. I. Taylor	5

All-Time Negro League All-Star Team: The Final Selection

Over the past 50 years, a number of all-time Negro league all-star teams have been constructed by various individuals, organizations, and panels. *The Pittsburgh Courier,* one of the leading Black newspapers in the United States, presented an all-time Negro league all-star team in 1952. The team was selected by former stars of the Negro league.

Pittsburgh Courier's All-Time Negro League All-Star Team:

Catcher: Josh Gibson, Biz Mackey
Pitcher: Joe Williams, Satchel Paige, Bullet Rogan, John Donaldson, Bill Foster, Dave Brown, Dick Redding
First Base: Buck Leonard, Ben Taylor
Second Base: Jack Robinson, Bingo DeMoss
Shortstop: Pop Lloyd, Willie Wells
Third Base: Oliver Marcelle, Judy Johnson
Outfield: Monte Irvin, Pete Hill, Oscar Charleston, Cool Papa Bell, Cristobal Torriente, Chino Smith
Utility: Martin Dihigo, John Beckwith, Sam Bankhead, Newt Allen
Manager: Rube Foster, Cum Posey

Cumberland Willis ("Cum") Posey, was often called the "Father of the Homestead Grays." Posey was a native-born Homesteader, first seeing the light of day in that Pennsylvania community on June 20, 1880. He grew up to become a baseball player, spending many years with the Homestead Grays when they were a semi-pro club. Eventually he progressed to manager, then owner. Under his leadership, the Grays became the top professional team in Negro league baseball. With home grown products like Josh

John Henry Lloyd is considered to be one of the top two shortstops, black or white, in baseball history. The other is Honus Wagner.

Gibson and Buck Leonard, popularly known as the "Thunder Twins," smashing long home runs on a regular basis, the Grays captured nine consecutive Negro National League championships from 1937 through 1945.

Cum Posey was a powerful force in Negro league baseball for over 55 years, from his first day as an outfielder for the Homestead Grays in 1911 until his death from lung cancer at the age of 70 in 1946. Thirteen years prior to his death, the 57-year-old baseball mogul selected his all-time Negro league all-star team.

Catcher: Josh Gibson, Biz Mackey

Pitchers: Joe Williams, Dick Redding, Eustaquio Pedroso, Bullet Joe Rogan, Satchel Paige, Dave Brown, Willie Foster

First Base: Ben Taylor, Buck Leonard

Second Base: Sammy Hughes

Shortstop: John Henry Lloyd

Third Base: Jud Wilson

Outfield: Cristobal Torriente, Oscar Charleston, Pete Hill

Utility: Dick Lundy (infielder), Chester Brooks (outfielder)

Manager: C. I. Taylor

Posey also proposed a batting order, and left us with a few of his own personal comments on many of the players he chose.

Batting Order

Charleston CF, Lloyd SS (Captain), Hill RF, Torriente LF, Wilson 3B, Gibson C or Mackey, Taylor 1B, Hughes 2B, Pitcher

Posey's Capsule Comments

Catcher: "Josh Gibson [is] the most famed batter of colored baseball history, a great thrower, fast, and who lately has developed into one of our smartest catchers.

"Biz Mackey was the leading catcher up until the rapid rise of Gibson.... He was a better man than Petway, Santop, Beckwith, Larry Brown, and other good catchers.

"There can be little argument over Joe Williams and Dick Redding in their prime, or Satchel Paige of 1931, 1932, 1933, and 1934. Bullet Rogan ... compares with any of the above pitchers and was in addition our greatest fielding pitcher.

"Ben [Taylor] did not have a weakness at the bat. Both [Taylor and Leonard] were ideal men on a ballclub, left hand first basemen, good ground-ball men with their heads up all the time.

"Sammy Hughes [was] a good hitter, crack fielder, and real baserunner. Scales could not cover enough ground at second base; DeMoss and Warfield were mediocre hitters.

"[Boojum] Wilson had no form whatsoever, but he had sure hands, got in front of everything, was fast, and had a very good arm. Wilson was the surest hitter, Colored or White, we have ever seen on any club.

"John Henry Lloyd is the best of all. His all-around ability overshadowed the great playing of Dick Lundy, Wells, Moore, and Stevens.

"Torriente could do everything. One day C. I. Taylor said, 'Mr. Posey, if I should see Torriente walking up the other side of this street, I would say, 'There goes a ballclub.'"

"Oscar Charleston ... appeared to actually smell where the ball was going to be hit.

"Pete Hill [was] probably the best hitter

Bullet Joe Rogan was one of the most versatile players ever to play in the Negro leagues; one of the leagues' three greatest pitchers, its best fielding pitcher, and his team's cleanup hitter. (Photograph courtesy Robert W. Peterson Collection, National Baseball Hall of Fame Library.)

of Rube Foster's championship clubs. He was the most consistent hitter of his time, and while a left handed batter, he hit both left and right handers equally well.

"Dick Lundy [is] the utility infielder.

"For utility outfielder we put Brooks, a great player who spent practically his whole baseball life with the Brooklyn Royal Giants. Some fans of the East rate Brooks the greatest Colored player of all time.

It should be noted that, at the time Posey selected his all-time team, Buck Leonard, a four-year veteran, was just approaching his prime and had not yet become the "Black Lou Gehrig," as he was later called. In his book, *Blackball Stars,* John B. Holway presented another Cum Posey All-Time All-Star Team, probably done at a later time. This team was the same as the team above, except that Buck Leonard was the first baseman, Martin Dihigo was the second baseman, and Ray Dandridge was the third baseman.

Years later, in 1993, the Negro League Baseball Museum in Kansas City, Missouri, polled their members to determine an all-time Negro league all-star team.

Negro League Baseball Museum Members' All-Time Negro League All-Star Team:

Catcher: Josh Gibson, Biz Mackey

Pitcher: Satchel Paige, Leon Day, Hilton Smith, Smokey Joe Williams, Bullet Rogan, Ray Brown

First Base: Buck Leonard, Mule Suttles

Second Base: Piper Davis, Newt Allen

Shortstop: Willie Wells, Artie Wilson

Third Base: Ray Dandridge, Judy Johnson

Outfield: Cool Papa Bell, Willard Brown, Oscar Charleston, Sam Jethroe, Turkey Stearnes, Martin Dihigo

Manager: Buck O'Neil, Candy Jim Taylor

The previous all-star team selections noted above all had limitations. In one case, only Negro league players were polled, and their choices had to have been influenced by their ingrained biases and personal relationships. Another all-star team, although a very important one, was the choice of just one man and was influenced by his personal relationships, both friendly and unfriendly. And finally, a third all-star team was the result of a more informal poll involving an organization whose members were interested in the Negro leagues, but were not required to have any expertise in the history of the league or its players.

The present study presents the ultimate all-time Negro league all-star team. It represents a necessary balance between active participants in the game and scholars who bring to the table a more subjective evaluation of the skills of the various players. Two outstanding panels of Negro league baseball experts, one panel consisting of 33 veterans of the Negro league wars, and the other panel consisting of 24 of the top Negro league historians and authors, were invited to submit their all-star selections. The choices of each panel were presented in the previous two chapters. The combined vote of the two panels was used to determine the ultimate all-time Negro league all-star team. The total number of votes each player received from the two panels is shown after the player's name.

Cool Papa Bell was the fastest runner in the Negro leagues. He was a brillant outfielder, a speedy baserunner, and an outstanding hitter.

Ultimate All-Time Negro League All-Star Team

Position	Player	Votes
Catcher:	Josh Gibson	36
	Biz Mackey	27
Pitcher:	Satchel Paige	37
	Willie Foster	24
	Smokey Joe Williams	16
	Bullet Joe Rogan	14
	Ray Brown	12

Satchel Paige was one of the best pitchers, black or white, in baseball history. He might have been the best ever.

Position	Player	Votes
	Leon Day	10
	Hilton Smith	10
First Base:	Buck Leonard	40

Position	Player	Votes
	Mule Suttles	13
Second Base:	Sammy T. Hughes	22
	Newt Allen	17
Shortstop:	Willie Wells	33
	John Henry Lloyd	21
Third Base:	Ray Dandridge	30
	Judy Johnson	17
Outfield:	Cool Papa Bell	30
	Oscar Charleston	27
	Turkey Stearnes	27
	Cristobal Torriente	19
	Wild Bill Wright	16
	Monte Irvin	15
Utility:	Martin Dihigo	24
	Sammy Bankhead	8

Buck Leonard received the most votes (40) of any player. He was closely followed by:

Satchel Paige 37, Josh Gibson 36, Willie Wells 33, Ray Dandridge 30, Cool Papa Bell 30, Martin Dihigo 29 (24 for utility and 5 for second base), Oscar Charleston 27, Turkey Stearnes 27, Biz Mackey 27.

Of those 10 players, 9 of them are presently members of the National Baseball Hall of Fame in Cooperstown, New York. Biz Mackey, the only member of the group not in the Hall of Fame, is

Oscar Charleston was one of the Negro league's superstars. He is considered by many to be its greatest all-around player.

expected to join the others in Cooperstown soon.

Combined Panel's Selections for the Greatest Player in Negro League History.

Josh Gibson 13
Oscar Charleston 8
Martin Dihigo 5

Combined Panel's Selections for the Greatest Manager in Negro League History

Rube Foster 17
Oscar Charleston 8

Smokey Joe Williams was voted the greatest pitcher in Negro league history in 1952, by former players. (Photograph courtesy John B. Holway.)

All-Time Negro League All-Star Team: Biographies

The all-time Negro league all-star team was selected by a combined panel of 57 Negro league veterans, all of whom played prior to the integration of organized baseball in 1945, and Negro league historians and authors.

The team consists of a total of 25 players, two for every position, seven pitchers, and two utility players. Two managers were also selected.

The biographies of many of the players were covered in a previous chapter. Players in the National Baseball Hall of Fame in Cooperstown, New York, were not covered, with the exception of Turkey Stearnes, who had not been elected to the Hall when the poll was taken. The biographies of the Hall of Fame players follow, by position. The biography of Sammy Bankhead, selected as an all-time all-star, is also included. It is an anomaly of the two polls that Bankhead was selected as a member of the all-time Negro league all-star team, yet was not chosen as one of the 20 candidates for the National Baseball Hall of Fame.

CATCHER: JOSH GIBSON

Josh Gibson may have been the greatest baseball player ever to step on a diamond. He died much too young, at the early age of 35, just three months before Jackie Robinson stepped on the grass at Ebbets Field, destroying the color barrier once and for all.

Gibson was a terrifying hitter, who hit for both average and distance.

His long home runs have become the source of almost mythical tales over the years, with his most famous belt supposedly the only fair ball ever hit out of Yankee Stadium. The 1930 home run has never been authenticated, but it lives on in legend.

The facts are that Josh Gibson, a powerful six-footer, who packed 215 pounds of solid muscle on his sleek frame, hit the ball wherever he played. He hit .351 in the Negro leagues over a 15-year career, with 52 home runs for every 550 at-bats. He also hit:

- .353 in the Cuban Winter League with 34 home runs a year,
- .355 in the Puerto Rican Winter League with 27 home runs a year, and
- .373 in the Mexican League with 54 home runs a year.

Some baseball experts have downplayed Gibson's defensive capabilities, but their evaluations are unfounded. According to knowledgeable Negro league authorities like Cum Posey and Roy Campanella, Gibson was an outstanding receiver. He was a good handler of pitchers, had a rifle for a throwing arm, and was a block of granite blocking the plate.

CATCHER: BIZ MACKEY

See pages 102–103.

PITCHER: SATCHEL PAIGE

Satchel Paige was a legend in his own time — and it was all justified. He entered the Negro leagues in 1927 and immediately turned the leagues upside down with his overpowering pitching. Throwing strictly a fastball, he dominated every league he pitched in for almost 30 years.

Paige's record in the Negro leagues, 147 victories against 92 losses, did not reflect his actual skill level. He was by far the greatest drawing card in Negro league history, and fans clamored to see him wherever he went. As a result, he pitched frequently, usually throwing for three or four innings, and then turning the ball over to a relief pitcher. Under those conditions, he failed to pitch the required five innings to qualify as the winning pitcher.

Satchel Paige pitched all over the western hemisphere 12 months every year. And he dominated the batters wherever he pitched. He set the Puerto

Rican Winter League record, winning 19 games against 3 losses and fanning 209 batters in 205 innings. He started 24 of the 56 games his team played.

The year 1934 gives a good example of Paige's pitching dominance. During the winter, he pitched for the Nashville Elite Giants in the California Winter League against major league and AAA minor league opposition, winning 16 games against only 2 losses. He followed that up by winning 13 games against 3 losses for the Pittsburgh Crawfords in the Negro National League.

The next year, he spent the summer pitching for a semi-pro team in Bismark, North Dakota, winning 30 games against only 2 losses. That winter, he went 11–0 in the California Winter League, for a combined record for the year of 41–2, in 408 innings.

To prove he didn't just prey on amateur talent, the 42-year-old veteran tossed two shutouts against the Chicago White Sox over a period of eight days, when he finally got his chance to pitch for the Cleveland Indians in 1948.

PITCHER: WILLIE FOSTER

Willie Foster is generally considered to be the greatest left handed pitcher in Negro league history. The brother of the legendary Rube Foster, Willie was groomed for stardom by his famous brother during his developing years. Over a memorable 15-year career, the 6'1", 195-pound southpaw won 146 games against 66 losses, for an outstanding .689 winning percentage.

Foster's stock in trade was pinpoint control and a variety of pitches all thrown with the same motion. He was a thinking man's pitcher who kept hitters off balance with a repertoire that included a fastball, a curve ball, a drop, and a change of pace.

The smooth-working southpaw also pitched in the winter leagues frequently. He pitched in Cuba in 1927–28, but his 6–8 record is deceptive. He was the ace of the Cuba club staff, but the team finished last in the league with a winning percentage of just .375.

He fared much better in the strong California Winter League. Incomplete statistics credit him with a 24–1 record over three seasons.

PITCHER: SMOKEY JOE WILLIAMS

One of the greatest pitchers in baseball history, black or white, strode out of central Texas during the first decade of the twentieth century to mesmerize that baseball world. After his blazing fastball left the semi-pro teams around San Antonio in shambles, the tall, lanky right hander joined the Chicago Giants in 1910, moving over the New York Lincoln Giants the following year.

During a storied 23-year career in the Negro leagues, including 13 years with the Giants and 8 years with the famed Homestead Grays, Smokey Joe compiled a 125–56 record. But it was his strikeout achievements that left fans and opposing players alike shaking their heads in disbelief. In 1917, he supposedly threw a 10-inning no-hitter at the National League champion New York Giants fanning 20 batters. Despite this achievement, his team lost 1–0 in the 10th on an error.

Seven years later, the man known as "Cyclone Joe" back home struck out 25 Brooklyn Bushwick batters in 11 innings of shutout relief, only to lose the game in the 12th on three consecutive base hits.

Williams's last memorable game occurred in 1930, when the 44-year-old veteran tangled with Chet Brewer of the Kansas City Monarchs in one of the first night games in professional baseball. The dim lights didn't do the hitters any favor, as the 6'4" fireballer sent them back to the bench one after another. In all, Smokey Joe fanned 27 batters in 12 innings of one-hit ball, finally winning 1–0 on a two-out single by Chaney White.

He also struck out 19 batters in a California winter league game in 1911.

PITCHER: BULLET JOE ROGAN

If Smokey Joe Williams was not the greatest pitcher in Negro league history, then maybe Bullet Joe Rogan was. Certainly Rogan was one of the top three along with Williams and Satchel Paige. Rogan was a small guy compared to the other two, standing only 5'7", but he packed 180 pounds of muscle on his frame, particularly on the upper half. He had broad shoulders, big arms, and a huge chest mounted on spindly legs.

Wilbur Rogan was an army man, who spent more than 10 years in military service in the United States and Hawaii. He was a well-disciplined soldier, a characteristic that served him well throughout his professional baseball career. He always stayed in top condition, and he was always planning ahead — to the next pitch, the next inning.

Bullet Joe didn't enter the Negro leagues until he was past his 30th birthday, but he still put together an excellent career record of 151–65, for a winning percentage of .699, fifth all-time. The tough little right hander had two advantages over his fellow pitchers Williams and Paige. He is generally recognized as the best-fielding pitcher in Negro league history — and he could hit. In fact, he was one of the few pitchers who batted cleanup on his team. He was a career .348 hitter in the Negro leagues, averaging 16 home runs for every 550 at-bats.

Like many of his compatriots, he usually played winter ball from October till March. He played in Cuba in 1924-25, going 9–4, for the Almendares Blues. Most years, however, he pitched in the California Winter League, with great success. Box scores uncovered to date credit him with an excellent 42–14 pitching record, a .362 batting average, and 30 doubles and 19 home runs for every 550 at-bats. Bullet Joe Rogan could do it all.

PITCHER: RAY BROWN

See pages 95–96.

PITCHER: LEON DAY

Leon Day was a stocky fastball pitcher, who anchored the Newark Eagles pitching staff during the late 30s and early 40s. He was considered to be the most consistent pitcher of the era, outshining such luminaries as Satchel Paige and Ray Brown. Unfortunately, Day's team happened to be in the same division as the Homestead Gray's, and were caught in the middle of the Grays' nine-year dynasty.

The 170-pound right hander went 6–0 in 1937, 12–4 two years later, and 11–4 in 42–43, before his career was interrupted by military service in World War II . On his return to baseball in 1946, he dazzled the home fans by tossing an opening day no-hitter at the Philadelphia Stars. In all, Day compiled a 68–30 record over an 11-year career, for a winning percentage of .694, the sixth-highest winning percentage in Negro league history.

Leon Day also paraded his skills outside the borders of the United States, pitching in Mexico, Puerto Rico, Cuba, Venezuela, and Canada. He went 24–20 in Mexico, including a clean 6–0 slate in 1940, and went 35–28 in Puerto Rico, 12–1 in Venezuela, and 8–4 in Cuba. He also won 19 games against 15 losses in the United States minor leagues after integration became

Leon Day, a member of the National Baseball Hall of Fame, starred for the Newark Eagles during the 30s and 40s.

the law of the land. By then, however, it was too late for him to reach the major leagues. He was already 34 years old when his chance came.

Day established strikeout records wherever he pitched. He set the Negro National League strikeout record by fanning 18 Baltimore Elite Giants in 1942. He holds the Negro league All-Star game strikeout record with 14 in 7 games. In 1942, he fanned 5 of the 7 batters he faced. He also established a Puerto Rican Winter League strikeout record with 19 in 1941. The Virginia native brought more to the ballpark than a pitching arm, however. He was an excellent hitter and could play any outfield or infield position with distinction. His Negro league statistics include a .287 batting average with 22 doubles, 9 triples, and 5 home runs a year. He pounded the ball at a .314 clip in Mexico. When not pitching, he often played second base or center field. His outstanding speed was an asset both in the outfield and on the bases.

PITCHER: HILTON SMITH

See pages 112–113.

FIRST BASE: BUCK LEONARD

Walter Fenner "Buck" Leonard was born in Rocky Mount, North Carolina, on September 8, 1907. He grew up to be one of the most feared batters in the Negro leagues. Teaming with Josh Gibson to form the devastating "Thunder Twins," he sparked the Homestead Grays to nine successive Negro National League pennants between 1937 and 1945 and two World Championships in the four World Series played.

Buck Leonard was a smooth-swinging left handed slugger who hit for both average and distance. Over a distinguished 16-year career, the 5'10", 180-pound bomber compiled a .335 batting average, with 24 home runs a year. His best year was 1948 when he led the league with 13 home runs in 157 at-bats and in hitting with an average of .395. He also

Buck Leonard, known as the "Black Lou Gehrig" is considered to be the all-time Negro league first baseman by many experts.

captured the batting championship in 1940 with an average of .383 and led the league in doubles and home runs as well. He put together other notable seasons where he hit .375, .345, and .333.

Leonard showcased his wares in several countries around the western hemisphere during the winter. He batted .326, with 20 home runs a year, for Torreon in the Mexican League between 1951 and 1953. He also hit .390 in Puerto Rico in 1941-42 and led the league in both doubles (17) and home runs (8) in just 118 at-bats. And he hit .284 in two years in Cuba.

When integration came, he gave organized ball a brief trial, playing 10 games for Portsmouth in the Piedmont League. Even though he was on the shady side of 45 at the time, he hit a solid .333 before hanging up his spikes.

Buck Leonard was known as a great clutch hitter, the one man you want at the plate when the game is on the line.

FIRST BASE: MULE SUTTLES

See pages 115–117.

SECOND BASE: SAMMY T. HUGHES

See page 100.

SECOND BASE: NEWT ALLEN

See pages 123–124.

SHORTSTOP: WILLIE WELLS

Willie Wells has many supporters as the greatest shortstop in Negro league history. He is definitely in the top four, along with John Henry Lloyd, Dobie Moore, and Dick Lundy. The irrepressible Wells began his professional baseball career as an 18-year-old shortstop with the St. Louis Stars in 1924. He quickly became one of the stars of the Negro National League with his all-around brilliance.

Wells was an outstanding defensive shortstop with wide range, a sure glove, and an accurate throwing arm. He offset a lack of strength in his throwing arm with quick reflexes and a fast release. In Mexico, where he spent several years, he was known as "El Diablo." Fans would often chant, "Don't hit the ball to shortstop. The Devil plays out there."

The man known as "Pepper" was more than a glove, however. He was one of the top hitters in the league, with a career batting average of .328 and 20 home runs a year. Although he weighed only 166 pounds, the 5'9" right handed batter hit the ball with authority. He led the league in home runs in 1929, hitting 29 in just 334 at-bats, beating out his teammate Mule Suttles who hit 20.

Willie Wells also starred in other leagues around the western hemisphere. He spent three summers in Mexico where he hit .323 with 11 home runs. He spent the winter months playing ball either in the Cuban Winter League or the California Winter League. He played seven years in Cuba, compiling a batting average of .320 with eight home runs. He led the league in home runs twice, in 1935-36 and 37-38. He also tormented white pitchers in California for eight years, batting .301 with 11 home runs. Against major league hurlers like Larry French, Buck Newsome, and Sloppy Thurston, Wells hit the ball at a .303 clip.

SHORTSTOP: JOHN HENRY LLOYD

John Henry Lloyd was the consummate short-fielder during the early part of the twentieth century. He and Honus Wagner were considered to be the two finest shortstops in the country. Connie Mack once said, "You could put both Lloyd and Wagner in a bag and shake it up, and whichever one you pulled out, you had the best."

Lloyd was called "El Cuchara" (the Shovel) in Cuba, because every time he fielded a ground ball in the hard-packed Havana infield, he came up, not only with the ball, but also with a glove full of dirt. He was a wizard on defense, gliding across the infield like a ghost, scooping up balls behind third base or second base, and taking another base hit away from the batter with a strong, accurate throw.

The 5'11", 180-pound left handed batter not only excelled on defense, he also excelled at the plate. He was one of the top batters in the Negro leagues, year after year, spraying hits to all corners of the ballpark. Not a long-ball hitter, Lloyd kept the fielders on their toes with well-placed hits to open spaces. He banged the ball at a .300 pace year after year, leading the league with a phenomenal .564 average in 1928, still the all-time single-season Negro league record. Over the course of a memorable 27-year career, the Atlantic City, New Jersey, native hit a resounding .337, with 21 doubles, 10 triples, and 5 home runs a year.

He was not only an outstanding hitter. He was also an adept bat handler who could bunt, hit-and-run, or swing away depending on the situation. And he was dangerous on the bases. His speed made him a threat to steal at any time, as well as take an extra base on a hit.

John Henry Lloyd played his winter ball primarily in Cuba, where he was always welcomed as a hero. In an illustrious 13-year Cuban career, the tall, lanky infielder set the standard for shortstops and hit .329 to boot, with an average of 19 doubles, 13 triples, and 2 home runs for every 550 at-bats. He led the league in doubles once, triples once, and, surprisingly, home runs once.

Ray Dandridge is generally considered to be the greatest all-around third baseman in Negro league history. (Photograph courtesy James A. Riley.)

THIRD BASE: RAY DANDRIDGE

Ray Dandridge, the squat third baseman for the Newark Eagles, was an outstanding all-around player. He was flawless on defense, with quick reflexes, a sure glove, and a cannon for an arm. His teammates said his legs were so bowed you could drive a train between them, but not a baseball. While with Newark, he joined with Mule Suttles, Willie Wells, and Dick Seay to form the Eagles famed "Million Dollar Infield."

The 5'7" infielder, regarded by many as the greatest third baseman in Negro league history, played in the Negro leagues for 17 years, compiling a lifetime batting average of .350 with 28 doubles, 10 triples, and 3 home runs. When integration finally came, the 35-year-old veteran joined the New York Giants farm team in Minneapolis, where he excelled. Sadly, he was never called up to the big club, because Giant owner Horace Stoneham had two black players already — Monte Irvin and Hank Thompson, and he was on the verge of calling up another one — Willie Mays. His age probably did him in. The Giants wanted to bring up the younger players. So Dandridge stayed in Minneapolis.

Dandridge's bad luck was the Millers's good luck. In 1949, Hooks Dandridge pounded American Association pitching for a .362 batting

average in 99 games and was voted Rookie of the Year. The following year
he led the league with 627 at-bats and 195 base hits, while batting .311 and
scoring 106 runs. He hit .324 in '51 and .291 in '52 before finishing his organized-ball career in the Pacific Coast League. Overall, he tattooed AAA
pitching for a .316 average for five years between the ages of 35 and 40.

Dandridge was another vagabond ballplayer who traveled with the sun.
In the winter, he headed south to Mexico, Cuba, or Puerto Rico. He had a
long career in the Cuban Winter League, playing there for 12 years in all and
compiling a lifetime batting average of .282, with four years over .300. He
also hit .347 for eight summer seasons in Mexico, from 1940 to 1948.

Ray Dandridge's playing statistics are impressive.

	At-Bats	Hits	Avg.
Negro leagues	1,160	406	.350
Cuban Winter League	2,129	601	.282
Mexican League	2,714	943	.347
Minneapolis-American Association	2,066	656	.318
Pacific Coast League (AAA)	254	68	.268
Totals	8,323	2674	.321

THIRD BASE: JUDY JOHNSON

Judy Johnson was another dazzling all-around third baseman. He is considered to be the best third baseman ever to play the game by many baseball
experts. Born William J. Johnson in Snow Hill, Maryland, on October 26,
1900, the tall, slender youngster was an all-around athlete in his school years.

In 1918, he left school and joined the professional baseball ranks,
spending a year with the Bacharach Giants and two years with the Madi-
son Stars, before taking over infield duties with the Hilldale Daisies in the
Eastern Colored League. In 1923 he settled in at third base and began to
build a legend. The Daisies too built a legend, walking away with the league
championship three successive years, between 1923 and 1925. In '24, the
Daisies played the powerful Kansas City Monarchs in the first Negro
League World Series, bowing to the K. C. nine 5–4 when the aging skip-
per of the Monarchs, Jose Mendez, shut them down 5–0 in the finale. The
next year, however, Hilldale got their revenge, whipping K. C. 5–1. Johnson rapped K. C. pitching to the tune of .323 in the two championships,
including .364 in 1924.

The Maryland native was the heart and soul of the Hilldale club between 1923 and 1929. In addition to stringing together seasons of .327, .364, and .302 between 1924 and 1926, he was also a defensive standout. Ted Page was quoted in John Holway's book *Blackball Stars* as saying, "Judy Johnson was the smartest third baseman I ever came across. A scientific ballplayer, [he] did everything with grace and poise. Played a heady game of baseball...." Other players, in the same book, seconded Page's comments. Willie Wells said "He had intelligence and finesse." And Jimmie Crutchfield volunteered that Johnson was "A steadying influence on the club. He had a great brain, could anticipate a play, knew what his opponents were going to do."

Judy Johnson played in the Negro leagues for 20 years, compiling a respectable .285 batting average. He journeyed to Cuba occasionally in the winter and hit .334 in the tough Cuban Winter League between 1926 and 1930.

OUTFIELD: COOL PAPA BELL

James "Cool Papa" Bell was one of the great center fielders in baseball history. He grew up tall and slender and as fast as greased lightning. After spending a couple of years as a pitcher, "Cool" found his rightful spot in center field. The 5'11", 150-pound speedster covered the outfield like a gazelle, running down fly balls with effortless grace. He also kept the baserunners honest with a strong, accurate throwing arm.

Bell could do it all. He was an electrifying batter, capable of hitting to all fields with decent power, or dragging bunts for base hits. A smooth left handed batter, Bell terrorized opposing pitchers in the Negro league for 25 years. During his career, he led the league in at-bats five times, runs scored once, doubles once, stolen bases five times, and batting average once. He hit .354 and .362 with the St. Louis Stars in 1925 and '26; .384 with the Detroit Wolves in 1932; .341 with the Pittsburgh Crawfords in '35; and .356, .379, and .429 with the Homestead Grays in '43, '44, and '46.

On the bases, Cool Papa became a mythical figure because of his feats. He was reported to have raced from first to third on a bunt, scored from second on a sacrifice fly, and stole two bases on the same pitch. Satchel Paige once declared that Bell was so fast he could shut off a light switch in their hotel room and be in bed before the room got dark.

When Bell retired, he left behind a career batting average in the Negro leagues of .328. He also played ball for five years in Cuba, hitting .292 and leading the league once each in doubles, home runs, and stolen bases. But it was on the West Coast where Bell got to demonstrate his talents to major league players. He spent twelve years in the California Winter League (CWL), batting against such big league pitchers as Larry French, Buck Newsome, and Sloppy Thurston. He hit .367 in the CWL and led the league in batting twice, with an average of .400 in 1924-25 and .362 in 1933-34.

OUTFIELD: OSCAR CHARLESTON

Oscar Charleston is one of the four or five players who are usually nominated as the greatest all-around player in Negro league history. Charleston was a superstar — a five-point player. He could hit, hit with power, run, field, and throw. In his youth, he had no equal in center field. He was fast, had extraordinary range, and had a strong, accurate throwing arm. He played a shallow center field, like Tris Speaker, but was able to run down any ball hit over his head, or to either side.

The 6', 190-pound left handed slugger entered the Negro leagues in 1915 at the age of 18. He was all fight and fire, with blazing speed. In the field, he was the ultimate defender. At bat, he was a deadly fastball hitter, who hit the ball to all fields. And on the bases, he was aggressive and fearless. As Jim Riley noted, "He was rough and tumble, sliding hard with spikes high."

Oscar Charleston played ball in the Negro leagues for 27 years, then managed for another 13 years. He left behind some eye-popping statistics. He hit a mighty .340 in almost 5,000 at-bats, while averaging 29 doubles, 13 triples, and 26 home runs a year.

The big slugger vacationed in Cuba most winters, spending 10 years there between 1920 and 1931, and he showed no mercy on the Cuban pitchers. He smashed the ball at a torrid .361 clip, second only to Jud Wilson in Cuban Winter League history. His offensive production included 29 doubles, 14 triples, and 10 home runs. He won the batting championship in 1930-31 with an average of .373. He also led the league in triples once, home runs once, and stolen bases twice.

Charleston played only one year in the California Winter League, but he left the opposing pitchers with nightmares of what might have been. In 23 games in 1921-22, he mauled major league pitchers like Slim Love, Bill Pertica, and Red Oldham for a .375 average.

OUTFIELD: TURKEY STEARNES

See pages 113–115.

OUTFIELD: CRISTOBAL TORRIENTE

See pages 118–119.

OUTFIELD: WILD BILL WRIGHT

See pages 121–123.

OUTFIELD: MONTE IRVIN

See pages 32–33.

UTILITY: MARTIN DIHIGO

Martin Dihigo may have been Cuba's most valuable export. He was certainly one of the most versatile players ever to step on a baseball diamond. He was one of the best pitchers of his era, winning more than 250 games all over the western hemisphere. He was also an outstanding center fielder and one of the best second basemen ever to play in the Negro leagues.

Dihigo played in the Cuban Winter League for 26 years. He won 106 games as a pitcher, with just 59 losses, and batted .293. In Mexico, during an illustrious 11-year career, the man they called "El Maestro" (the Master) in his homeland, went 119–57 on the mound and hit a solid .317 with 16 home runs a year. In 1938, he was a one-man army in Mexico. He won the batting championship with a .387 average, won the pitching title with an 18–2 record, and led the league in earned run average (0.90) and strikeouts (184 in 167 innings). His best year pitching-wise was 1942 when he went 22–7, led the league with a 2.53 ERA, and hit .319. During the infamous Dominican Republic Summer League, the big right hander compiled a 6–4 record and batted .351, with 4 home runs in 25 games. He also pitched in Venezuela, where he ran up a perfect 6–0 record in 1933, with a minuscule 0.15 earned run average.

Somehow "El Maestro" also managed to play in the Negro leagues for 12 years, primarily with the New York Cubans. As a second baseman and center fielder, Dihigo batted .299 with 19 home runs a year. On the mound he went 29–26. He was selected as the all-time Negro league second baseman by many Negro league experts.

Overall, the graceful 6'3", 190-pound all-star won 260 games against 146 losses, for an outstanding winning percentage of .640. He also put together a .300 batting average, with good long-ball power. Fittingly he was elected to the Hall of Fame in four countries—Venezuela, Mexico, Cuba, and the United States.

UTILITY: SAMMY BANKHEAD

Sammy Bankhead was one of five baseball-playing brothers. One member of his family, Dan Bankhead, pitched briefly for the Brooklyn Dodgers in the early 50s. Dan's main claim to fame was that he hit a home run in his first major league time at bat.

Sam Bankhead was an outstanding all-around shortstop for several Negro league teams, most notably the Pittsburgh Crawfords and the Homestead Grays during a 21-year career that ended in 1951. The oldest of the Bankhead boys was a hustler, who did everything he could to win a ball game. At shortstop, he had a wide range and a cannon for an arm. He could throw out baserunners from anywhere on the infield.

He was a good hitter with above average power and was noted as a clutch hitter. It was Bankhead who, in the tension-packed final game of the Dominican Republic Summer League, hit the pennant-winning home run off Chet Brewer. Over the course of his Negro league career, the 5'8", 170-pound batter hit a respectable .285, with seven home runs for every 550 at-bats.

Sammy Bankhead spent two summers in Mexico, in 1940 and 1941. Playing with Monterrey, he scorched the ball at a .335 clip, with 28 doubles, 16 triples, and 11 home runs a year. His 32 stolen bases led the Mexican League in 1940. He also played winter ball in Cuba, Puerto Rico, and California. He led the Cuban Winter League in batting in 1937-38, with an average of .366. He also led the league in hits and runs scored. Overall, he hit .297 for four years in Cuba, with two years over .300 and two years in the low .200s. In Puerto Rico, he compiled a four-year average of .311. He led the league in home runs (3 in 155 at-bats) and stolen bases (12) during the 1945-46 season. In his two years in the California Winter League, competing against major league pitchers and Pacific Coast League pitchers, the right hander hit a resounding .351, with 32 doubles, 18 triples, and 16 home runs a year.

Appendix I—
The Players Panel: The Voters

Armstead, James
SURVEYS: Hall of Fame
YEARS PLAYED: 1938–1949
TEAMS: Indianapolis ABC's, St. Louis Stars, Baltimore Elite Giants, Philadelphia Stars
POSITIONS PLAYED: OF, P
RESIDENCE: New Rochelle, NY
COMMENTS: Hit .294 in 1940.

Barnhill, Herbert
NICKNAME: Herb
SURVEYS: Hall of Fame, All-Time All-Star Team
HEIGHT: 6'
WEIGHT: 175 lbs.
Bats right Throws right
YEARS PLAYED: 1938–1946
TEAMS: Jacksonville Red Caps, Cleveland Bears, Kansas City Monarchs, Chicago American Giants
POSITIONS PLAYED: C
RESIDENCE: Jacksonville, FL

Bell, James Thomas
NICKNAME: Cool Papa
SURVEYS: All-Time All-Star Team (from The "All-Stars" All-Star Baseball Handbook)
BORN: May 17, 1903, Starkville, MS

DIED: March 7, 1991, St. Louis, MO
HEIGHT: 5' 11"
WEIGHT: 150 lbs.
Bats both Throws left
YEARS PLAYED: 1922–1946
TEAMS: St. Louis Stars, Detroit Wolves, Kansas City Monarchs, Homestead Grays, Pittsburgh Crawfords, Memphis Red Sox, Chicago American Giants
POSITIONS PLAYED: OF, 1B, P
NATIONAL BASEBALL HALL OF FAME: 1974
COMMENTS: .328 career batting average

Biot, Charles Augustus Jr.
NICKNAME: Charlie
SURVEYS: All-Time All-Star Team
BORN: October 18, 1917, Orange, NJ
DIED: March 10, 2000, East Orange, NJ
HEIGHT: 6' 3"
WEIGHT: 180 lbs.
Bats right Throws right
YEARS PLAYED: 1939–1941
POSITIONS PLAYED: OF
TEAMS: Newark Eagles, New York Black Yankees, Baltimore Elite Giants

Carter, Marlin Theodore
NICKNAME: Mel, Pee Wee
SURVEYS: All-Time All-Star Team
BORN: December 27, 1912, Haslam, TX
DIED: December 20, 1993, Memphis, TN
HEIGHT: 5' 7"
WEIGHT: 159 lbs.
Bats left Throws right
YEARS PLAYED: 1932–1948
TEAMS: Monroe Monarchs, Memphis Red Sox, Cincinnati Tigers, Chicago American Giants
POSITIONS PLAYED: 3B, SS, 2B
COMMENTS: Played two years in organized ball after the color barrier was lifted. Played with the Rochester Royals, retiring at the age of 38.

Cash, William Walker
NICKNAME: Ready
SURVEYS: Hall of Fame, All-Time All-Star Team
BORN: February 21, 1919, Round Oak, GA
HEIGHT: 6' 2"
WEIGHT: 195 lbs.

Bats right Throws right
YEARS PLAYED: 1943–1950
TEAMS: Philadelphia Stars
POSITIONS PLAYED: C, OF, 3B, 1B
RESIDENCE: Philadelphia, PA

Davis, Ross
NICKNAME: Satchel, Schoolboy
SURVEYS: Hall of Fame, All-Time All-Star Team
BORN: ca. 1919
Bats right Throws right
YEARS PLAYED: 1940–1947
TEAMS: Baltimore Elite Giants, Cleveland Buckeyes
POSITIONS PLAYED: P
RESIDENCE: Long Beach, FL

Day, Leon
SURVEYS: All-Time All-Star Team
BORN: October 30, 1916, Alexandria, VA
DIED: March 13, 1995, Baltimore, MD
HEIGHT: 5' 9"
WEIGHT: 170 lbs.
Bats right Throws right
YEARS PLAYED: 1934–1950
TEAMS: Baltimore Black Sox, Brooklyn Eagles, Newark Eagles, Baltimore Elite
    Giants
POSITIONS PLAYED: P, 2B, OF
NATIONAL BASEBALL HALL OF FAME: 1995
COMMENTS: Compiled a record of 68–30 during his Negro League career. Entered
    organized baseball in 1951, going 1–1 with a 1.58 ERA with Toronto in the
    AAA International League.

Dials, Oland Cecil
NICKNAME: Lou
SURVEYS: All-Time All-Star Team
BORN: January 10, 1904
DIED: April 5, 1994, Modesto, CA
HEIGHT: 5' 10"
WEIGHT: 185 lbs.
Bats left Throws left
YEARS PLAYED: 1925–1936
TEAMS: Chicago American Giants, Birmingham Black Barons, Memphis Red Sox,
    Detroit Stars, Hilldale Daisies, Homestead Grays, Columbus Redbirds, Cleve-
    land Giants, New York Black Yankees

POSITIONS PLAYED: 1B, OF
COMMENTS: Good hitter, decent power

Doby, Lawrence Eugene
SURVEYS: Hall of Fame
BORN: December 13, 1923, Camden, SC
HEIGHT: 6' 1"
WEIGHT: 175 lbs.
Bats left Throws right
YEARS PLAYED: 1942–1947
TEAMS: Newark Eagles
POSITIONS PLAYED: 2B, 3B
NATIONAL BASEBALL HALL OF FAME: 1998
COMMENTS: First black player in the American League 1947.
RESIDENCE: New Jersey

Duckett, Mahlon Newton
NICKNAME: Mal
SURVEYS: Hall of Fame, All-Time All-Star Team
BORN: December 20, 1922, Philadelphia, PA
HEIGHT: 5' 10"
WEIGHT: 170 lbs.
YEARS PLAYED: 1940–1950
TEAMS: Philadelphia Stars, Homestead Grays
POSITIONS PLAYED: 2B, SS, 3B
RESIDENCE: Philadelphia, PA

Fennar, Albertus Avant
NICKNAME: Cleffie, Al
SURVEYS: Hall of Fame
BORN: May 12, 1911, Wilmington, NC
HEIGHT: 5' 8"
WEIGHT: 170 lbs.
YEARS PLAYED: 1931–1934
TEAMS: Harlem Stars, New York Black Yankees, Brooklyn Royal Giants, Atlantic
    City Bacharach Giants, Cuban Stars
POSITIONS: SS, 3B, 2B
RESIDENCE: Palm Bay, FL

Fernandez, Bernard
SURVEYS: Hall of Fame, All-Time All-Star Team
BORN: Cuba
YEARS PLAYED: 1938–1949
TEAMS: Atlanta Black Crackers, Jacksonville Red Caps, Pittsburgh Crawfords, New
    York Black Yankees

POSITIONS: P
RESIDENCE: Philadelphia, PA

Fernandez, Rodolfo
SURVEYS: Hall of Fame, All-Time all-Star Team
BORN: June 27, 1911, Guanabacoa, Havana, Cuba
DIED: September 6, 2000, New York City
HEIGHT: 6' 1"
WEIGHT: 190 lbs.
Bats right Throws right
YEARS PLAYED: 1932–1943
TEAMS: New York Cubans
CUBAN BASEBALL HALL OF FAME: 1966
RESIDENCE: New York City, NY
COMMENTS: Pitched in the Cuban Winter League 1931–1944, won 50 games against 38 losses.

Glenn, Stanley Rudolf
NICKNAME: Doc
SURVEYS: All-Time All-Star Team
BORN: September 19, 1926, Wachatreague VA
HEIGHT: 6' 3"
WEIGHT: 200 lbs.
YEARS PLAYED: 1944–1950
TEAMS: Philadelphia Stars
POSITIONS PLAYED: C
RESIDENCE: Yeadon, PA
COMMENTS: Played four years in organized baseball after the color barrier was broken.

Grace, William
NICKNAME: Willie
SURVEYS: Hall of Fame, All-Time All-Star Team
BORN: June 30, 1918, Memphis, TN
HEIGHT: 6'
WEIGHT: 170 lbs.
Bats both Throws left
YEARS PLAYED: 1942–1950
TEAMS: Cincinnati Buckeyes, Cleveland Buckeyes, Louisville Buckeyes, Houston Eagles
POSITIONS: OF, P
RESIDENCE: Erie, PA
COMMENTS: Played one year of organized baseball with Erie in the Middle Atlantic League in 1951.

Hyde, Cowan F.

NICKNAME: Bubba
SURVEYS: All-Time All-Star Team
BORN: April 10, 1908, Pontotoc, MS
HEIGHT: 5' 8"
WEIGHT: 150 lbs.
Bats right Throws right
YEARS PLAYED: 1927–1950
TEAMS: Memphis Red Sox, Birmingham Black Barons, Indianapolis Athletics, Cincinnati Tigers, Chicago American Giants
POSITIONS: OF, 2B
COMMENTS: Played in organized baseball from 1949 through 1953.

Irvin, Monford Merrill

NICKNAME: Monte
SURVEYS: Hall of Fame, All-Time All-Star Team
BORN: February 25, 1919, Halesburg, AL
HEIGHT: 6' 1"
WEIGHT: 190 lbs.
Bats right Throws right
YEARS PLAYED: 1937–1948
TEAMS: Newark Eagles
POSITIONS: OF, SS, 3B
NATIONAL BASEBALL HALL OF FAME: 1973
Mexican Baseball Hall of Fame
RESIDENCE: Florida

Johnson, Charles

SURVEYS: Hall of Fame
YEARS PLAYED: 1932–1933
TEAMS: Chicago American Giants
RESIDENCE: Chicago, IL

Johnson, Joshua

NICKNAME: Josh, Brute
SURVEYS: Hall of Fame, All-Time All-Star Team
BORN: January 24, 1913, Evergreen, AL
DIED: August 12, 1999, Springfield, IL
HEIGHT: 6' 1"
WEIGHT: 195 lbs.
Bats right Throws right
YEARS PLAYED: 1934–1942
TEAMS: Homestead Grays, New York Black Yankees, Cincinnati Tigers, Brooklyn Royal Giants

POSITIONS: C, OF, P

Leonard, Walter Fenner
NICKNAME: Buck
SURVEYS: All-Time All-Star Team
BORN: September 8, 1907, Rocky Mount, NC
DIED: November 27, 1997, Rocky Mount, NC
HEIGHT: 5' 10"
WEIGHT: 185 lbs.
Bats left Throws left
YEARS PLAYED: 1933–1950
TEAMS: Brooklyn Royal Giants, Homestead Grays
POSITIONS: 1B, OF
NATIONAL BASEBALL HALL OF FAME: 1972

Lindsay, William Hudson
NICKNAME: Red
SURVEYS: Hall of Fame
YEARS PLAYED: 1931–1932
TEAMS: Hilldale Daisies
RESIDENCE: Philadelphia, PA

Manning, Maxwell
NICKNAME: Max, Dr. Cyclops
SURVEYS: Hall of Fame
BORN: November 18, 1918, Rome, GA
HEIGHT: 6' 4"
WEIGHT: 185 lbs.
Bats left Throws right
YEARS PLAYED: 1938–1949
TEAMS: Newark Eagles, Houston Eagles
POSITIONS: P
RESIDENCE: Pleasantville, NJ

Matthews, Francis Oliver
NICKNAME: Fran, Matty
SURVEYS: Hall of Fame
DIED: August 24, 1999, Los Angeles, CA
HEIGHT: 5' 9"
WEIGHT: 170 lbs.
Bats left Throws left
YEARS PLAYED: 1938–1945
TEAMS: Newark Eagles, Baltimore Elite Giants, Boston Royal Giants
POSITIONS: 1B, OF

Miles, John Jr.
NICKNAME: Mule, Sonnyboy
SURVEYS: All-Time All-Star Team
BORN: August 11, 1922, San Antonio, TX
HEIGHT: 6' 3"
WEIGHT: 228 lbs.
Bats right Throws right
YEARS PLAYED: 1946–1948
TEAMS: Chicago American Giants
POSITIONS: OF, 3B
RESIDENCE: San Antonio, TX

Moore, James Robert
NICKNAME: Red
SURVEYS: Hall of Fame, All-Time All-Star Team
BORN: November 18, 1916, Atlanta, GA
DIED: 1994, Vienna, WV
HEIGHT: 5' 10"
WEIGHT: 165 lbs.
Bats left Throws left
YEARS PLAYED: 1936–1940
TEAMS: Atlanta Black Crackers, Newark Eagles, Indianapolis ABC's, Baltimore
      Elite Giants
POSITIONS: 1B

O'Neil, John Jordan Jr.
NICKNAME: Buck, Foots, Nancy
SURVEYS: Hall of Fame, All-Time All-Star Team
BORN: November 13, 1911, Carabelle, FL
HEIGHT: 6' 2"
WEIGHT: 190 lbs.
Bats right Throws right
YEARS PLAYED: 1937–1955
TEAMS: Memphis Red Sox, Kansas City Monarchs
POSITIONS: 1B, OF, Mgr.
RESIDENCE: Kansas City, MO

Pennington, Arthur David
NICKNAME: Art, Superman
SURVEYS: All-Time All-Star Team
BORN: May 18, 1923, Memphis, TN
HEIGHT: 5' 11"
WEIGHT: 195 lbs.
Bats both Throws right
YEARS PLAYED: 1940–1950

TEAMS: Chicago American Giants, Pittsburgh Crawfords
POSITIONS: OF, IF, P
RESIDENCE: Cedar Rapids, IA
COMMENTS: Played in organized ball from 1949 to 1959.

Porter, Andrew
NICKNAME: Andy, Pullman
SURVEYS: All-Time All-Star Team
BORN: March 7, 1911, Little Rock, AR
HEIGHT: 6' 4"
WEIGHT: 190 lbs.
Bats right Throws right
YEARS PLAYED: 1932–1950
TEAMS: Cleveland Cubs, Nashville Elite Giants, Washington Elite Giants, Baltimore Elite Giants
POSITIONS: P

Radcliffe, Theodore Roosevelt
NICKNAME: Double Duty
SURVEYS: Hall of Fame, All-time All-Star Team
BORN: July 7, 1902, Mobile, AL
HEIGHT: 5' 10"
WEIGHT: 190 lbs.
Bats right Throws right
YEARS PLAYED: 1928–1950
TEAMS: Detroit Stars, St. Louis Stars, Homestead Grays, Pittsburgh Crawfords, Columbus Bluebirds, Cleveland Giants, New York Black Yankees, Chicago American Giants, Brooklyn Eagles, Cincinnati Tigers, Memphis Red Sox, Birmingham Black Barons, Kansas City Monarchs, Louisville Buckeyes
POSITIONS: C, P, Mgr.
RESIDENCE: Chicago, IL

Redd, Ulysses Adolph
NICKNAME: Hickey, Cherry
SURVEYS: Hall of Fame, All-Time All-star Team
YEARS PLAYED: 1940–1941
TEAMS: Birmingham Black Barons, Chicago American Giants
POSITIONS: SS, 2B, 3B
RESIDENCE: Baton Rouge, LA

Robinson, William
NICKNAME: Bobby
SURVEYS: Hall of Fame
BORN: October 25, 1903, Mobile, AL

HEIGHT: 6' 0"
WEIGHT: 170 lbs.
Bats right Throws right
YEARS PLAYED: 1925–1942
TEAMS: Indianapolis ABC's, Cleveland Elites, Chicago American Giants, Birmingham Black Barons, Memphis Red Sox, Detroit Stars, Baltimore Black Sox, Cleveland Stars, Cleveland Giants, Cleveland Red Sox, St. Louis Stars
POSITIONS: 3B, SS
RESIDENCE: Chicago, IL

Sampson, Thomas
NICKNAME: Tommy, Toots
SURVEYS: Hall of Fame, All-Time All-Star Team
BORN: August 31, 1914, Calhoun, AL
HEIGHT: 6' 1"
WEIGHT: 180 lbs.
Bats right Throws right
YEARS PLAYED: 1940–1949
TEAMS: Birmingham Black Barons, Chicago American Giants
POSITIONS: 2B, 1B, OF
RESIDENCE: Elizabeth City, NC

Simpson, Herbert Harold
NICKNAME: Herb, Briefcase
SURVEYS: Hall of Fame, All-Time All-Star Team
YEARS PLAYED: 1942–1951
TEAMS: Chicago American Giants, Birmingham Black Barons, Homestead Grays
POSITIONS: P, 1B, OF
RESIDENCE: New Orleans, LA

Smith, Hilton Lee
SURVEYS: All-Time All-Star Team
BORN: February 27, 1912, Giddings, TX
DIED: November 18, 1983, Kansas City, MO
HEIGHT: 6' 2"
WEIGHT: 180 lbs.
Bats right Throws right
YEARS PLAYED: 1932–1948
TEAMS: Monroe Monarchs, Kansas City Monarchs
POSITIONS: P, OF, 1B
NATIONAL BASEBALL HALL OF FAME: 2001

Summers, Lonnie
NICKNAME: Carl
SURVEYS: All-Time All-Star Team

BORN: August 2, 1915, Davis, OK
DIED: August 24, 1999, Los Angeles, CA
HEIGHT: 6'
WEIGHT: 202 lbs.
Bats right Throws right
YEARS PLAYED: 1938–1949
TEAMS: Baltimore Elite Giants, Chicago American Giants

Tinker, the Rev. Harold C., Sr.

NICKNAME: Hooks
SURVEYS: Hall of Fame
BORN: 1905, Pittsburgh, PA
DIED: November 27, 2000, Pittsburgh, PA
HEIGHT: 5' 10"
WEIGHT: 170 lbs.
Bats right Throws right
YEARS PLAYED: 1928–1931
TEAMS: Pittsburgh Crawfords
POSITIONS: OF, Mgr.

Turner, James

NICKNAME: Lefty
SURVEYS: Hall of Fame, All-Time All-Star Team
DIED: 2000
YEARS PLAYED: 1940–1942
TEAMS: Indianapolis Crawfords, Baltimore Elite Giants
POSITIONS: 1B
RESIDENCE: Palatka, FL

Vasquez, Armando Bernando

SURVEYS: Hall of Fame, All-Time All-Star Team
BORN: August 20, 1922, Guines, Cuba
HEIGHT: 5' 8"
WEIGHT: 160 lbs.
YEARS PLAYED: 1944–1952
TEAMS: Indianapolis Clowns
POSITIONS: P, 1B
RESIDENCE: New York City, NY
COMMENTS: Played in organized ball from 1950 to 1954

Walker, Edsall

NICKNAME: Big
SURVEYS: All-Time All-Star Team
BORN: September 15, 1913, Catskill, NY

DIED: February 19, 1997, Albany, NY
HEIGHT: 6'
WEIGHT: 215 lbs.
YEARS PLAYED: 1936–1945
TEAMS: Homestead Grays, Philadelphia Stars, Newark Eagles, New York Black Yankees
POSITIONS: P

Webb, Normal
NICKNAME: Tweed
SURVEYS: Hall of Fame, All-Time All-Star Team
BORN: 1905, St. Louis, MO
DIED: April 27, 1995, St. Louis, MO
HEIGHT: 5' 9"
WEIGHT: 150 lbs.
Bats right Throws right
YEARS PLAYED: 1926
TEAMS: Fort Wayne Pirates
POSITIONS: OF, IF
COMMENTS: Webb was the foremost Negro League historian, having followed the league from 1910 until its demise.

Williams, Walter T.
SURVEYS: Hall of Fame
YEARS PLAYED: 1937–1939
TEAMS: Newark Eagles, Philadelphia Stars, Washington Black Senators
POSITIONS: P
RESIDENCE: Silver Springs, MD

Wilson, Earl, Sr.
SURVEYS: Hall of Fame, All-Time All-Star Team
YEARS PLAYED: 1938
TEAMS: Birmingham Black Barons
RESIDENCE: San Diego, CA

Appendix II —
The Historians Panel:
The Voters

Alvelo, Luis
SURVEYS: Hall of Fame
MEMBER: SABR, Negro Leagues Baseball Museum
RESIDENCE: Caguas, PR
COMMENTS: Luis Alvelo is one of Puerto Rico's foremost baseball historians. He has followed the game in Puerto Rico since the 1930s.

Bolton, Todd P.
SURVEYS: Hall of Fame, All-Time All-Star Team
MEMBER: SABR's Negro Leagues Committee, National Baseball Hall of Fame, Negro League Baseball Museum
INTERESTS: Negro Leagues, Latin America
OCCUPATION: Branch chief, National Park Service
RESIDENCE: Smithsburg, MD

Bozzone, Richard H.
SURVEYS: Hall of Fame, All-Time All-Star Team
MEMBER: SABR's Negro Leagues Committee
INTERESTS: Minor leagues, Negro Leagues, biographical research, nineteenth-century baseball,
OCCUPATION: Postal Service
RESIDENCE: Tolland, CT.

Clark, Richard C.
NICKNAME: Dick

SURVEYS: Hall of Fame, All-Time All-Star Team
MEMBER: SABR, Chairman SABR Negro Leagues Committee
INTERESTS: Minor leagues, Negro Leagues, nineteenth-century baseball
OCCUPATION: Manufacturer's representative
RESIDENCE: Ypsilanti, MI
COMMENTS: Dick Clark is the co-editor of *The Negro Leagues Book* and co-editor
of Negro League Statistics for *Baseball Encyclopedia*, 8th edition.

Eastland, Jeff
SURVEYS: Hall of Fame, All-Time All-Star Team
MEMBER: SABR's Negro Leagues Committee
INTERESTS: Negro Leagues, Latin America, Hall of Fame, nineteenth-century base-
ball, ballpark history
OCCUPATION: Antiques dealer
RESIDENCE: Falmouth, VA
COMMENTS: Jeff Eastland is a guest lecturer on the Negro Leagues. He has a large
Negro League photo collection. His expertise includes both Negro Leagues
and Latin American baseball.

Finkel, Jan
SURVEYS: Hall of Fame, All-Time All-Star Team
MEMBER: SABR's Negro Leagues Committee
INTERESTS: Negro Leagues, baseball records
OCCUPATION: Retired English professor, investment analyst
RESIDENCE: Demarest, NJ
COMMENTS: Jan Finkel is a guest lecturer on baseball, Hall of Fame, and Negro
Leagues.

Garrett, Thomas R.
NICKNAME: Tom
SURVEYS: Hall of Fame, All-Time All-Star Team
MEMBER: SABR's Negro Leagues Committee
INTERESTS: Minor leagues, Negro Leagues, biographical research
OCCUPATION: Special education specialist
RESIDENCE: Suffolk, VA

Heaphy, Leslie
SURVEYS: Hall of Fame, All-Time All-Star Team
MEMBER: SABR's Negro Leagues Committee, North American Society of Sports
History
INTERESTS: Sport history, women in sports
OCCUPATION: Assistant professor of history, Kent State University
RESIDENCE: Canton, OH
COMMENTS: Leslie Heaphy is the chairperson for SABR's Women in Baseball

Committee. She is presently working on a book on the history of the Negro Leagues.

Hogan, Lawrence D.

SURVEYS: Hall of Fame
MEMBER: SABR's Negro Leagues Committee
INTERESTS: Negro Leagues, ballpark history, Hall of Fame
OCCUPATION: Professor of history at Union County College, N.J.
RESIDENCE: Fanwood, NJ
COMMENTS: Larry Hogan is heavily involved in Negro League projects; writing, creating exhibits, and producing video documentaries. He is secretary to the John Henry Pop Lloyd Committee in Atlantic City, NJ.

Holway, John B.

SURVEYS: Hall of Fame, All-Time All-Star Team
MEMBER: SABR's Negro Leagues Committee
INTERESTS: Negro Leagues, baseball records, statistical analysis, Latin America
OCCUPATION: Writer
RESIDENCE: Springfield, VA
COMMENTS: John Holway is one of the Negro League's foremost historians and authors. His books on Negro League legends include the acclaimed *Blackball Stars*. His 30 years of painstaking research has provided the baseball world with the most complete career statistics ever compiled on Negro League players.

Hunsinger, Lou, Jr.

SURVEYS: Hall of Fame, All-Time All-Star Team
MEMBER: SABR's Negro Leagues Committee
INTERESTS: Minor leagues, Negro Leagues, nineteenth-century baseball, ballpark history, women in baseball.
OCCUPATION: News reporter for the *Williamsport Sun-Gazette.*
RESIDENCE: Williamsport, PA
COMMENTS: Lou Hunsinger is the co-author of *Williamsport's Baseball Heritage.*

Keetz, Frank

SURVEYS: All-Time All-Star Team
MEMBER: SABR
INTERESTS: Minor leagues, socio-economic aspects, black baseball in Schenectady
OCCUPATION: Retired teacher, author
RESIDENCE: Schenectady, NY

Kelley, Brent

SURVEYS: Hall of Fame, All-Time All-Star Team
MEMBER: SABR's Negro Leagues Committee, Negro League Baseball Museum.

INTERESTS: Minor leagues, Negro Leagues, baseball records, biographical research, Hall of Fame

OCCUPATION: Writer

RESIDENCE: Paris, KY

COMMENTS: Brent Kelley is a prolific writer and interviewer, with over 400 magazine articles, plus several books, including *Voices from the Negro Leagues.*

Kleinknecht, Merl F.

SURVEYS: Hall of Fame, All-Time All-Star Team

MEMBER: SABR's Negro Leagues Committee

INTERESTS: Minor leagues, Negro Leagues, nineteenth-century baseball, Latin America

OCCUPATION: Publisher of high school sports record manuals

RESIDENCE: Galion, OH

COMMENTS: Merl Kleinknecht is a founding member of SABR's Negro Leagues Committee and two-term Committee Chairman. He has published numerous articles on the Negro Leagues.

Knorr, Theodore

NICKNAME: Ted, Tee

SURVEYS: Hall of Fame, All-Time All-Star Team

MEMBER: SABR's Negro Leagues Committee

INTERESTS: Negro Leagues, statistical analysis, socio-economic aspects

OCCUPATION: Grants administrator

RESIDENCE: Harrisburg, PA

COMMENTS: Ted Knorr is the founder and coordinator of the SABR Negro League Committee Research Conference.

Lawrence, David A.

SURVEYS: Hall of Fame, All-Time All-Star Team

MEMBER: SABR's Negro Leagues Committee

INTERESTS: Negro League history, particularly the Eastern Colored League.

RESIDENCE: Saratoga, CA

COMMENTS: David Lawrence holds a Ph.D. in aesthetics from Stanford University.

Lester, Larry

SURVEYS: Hall of Fame, All-Time All-Star Team

MEMBER: SABR's Negro Leagues Committee, Negro Leagues Baseball Museum

INTERESTS: Negro Leagues, baseball research, statistical analysis, nineteenth-century baseball

OCCUPATION: Owner, NoirTech Research, Inc.

RESIDENCE: Raytown, MO.

COMMENTS: Larry Lester is one of the country's leading authorities on the Negro Baseball Leagues. He has written extensively on the Negro Leagues, and is co-editor of *The Negro Leagues* book.

Malloy, Jerry
SURVEYS: Hall of Fame
MEMBER: SABR's Negro Leagues Committee
INTERESTS: Negro Leagues, biographical research, nineteenth-century black Baseball, Black baseball in the military, women in baseball
DIED: September 6, 2000, in Mundelein, IL
RESIDENCE: Mundelein, IL
COMMENTS: Jerry Malloy edited and introduced *Sol White's History of Colored Baseball*. He also wrote articles for several publications. He was an expert on Negro League history.

McNeil, William F.
NICKNAME: Bill, Mick
SURVEYS: Hall of Fame, All-Time All-Star Team
MEMBER: SABR
INTERESTS: Negro Leagues, Latin American baseball, Japanese baseball, Brooklyn and Los Angeles Dodgers
OCCUPATION: Writer
RESIDENCE: Pittsfield, MA

Miller, Sammy J.
SURVEYS: Hall of Fame, All-Time All-Star Team
MEMBER: SABR's Negro Leagues Committee
INTERESTS: Negro Leagues
OCCUPATION: Writer
RESIDENCE: Florence, KY
COMMENTS: Sammy Miller is the editor of the Negro League's monthly newsletter, *The Negro League Courier*. He is actively engaged in many Negro League projects, serving as consultant, writer, panelist, editor, and interviewer.

Morris, Rick
SURVEYS: Hall of Fame, All-Time All-Star Team
MEMBER: SABR's Negro Leagues Committee
INTERESTS: Negro Leagues, nineteenth-century baseball
OCCUPATION: Filmmaker
RESIDENCE: King of Prussia, PA
COMMENTS: Rick Morris is a dedicated interviewer, who has conducted dozens of interviews with former Negro League players as well as their white opponents. He is presently working on a Negro League film documentary.

Newland, Eric
SURVEYS: Hall of Fame, All-Time All-Star Team
MEMBER: SABR's Negro Leagues Committee
INTERESTS: Negro Leagues, Hall of Fame, women in baseball

OCCUPATION: TV producer, interviewer
RESIDENCE: Katonah, NY
COMMENTS: Eric Newland has one of the largest collections of baseball player interviews.

Overmyer, James E.

NICKNAME: Jim
SURVEYS: Hall of Fame
MEMBER: SABR's Negro Leagues Committee, SABR's Business of Baseball Committee
INTERESTS: Negro Leagues, nineteenth-century baseball, socio-economic aspects
OCCUPATION: Postal Service
RESIDENCE: Lenox, MA
COMMENTS: Jim Overmeyer has authored several publications on Negro League baseball, including *Effa Manley and the Newark Eagles.*

Peterson, Robert W.

NICKNAME: Bob
SURVEYS: Hall of Fame
MEMBER: SABR
INTERESTS: Negro Leagues
OCCUPATION: Writer, editor
RESIDENCE: Ramsey, NJ
COMMENTS: Bob Peterson was a pioneer in the field of Negro baseball history. His book, *Only the Ball Was White,* first published in 1970, and still being reissued, introduced a generation of baseball researchers to the shadowy world of black baseball.

Riley, James A.

NICKNAME: Jim
SURVEYS: Hall of Fame, All-Time All-Star Team
MEMBER: SABR's Negro Leagues Committee
INTERESTS: Negro Leagues, statistical analysis, biographical research, Hall of Fame
OCCUPATION: Writer, editor, publisher
RESIDENCE: Rockledge, FL
COMMENTS: Jim Riley's mammoth effort, *The Biographical Encyclopedia of the Negro Baseball Leagues,* is the primary reference work on the forgotten men of that long-ago era.

Sanford, Jay

SURVEYS: Hall of Fame
MEMBER: SABR's Negro Leagues Committee, Colorado Historical Society
INTERESTS: Negro Leagues, biographical research, nineteenth-century baseball
OCCUPATION: Director wholesale lending/mortgage

RESIDENCE: Arvada, CO

COMMENTS: Jay Sanford is a long time sports historian, researcher, guest lecturer, and writer. He also owns a large baseball photo collection of both major league players and Negro League players.

Valero, Eduardo

SURVEYS: All-Time All-Star Team

MEMBER: SABR, chairperson of SABR's Latin America Committee, Puerto Rico Sports Hall of Fame, Puerto Rico Baseball Hall of Fame

INTERESTS: Latin American baseball, Negro Leagues

OCCUPATION: Sports journalist, historian

RESIDENCE: Santurce, PR

COMMENTS: Eduardo Valero has followed baseball in Puerto Rico since the 1940s. His friends have included many Negro League players like Raymond Brown, Josh Gibson, and Leon Day.

Wilson, Lyle K.

SURVEYS: Hall of Fame, All-Time All-Star Team

MEMBER: SABR's Negro Leagues Committee

INTERESTS: Negro Leagues

OCCUPATION: Attorney

RESIDENCE: Mill Creek, WA

COMMENTS: Lyle Wilson has contributed several articles on black baseball to SABR's publications, *The National Pastime* and *The Baseball Research Journal.*

Bibliography

Acocella, Nick, and Donald Dewey. *The All-Stars.* New York: Avon Books, 1986.

Bak, Richard. *Turkey Stearnes and the Detroit Stars.* Detroit: Great Lakes Books, 1994.

Bankes, James. *The Pittsburgh Crawfords.* Dubuque, Iowa: William C. Brown Publishers, 1991.

Bruce, Janet. *The Kansas City Monarchs.* Lawrence: University Press of Kansas, 1985.

Campanella, Roy. *It's Good to Be Alive.* New York: Signet Books, 1959.

Carter, Craig, ed. *Daguerreotypes.* 8th ed. St. Louis: The Sporting News Publishing Co., 1990.

Chadwick, Bruce. *When the Game Was Black and White.* New York: Abbeville Press Publishers, date?.

Cisneros, Pedro Treto, ed. *Enciclopedia del Béisbol Mexicano.* Mexico: Revistas Deportivas, date?.

Clark, Dick, and Larry Lester, eds. *The Negro Leagues Book.* Cleveland, Ohio: Society for American Baseball Research, 1994.

Hoie, Bob, and Carlos Bauer, comps. *The Historical Register.* San Marino, Calif.: Baseball Press Books, 1998.

Holway, John B. *Black Diamonds.* New York: Stadium Books, 1991.

_____. *Blackball Stars.* Westport, Conn.: Meckler Books, 1988.

_____. *Josh and Satch.* New York: Carroll and Graf Publishers, 1991.

_____. *Voices from the Great Black Baseball Leagues.* New York: Da Capo Press, 1992.

Johnson, Lloyd, and Miles Wolff, eds. *The Encyclopedia of Minor League Baseball.* Durham, N.C.: Baseball America, Inc., 1993.

Keetz, Frank M. *The Mohawk Colored Giants of Schenectady.* Schenectady, N.Y.: 1999.

Kelley, Brent. *Voices from the Negro Leagues.* Jefferson, N.C.: McFarland, 1998.

Malloy, Jerry, comp. *Sol White's History of Colored Base Ball.* Lincoln, Neb.: University of Nebraska Press, 1995.

McNary, Kyle P., *Ted "Double Duty" Radcliffe.* St. Louis Park, Minn.: McNary Publishing, 1994.

McNeil, William F. *Baseball's Other All-Stars.* Jefferson, N.C.: McFarland, 2000.

_____. *The King of Swat.* Jefferson, N.C.: McFarland, 1997.

Nemec, David. *The Great American Baseball Team Book.* New York: Penguin, 1992.

O'Neil, Buck. *I Was Right on Time.* New York: Simon & Schuster, 1996.

Paige, LeRoy ("Satchel"). *Maybe I'll Pitch Forever.* Lincoln: University of Nebraska Press, 1993.

Peterson, Robert. *Only the Ball Was White.* New York: McGraw-Hill, 1984.

Ribowsky, Mark. *The Power and the Darkness.* New York: Simon & Schuster, 1996.

Riley, James A. *The Biographical Encyclopedia of the Negro Baseball Leagues.* New York: Carroll & Graf Publishers, 1994.

_____. *Dandy, Day, and the Devil.* Cocoa, Fla.: TK Publishers, 1987.

Robinson, Jackie. *I Never Had It Made.* Hopewell, N.J.: Ecco Press, 1995.

Rogosin, Donn. *Invisible Men.* New York: Macmillan, 1983.

Society for American Baseball Research. *Minor League Baseball Stars.* Cleveland: Society for American Baseball Research. Vol. 1, 1978. Vol. 2, 1985. Vol. 3, 1992.

Thorn, John, et al., eds. *Total Baseball,* 5th ed. New York: Viking Penguin, 1997.

Van Hyning, Thomas E. *Puerto Rico's Winter League.* Jefferson, N.C.: McFarland, 1995.

Index